An Aleutian Ethnography

by Lucien M. Turner

edited by
Raymond L. Hudson

UNIVERSITY OF ALASKA PRESS
FAIRBANKS
2008

University of Alaska Press
P.O. Box 756240
Fairbanks, AK 99775-6240

ISBN 978-1-60223-028-6 (cloth)

Library of Congress Cataloging-in-Publication Data:

Turner, Lucien M. (Lucien McShan)
An Aleutian ethnography / by Lucien M. Turner ; edited by Raymond L. Hudson.
p. cm.
Includes bibliographical references.
ISBN 978-1-60223-028-6 (cloth : alk. paper) — ISBN 978-1-60223-039-2 (pbk.) 1. Aleuts—History. 2. Aleuts—Material culture. 3. Aleuts—Social life and customs. 4. Ethnography—Alaska—Aleutian Islands. 5. Material culture—Alaska—Aleutian Islands. 6. Aleutian Islands (Alaska) —History. 7. Aleutian Islands (Alaska) —Social life and customs. I. Hudson, Raymond L. II. Title.
E99.A34.T874 2008
979.8'00497—dc22
2008007424

Cover and interior design by Alcorn Publication Design

This publication was printed on acid-free paper that meets the minimum requirements for ANSI / NISO Z39.48–1992 (R2002) (Permanence of Paper for Printed Library Materials).

Printed in China

An Aleutian Ethnography

Table of Contents

List of Illustrations

Color Plates

See Color Insert following page 82

Tables

Acknowledgments

The late Lydia T. Black first drew my attention to Turner through the examples of basketry he collected at Atka. L. Wayne Turner, grandson of Lucien M. Turner, contributed family papers and drawings along with considerable enthusiasm for this project. Without his assistance and gentle nudging, the project would not have been completed. Debra Corbett, archaeologist for the U.S. Fish and Wildlife Service in Anchorage, and Stephen Loring, of the Arctic Studies Center, Smithsonian Institution, encouraged the preparation of Turner's Aleutian work. I have benefited immensely from Loring's study of Turner's Canadian years. Corbett has long recognized the value of Turner's work, especially for the Near Islands. The *Descriptive Catalogue of Ethnological Specimens Collected by Lucien M. Turner in Alaska* is in the National Anthropological Archives, Smithsonian Institution, which kindly permitted its use in this publication. I am indebted to the Smithsonian Institution Archives and the Blacker-Wood Library, McGill University, for use of their collections of Turner material. Middlebury College Library kindly made their government documents and rare books collections available. The Geography and Map Division, the Library of Congress, provided copies of Turner's maps of the Near Islands. Felicia Pickering guided me through the Turner collections in the ethnology and archaeological collections at the Smithsonian and arranged for photographs of objects. All object photography was by Donald E. Hurlbert, Smithsonian Institution, unless otherwise noted. The objects are in the collection of the Department of Anthropology, National Museum of Natural History (NMNH), Smithsonian Institution. The Aleutian Pribilof Islands Restitution Trust provided funding for photographs through a grant to the Museum of the Aleutians. Conversations with Marvin Collins about the early history and shipping practices of the A.C. Company have been illuminating. I want to thank Jeffery Dickrell of Unalaska for discussions about Turner over the years and for a copy of the *Contributions* so battered that I felt no guilt in marking it up. Finally, special thanks go to my wife, Shelly, for her patience as I plunged into yet another project about a place so far away but for which we both harbor such close affection.

A Note on the Term *Aleut*

In recent years the Association of *Unangan/Unangas* Educators has urged the abandonment of the term *Aleut*. "The time has come to reclaim our name for ourselves," the association stated in an introduction to a superb manual on Aleutian plants. "Elders often use 'Aleut' but want to hear us say 'Unangan' (Eastern) or 'Unangas' (Western). It is a matter of habit."[1] These terms—with a shared singular and possessive, *Unangax̂* and *Unangam*—refer to "the people of the pass."[2] The term *Aleut* is said to have originated either with residents on islands off Kamchatka or with those on the far western Aleutians.[3] However, Turner, who spent eleven months on Attu, did not find it in use among Attuans. "The term Aleut applied to the people of the Aleutian Islands," he wrote, "is one of very unsatisfactory origin and similarly of signification. . . . The word Aleut is recognized among those people as one of unknown quantity." Over millennia, the people developed significant cultural variations and identified themselves with regional names, including the *Sasaignan* of the Near Islands, the *Niiĝuĝis* of the Andreanofs, the *Qawalangin* and *Qigiiĝun* of the Fox Islands. Turner wrote that *Unangan* was an eastern term that "was afterward extended to include the western Aleut." Nevertheless, he and his contemporaries used *Aleut* in their writings. I have, for the sake of consistency, done the same in the introduction unless referring to the Unangan/Unangas of today.

Introduction

Lucien M. Turner and Late-Nineteenth-Century Aleutian Ethnography

Raymond L. Hudson

On October 5, 1880, thirteen years after the United States purchased Alaska from Russia, Lucien M. Turner, a poorly paid member of the United States Signal Service for whom natural history and ethnography were passions, braced himself as a series of gusts hammered the government house at Attu. He had arrived at the most western settlement in the Aleutian Islands three months earlier during a period of warm, calm weather. His Aleut neighbors were snug in their sod-banked barabaras over whose low, curved roofs the wind swept without disturbance. Turner's wooden walls and peaked roof were blunt targets as the wind rose to "a furious gale."[1]

He had been in the Aleutians since early May 1878, when he established headquarters at Unalaska Village on the island of the same name.[2] This settlement, also known as Iliuliuk, was the commercial and religious center for the eastern Aleutians. After establishing himself at Unalaska, he had made a brief visit to Nushagak (Fort Alexander in Bristol Bay) and returned to Unalaska in early July. Later that month he had visited Belkofski on the Alaska Peninsula, where he had unsuccessfully attempted to establish a meteorological station. On a visit north to St. George and St. Paul in the Pribilof Islands he had secured the assistance of H. H. McIntyre, superintendent for the Alaska Commercial Company's fur seal operations. Back at Unalaska near the end of August, he remained until May 1879, when he traveled to Atka in the central Aleutians. Returning to Unalaska in September he again wintered at the largest settlement before sailing in June 1880 to Attu, at the far western tip of the chain.

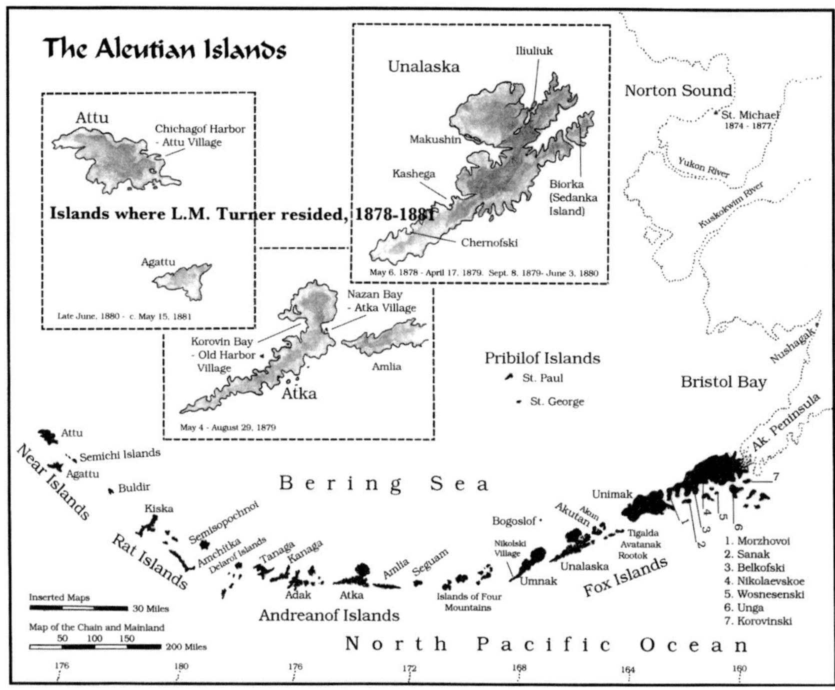

FIG. 1. Map of the Aleutian Islands showing locations where Turner resided, 1878–1881.

Uncertain whether or not the men of the A.C. Co. would safeguard his collections—he had found them deliberately unfriendly at times—he had brought to Attu all the plants gathered and pressed in the eastern and central islands. Clear, warm days with no precipitation had ended July, but an unusual three-day gale out of the northwest had ushered in August. The violent rain had gradually subsided, restoring the usual mixture of fog, light rain, and moderate winds for the remainder of August and the full month of September. On October 1 hard rain had accompanied a northerly gale. The temperature had dropped and the next day's showers had been interrupted by "spits of snow" as high winds continued. The wind and temperature had moderated on the 3rd but on the 4th heavy snow draped the mountains surrounding the village. By October 5 a grand Aleutian storm was in full glory.

The door and window of Turner's house pulsed as hurricane-force gusts crested the gale. A turbulent surge slashed the roof, opening it like a wound. As boards twisted loose, the house turned into a funnel for wind and rain. "All of my specimens of natural history," Turner lamented, "were ruined."[3] Most of his records written in ink were obliterated in the deluge that engulfed the dwelling, now a sieve of sticks. When he was able to get outside he found the wind gauge ripped from its base, hurled to the ground and bent out of shape. It would take him two weeks to repair the dwelling, but by October 17, when the steamer *Dora* arrived from Unalaska, he had reinforced the structure enough to face the winter—when really unpleasant weather could be expected.

Years later as he drafted an introduction to the Aleutian Islands, he got as far as describing a typical shoreline when the storm at Attu again burst into his mind, blasting his hapless sentence in all directions: "The shores are mostly abrupt or precipitous," he began, "difficult of approach except where the deeply indented coast has preserved the falling masses of rock and stones rolled into shingle and boulders of all sizes by the constant lashings of the sea waves impelled by the relentless fury of an ever changing atmosphere producing violent storms of long duration that cause the very foundations of the mountain bases to tremble under the crushing impetuosity of the surging billows of an ever angry ocean."[4]

Undoubtedly the destruction of so much of his collection contributed to the deficiencies of his final report. Cautioning readers against Turner's botanical information, Eric Hultén noted that Turner was not a botanist, and "as he apparently added information about the occurrence of the plants on the Aleutian Islands from memory without being able adequately to identify them, this list . . . is very unreliable and contains numerous errors. It is to be regretted that it can not be used as a reliable source of information for the distribution of the plants on the islands."[5] "Where he is the only one to report a plant from a particular station," Hultén advised, "a note of interrogation should be added."[6] Consequently it makes sense to ask how far Turner's ethnographic information can be trusted without independent confirmation from other observers.

Turner in Alaska

Lucien McShan Turner was born in Mainville, Ohio, on June 20, 1847.[7] While he was still a child his parents moved to Mt. Carmel, Illinois, where he grew up exploring the countryside and developing an enthusiasm for birds and natural history. A neighbor, Robert Ridgway, three years his

Fig. 2. Turner's family home in Mt. Carmel, Illinois. *L. Wayne Turner Collection.*

junior, shared Turner's interests and together they collected and mounted birds. With the coming of the War Between the States, Turner enlisted. He served with Company I, 80th Regiment of the Indiana Volunteers, and then transferred to his father's unit, Company H, 136th Regiment. Two of Lucien's brothers also served in the war. Turner returned to Mt. Carmel to work as a farmhand and bricklayer. In 1869 he married Mary Elizabeth Lutz. They had twin sons in March 1872, one of whom died eighteen months later. Turner's education was sufficient to enable him to open a private elementary school and later to teach in the local high school.

In the meantime, Ridgway had become a professional ornithologist. Something of a prodigy, at the age of fourteen he had come to the attention of Spencer Baird, secretary of the Smithsonian Institution. Ridgway spent three years doing fieldwork, starting at age seventeen. He published his first note on birds at eighteen and found occasional employment with the Smithsonian's National Museum. In 1874 he became a designated ornithologist. In 1880 he was appointed curator of birds and held this position until his death in 1929.[8]

Following the purchase of Alaska in 1867, the U.S. Army's Signal Corps stationed observers in the territory to broaden the base of meteorological and tidal data. The Smithsonian recommended men who were willing to

Fig. 3. L. M. Turner, 1874. *L. Wayne Turner Collection.* This was taken by Bradley & Rulofson in San Francisco about the time Turner departed on his first trip to Alaska.

spend their free time making collections for the institution, and once they passed the physical and technical examinations required by the corps they were enlisted. Through Ridgway's connections with Baird, Turner received an appointment in January 1874. Baird, on Henry Elliott's recommendation, initially considered sending him to Nulato, "the best station & most comfortable," but eventually directed him to St. Michael, an outpost on Norton Sound east of the mouth of the Yukon River, which Baird thought "would be more interesting, both in a meteorological & zoological point of view."[9]

In April Turner traveled with his wife and son to San Francisco, where officers of the A.C. Co. told him his family could not accompany him north. This separation was the first of many that would strain the marriage and contribute to its dissolution. Turner carried a letter of introduction from Baird to William Healey Dall, who had been part of the team exploring the interior of Alaska for the Western Union Telegraph Expedition from 1865 to 1868. Between 1871 and 1874 he had spent over sixteen months in the

Fig. 4. Mary and Jesse Turner in arctic clothing, c. 1874. *L. Wayne Turner Collection.* This was probably taken in San Francisco about the time Mary Turner learned she and her son could not accompany Lucien to Alaska.

Aleutians working for the U.S. Coast Survey, all the while establishing an enduring association with the Smithsonian. After Dall helped him select clothing suitable for Alaskan weather, Turner sailed from San Francisco on the *Eustice* on April 18.[10] It was a stormy voyage, and he arrived at Unalaska very weak from seasickness. People traveling to and from any point along the northwestern coast of Alaska invariably stopped at this ice-free port while goods were offloaded or loaded and the travel needs of government officials, company employees, various clergy, and private travelers were coordinated. The A.C. Co.'s district headquarters there oversaw stations throughout the islands, the Alaska Peninsula, and along the Kuskokwim River. Although St. Michael was the center for their northern activities, even its furs were frequently shipped south through Unalaska. For five days Turner busied himself making collections of birds before again setting sail. On May 17 he stopped briefly at St. Paul in the Pribilof Islands, and, finally, after a voyage of thirty-eight days from San Francisco, he arrived at St. Michael on May 25, 1874.

He remained there until Edward W. Nelson, another young employee of the Signal Corps, arrived on June 19, 1877, as his replacement. During the

This is an Indian account
Indian This means sent
Russian
hands of tobacco
ax
hatchet
double gun
single
knife
hat
gun cap
comb
spoon
sheeting
shirt
lead ladles
bear trap
fox trap
sausage cutter
chain
bars lead
mould
cup
can powder
file
Keep this

Fig. 5. "An Indian account." *L. Wayne Turner Collection.* This was collected by Turner, probably at St. Michael.

next month Turner introduced Nelson to the area. Together they visited the nearby village and initiated what would become Nelson's extraordinary collection of ethnographic items.[11] After Turner returned to the States, he spent time at the Smithsonian working with his St. Michael collections. He rejoined his wife and son at Mt. Carmel, but the stay was short. In March 1878 he re-enlisted in the Signal Corps and left for Alaska once again, this time to the Aleutian Islands. Five months later his son Eugene was born.

TABLE 1: Turner's Stay in the Aleutian Islands

1878	
6 May	Arrived Unalaska
6 June*–6 July*	Visited Nushagak, and the Kuskokwim/Ugashik regions
10 July*–20 July*	Visited Nushagak, Sanak, and Belkofski, with a stop in Akutan
20 July–2 August	Unalaska
2 August +–18 August +	Visited St. George and St. Paul
? August–? September	Visited Bristol Bay, again stopping at Akutan and other points
2 September–31 December	Unalaska
1879	
1 January–1 May	Unalaska
4 May–29 August	Atka
8 September–31 December	Unalaska
1880	
1 January–3 June	Unalaska
mid-June	Visited Chernofski and Atka
? July–31 December	Attu
1881	
1 January–15 ? May	Attu
mid-May–7 ? June	Visited Amchitka
18 June–22 July	Unalaska
22 July	Departed Unalaska for San Francisco

The majority of dates were taken from Turner's monthly abstracts and notes on birds in *Contributions.* Those marked with a * indicate a date Turner was named in the Alaska Commercial Company log, 1878–79. Those with a + indicate the day the log recorded a vessel sailed to that destination but Turner was not specifically mentioned.

Turner would spend a continuous three years and three months in the Aleutians, living at the three primary settlements: Unalaska, Atka, and Attu.

Unalaska

Turner's stay at Unalaska was punctuated by stormy weather and an increasingly tumultuous relationship with the Alaska Commercial Company. When he finally returned to San Francisco in the summer of 1881, he discovered that a defamatory article against him had appeared in the police gazette. He was incensed and wrote to Baird, blaming the A.C. Co. and determined to "expose their entire affair in Alaska."[12] Eight months later, as he was transmitting his *Contributions to the Natural History of Alaska*, he thanked numerous people by name. "In the Unalashkan District I can but remember with pleasure the facilities afforded me by the Western Fur and Trading Company through their agents, Mr. John Hague, and especially to Mr. Robert King, agent of the district. To the gentlemen composing the Alaska Commercial Company, in San Francisco," he continued with a notable absence of warmth or personal names, "I take pleasure in acknowledging the many favors extended me with extreme courtesy at Saint Michael's and during the first year of my stay at Unalashka."[13] What, one might ask, had happened during his remaining two years and three months in the Aleutians?

Briefly, he had butted heads with a company of unsurpassed power and influence. At the transfer of Alaska from Russia to the United States, men associated with what would become the Alaska Commercial Company had swept across the territory laying claim to every fur-trapping outpost in sight. They had purchased property and supplies from the Russian-American Company and had taken immediate steps to hire many of the departing company's employees. Originally incorporated as Hutchinson, Kohl and Company, the firm became the Alaska Commercial Company in October 1868. In the Aleutians, a few smaller companies initiated attempts to compete, and this produced ten years of relative economic prosperity for Aleut people.

"I first visited these people in 1868, the year after the purchase [as a first lieutenant aboard the *Wayanda* under Captain J. W. White]," wrote Captain George W. Bailey of the U.S. Revenue Cutter Service in 1879.

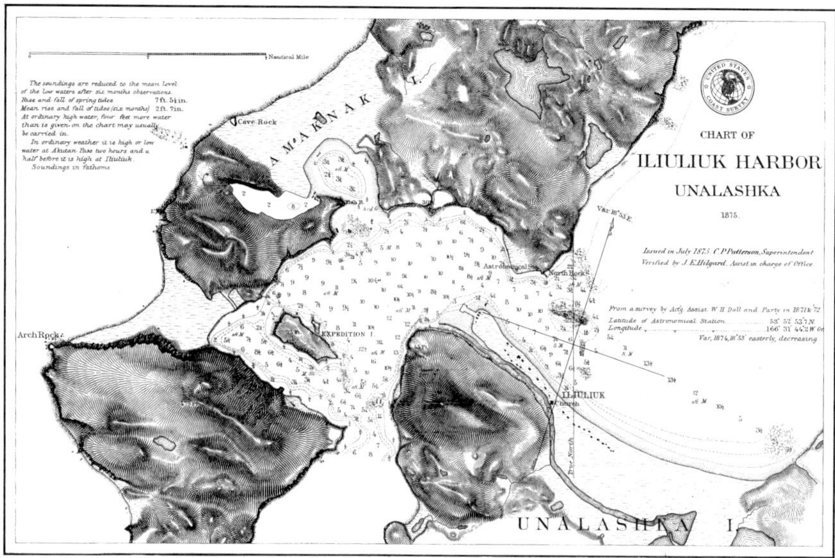

Fig. 6. Chart of Iliuliuk Harbor, Unalashka, 1875. *Courtesy NOAA's Historic Chart Collection (Chart 23).* This chart, drawn by H. Lindenkohl, was based on surveys by W. H. Dall in 1871–1872. Note the wharf that was constructed in 1873.

> Then many of the old rules and customs governing them were still adhered to; but, as soon as the different trading companies came among them, there was of course a competition for the trade. The price of furs went up to a ruinous figure for the traders, only the wealthiest ones being now left to continue the trade. The people consequently reaped the harvest. Money was plenty with them, and everything for sale in the way of life's luxuries was indulged in by them. This naturally introduced an entire change in their mode of living, the good times continuing sufficiently long to create certain wants never before known. They adopted the European style of dress, began to furnish their houses with articles never before considered necessary, thinking no doubt . . . that the improvement in their condition would be permanent.[14]

In August 1873 the A.C. Co. built a wharf seventy feet long and forty feet wide at the tip of the Iliuliuk peninsula at Unalaska. That same year they erected three additional warehouses and, by February 1874, the Company

House was being built, in front of which would stand a tall flagpole surrounded by Russian cannons. This two-and-a-half-story building with back wings enclosing a small courtyard would dominate not only the landscape but the economic and social life at Unalaska for decades. It surpassed even the Orthodox church in size and prominence. The church had been built in 1858 under Father Innokentii Shaiashnikov. (In 1896 a cathedral would replace this church and the Company House would begin a gradual slide leading to its razing about the time the church was declared a National Historic Landmark seventy years later.) The Company House held the firm's headquarters, apartments for the general agent and for visitors, and large rooms for entertainment. When Dall visited in July 1874, he noted the new building, some small houses the company had built for sea otter hunters, new fences, and a boardwalk from the "shore to the wharf—and various other improvements."[15]

In 1870 the company had secured a twenty-year lease of the fur seal–rich Pribilof Islands from which competitors had been driven out, kicking and screaming in various newspapers and calling for government investigations. By the time Turner arrived in 1878, the A.C. Co. was clearly the undisputed master of Alaska and especially of the Aleutians. Conditions for Aleut people had altered, as Captain Bailey noted in 1879:

> In a few years a change came; the traders of small capital went to the wall; the prices paid for furs went down to a living figure for those that remained; the hunter's profits became correspondingly less, and, in order to keep up his income, he had to be more constantly employed. This constant hunting has reduced the number of animals in some localities, and today a large proportion of these people are very poor.[16]

Turner drew a rough map of Unalaska and enclosed it in one of his letters to his family. It was probably made during the winter of 1878–79 and shows the peninsula or village spit formed by the bay—the "ocean"—and the Iliuliuk Creek. The hill behind the village is today known as Haystack.

The "high[h]ouse" was the company headquarters, the "company house," and between it and the store (written upside down) was a plank walk leading to warehouses at the wharf. There was a waterline running from a small reservoir halfway up Haystack to the A.C. Co. Turner noted

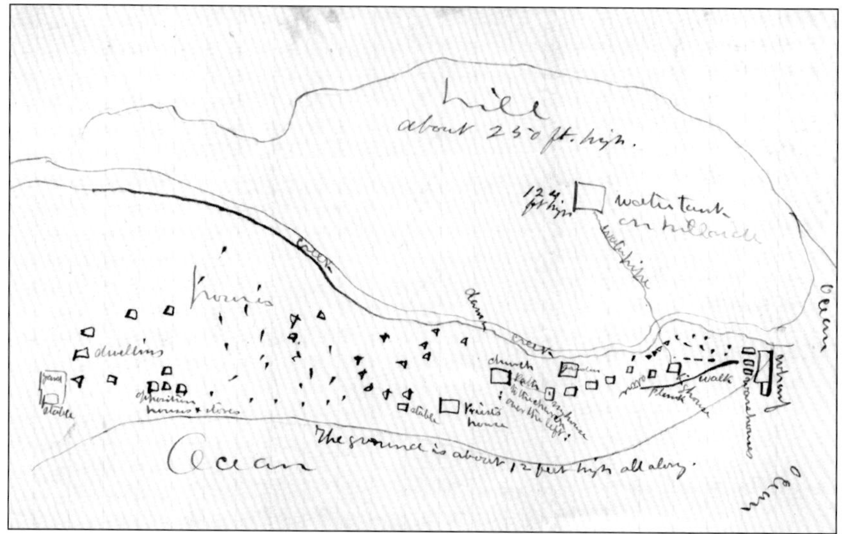

Fig. 7. Sketched map of Unalaska Village, 1878–1879. *L. Wayne Turner Collection.* Turner made this drawing from the perspective of someone entering the harbor in a vessel and consequently north is at the bottom of the drawing.

a "dam" midway along the creek. This may have been the site of a weir, similar to those recorded at Nikolski and Attu (see chapter 11). Turner's initial dwelling, the U.S. Custom House, was in front of the church. To the east and in front of the church was the home of Father Innokentii Shaiashnikov. Beyond that was a stable that probably belonged to the A.C. Co., although the priest at times kept cattle himself. The Western Fur and Trading Company, the "opposition," sat farther east along the front beach with another stable nearby. Aleut dwellings were primarily located east of the church, with a few to the west on the creek side of the A.C. Co. property. Turner sketched the Church of the Holy Ascension as it stood just outside the door of the custom house.

The general agent for the company from 1873 to 1880 was Alfred Greenbaum.[17] A member of a generation younger than the founders of the company, Greenbaum had family ties to major stockholders. His uncle was Louis Sloss, one of the original partners and first president of the A.C. Co. Visitors to Unalaska found Greenbaum a well-disposed and helpful person. "Mr. G.," wrote Ivan Petroff in his journal while collecting material for Bancroft's history of Alaska in 1878, "has been exceedingly kind and accommodating in furnishing me means of transportation and otherwise

Fig. 8. Church of the Holy Ascension, c. 1878. *L. Wayne Turner Collection.* Drawing by L. M. Turner. This building was erected under the priest Innokentii Shaiashnikov in 1858 and replaced the first church, built in 1825. Both structures were on the site of a chapel constructed around 1808.

assisting me in my exploration."[18] Turner would discover another side to the agent's personality.

During his first summer in the Aleutians, Turner had close association with the general agent. Both men traveled on the schooner *Eudora* to and from Bristol Bay, arriving at Unalaska on July 6, 1878. They boarded the same schooner four days later for a trip to Nushagak, Belkofski, and Sanak (where they were dropping off a party of sea otter hunters with their baidarkas). They returned on July 20. The agent, however, had been "full of business" and would not wait even an hour for Turner to make collections.[19]

The trips had been successful for Greenbaum, if not for Turner. From the first, the agent returned with $2,033.36 worth of assorted furs. The second trip resulted in $3,241 in sea otter pelts.[20] (On July 8, the store received $1,307.75 worth of furs from Atka, and $999.94 from Attu.) As the general agent was preparing to sail to San Francisco for the winter, Aleuts came to the Company House on November 12, 1878, for a farewell tea. Greenbaum returned to Unalaska in the spring and began considering a move to Morzhovoi, a prosperous sea otter–hunting village on the Alaska Peninsula, where in July 1879 he purchased a house from the local priest, Father Mosei Salamatov.

FIG. 9. Turner's drawing of the *Eudora* "across from Nushagak." *L. Wayne Turner Collection.* The *Eudora* was built by Matthew Turner of San Francisco. He was a prodigious shipbuilder who designed and constructed more than two hundred vessels, several of which were used by the A.C. Company. The *Eudora* was named for the daughter of John F. Miller, president of the A.C. Company.

Turner found Unalaska "a perfect desert" as far as making collections of birds. "Weeks at a time in summer," he wrote, "and not a bird in sight."[21] He requested $50 to $75 from Baird to purchase items from local Aleuts and to pay traders who, while employed by the company, demanded money for any outside work. On August 7 he met Ivan Petroff, who was doing double duty as government census collector and a researcher for H. H. Bancroft, who was including Alaska in his series of histories of the West. Bancroft wrote that Petroff had found Turner "a valuable informant on many subjects."[22] The impression is given that this information was supplied during the time both men were at Unalaska (August to October 1878). Turner, however, had just arrived, and if he gave Petroff information it was probably about the St. Michael region. No correspondence between the two men has been located. Petroff's only comment was that "Mr. T. has made a thorough study of the Innuit and Tinneh languages and also of the habits and traditions of all tribes belonging to these families. He intends to pass five more years in this region in order to complete his studies."[23]

Turner's relations with the company deteriorated during the winter of 1878–79, and he looked forward to visiting Atka and Attu. He went so far as to request a transfer to Attu from General William B. Hazen, chief signal officer. In the meantime, he worked with André Lodoshnikoff, the second priest of the village, and with "an intelligent man of the community" to assemble his "Alyut Vocabulary." The most important surviving document from his first stay at Unalaska, it contains 842 Aleut-English words and one hundred pages of demonstratives, numerals, and sentences.[24]

Turner described his winter in a letter to Baird:

> The past winter was one round of drunkenness and carousing. I had never seen such sights as I witnessed last winter. It is worth all of a man's reputation to live here unless he is fearlessly independent, though the latter course leads much to be talked about. I have been ridiculed, maligned and slandered until I was at times nearly exasperated beyond the extremity of forgetfulness and do some plain knocking-down; good-sense prevailed on me to not adopt such a course. All of these things were done because I would not join those men (?) in their dissipations. Obstacles have been placed in my way to hinder me from prosecuting both my official work and that of collecting. A proposition was made to me to go in with a certain man to do something that would injure the Alaska Com. Co. and eventually prove disastrous to me. This proposition was made by a man then and now in their employ.
>
> Mr. Greenbaum (their agent) is a man of violent temper, very rash and cruelly unjust. He has accused me of things that I offered to prove I was not the author of; but in his ungovernable temper refused to listen or allow me to speak: while the things were told by a man in their employ and told in the presence of the agent of the Opposition company.[25]

He went into more detail in a letter to Ridgway, to whom he wrote as a confidant. They had, after all, been friends since childhood. "This Unalaska is one of the worst places on the face of the globe," he declared. He described, but did not name, two white men whom he had to periodically rescue after one or the other had fallen into a drunken stupor and might have frozen to death. One, he said, was "one of the kind of men who boasts that he can cast off his evil ways as he would a suit of clothes. He can't do it." The other used the most obscene language Turner had ever heard. This man, somewhat elderly and gray-haired, had subsequently tried to turn the company agent against him. "I have tried to render myself oblivious to all that goes on there," Turner wrote, "but it was very hard for me to do it."[26] Three years later he would tell Ridgway that the men at Ungava, Québec, were "a pleasant contrast to the drunken scamps of Alaska."[27]

In March Turner witnessed a particularly brutal act.

> A native had his arm (ulnar bone) broken, and otherwise inhumanly beaten, on the 17th of March 1879, for selling some skins to the Opposition company while the native himself had but one skin belonging to himself, the other skins he sold belonged to other natives who commissioned him to sell them for them.[28] I examined the man's arm and know that it was broken, I saw him in less than three hours after he had received the beating. The beating was done by the man left in charge as agent while Greenbaum went to San Francisco.[29]

With the return of Greenbaum in the spring, Turner asked for transportation on a company vessel to Attu. The agent assured him no vessel would be traveling that far west.

Atka

The company schooner *St. George*, however, was able to provide passage to Atka, and from May 4 to August 29, 1879, Turner lived in the Central Aleutians. Two days after arriving, he shipped five boxes of "specimens," along with a quick note to Baird, aboard the departing *St. George*.[30] At least a portion of the collection was accessioned at the Smithsonian on December 16 (number 79A00065). Sixty-one ivory carvings were listed (of which forty-nine remain). They include pegged human figures, men in kayaks hunting seals and walrus, animals, birds, "ear rings," cleats in the shape of paired otters, and exquisite miniature staffs. Everything was assigned an Atkan or Aleutian provenance, but this is problematical for a number of reasons. One is the unlikelihood of Turner amassing such a magnificent collection during his first forty-eight hours on shore while the subsequent four months produced no other ivory work at all. I suspect much that was included in this shipment was gathered during his travels with Greenbaum and during his residence at Unalaska. He had requested funds from Baird to purchase items. We know, from his later comments, that he was reluctant to leave his collections where men from the A.C. Co. might gain access to them. Several of the pieces depict skin boats of the Nunivak Island style with a marked similarity to ivory models collected prior to 1846 in the Nushagak Basin and Bristol Bay regions and that are today in the Etholén collection.[31] Furthermore, the doll-like pegged human figures are unlike the realistic figurines in the Etholén collection that were collected at Atka during the first half of the nineteenth century. Other items, however, such as the carved birds and stylized sea otter cleats, strongly suggest an Aleutian origin. The extraordinary miniature staffs, topped with finely carved birds, have been identified both as tattoo needle handles[32] and by Henry Collins as models "of the Aleut staffs carved of wood and placed in front of a house where a death has occurred."[33] This, however, was not a practice known in the Aleutians. The collection warrants a thorough study.

Henry Dirks, a German immigrant and veteran of the Civil War, who had worked for the A.C. Co. as a carpenter, had been sent to Atka as their agent in June 1878. Eventually, he established one of the leading families in that village. However, he apparently was not there (or was planning to accompany the sea otter hunters during their extended absence from the village) as Turner noted he was unable to find "a white man permanently at that place" and so "was necessitated to remain there until September, 1879." After a visit on June 27, a member of the U.S. Revenue Cutter *Richard Rush* wrote to the *Alaska Appeal* (edited by Ivan Petroff in San Francisco) that at Atka "Mr. Turner is in charge in Mr. Derke's absence. No one else there except a few old women and children."[34]

As of late June it had been raining almost daily since his arrival. "Deluges of rain and sheets of snow . . . and fearful winds" had kept him imprisoned indoors for much of the time. It rained heavily on the fourth of July when Turner heard a rarity in the Aleutians: thunder. He found himself somewhat isolated and at loose ends during weeks when the men were off hunting and the rest of the village was busy with subsistence activities.

> I passed the summer at Atka where I collected many specimens of all but birds, the latter being very scarce during the summer months as they breed on the outlying rocks and islets that are inaccessible in the only means (a large heavy boat) at my disposal: Beside this there was not a man at the village for over two months of the three and a half months that I was there. The

> able men were sea-otter hunting far to the westward and the old men at a distance preparing fish for the summer. I never was so lonesome in my life. I was everything around the house at once, cook etc. . . .[35]

He taught himself to bake bread and relayed the experience to Ridgway. It took four days to get ready and then he waited three days for the yeast to activate.

> I then took flour until I began to accuse myself of extravagance, then the way that bread or dough . . . and I did wrestle for mastership. I had to get on my knees to keep the dough from getting under my chin. It tried to get all over me and it did in spots. Well, Robert[,] the needing was the worst and the kneading the hardest. I finally succeeded in surrounding two chunks, put them into a pan and then into the stove and sprang for the clock. I had seen or heard that the bread (dough) should be baked an hour. At 60 minutes I took them out and thought they felt heavy, but supposed they would *dry out*. I wrapped them in a cloth to cool. . . . For supper I opened my treasures and found the loaves about the size, shape, color (sock off) of your hoof and fully as hefty. The stuff tasted good.[36]

His second attempt was better and the third, a success. "Now my bread," he told his friend, "is fit food for the gods."

Turner, who read French,[37] used his time to study Russian. He wrote Ridgway that he was speaking virtually no English ("excepting a few *harmless* expletives, I say harmless because they seem to do so little good"[38]). He practiced the language with local residents. "My teeth chatter," he wrote, "over some of the sesquipedalian polysyllabic conglomerations of this fearfully compound language." Nevertheless, his fluency in speaking, reading, and writing was growing. He was also learning Aleut. To Ridgway, he was diffident as to why he was studying these languages. However, he briefly explained his reason to Baird. "I have decided to spend several years yet in this country which will permit me to work out a to me very interesting problem. . . . [ellipses in the original]," he told the secretary, "the origin of these people and I believe I am on the direct course. I am rapidly acquiring the different languages spoken here and a thorough knowledge of these alone will solve it."[39] When, two years later, Turner applied for a job as a special government agent to Alaska, he noted his fluency in Russian, Eskimo, and "two Aleutian languages."[40]

His four months at Atka were notable for collections of basketry and gut sewing. In addition to a large number of baskets (selected, in part, so as to fit inside each other for convenience in shipping), there is a series of more than thirty circular woven placemats that constitute a technical tour de force.[41] Small gut workbags, numbering more than forty, display a range of sewing and decorative techniques. I suspect both the workbags and the circular mats were commissioned by Turner. (See Appendix 2.)

Unalaska Again

He returned to Unalaska on September 7, 1879, aboard the *St. George*, along with Alfred Greenbaum, Father Innokentii Shaiashnikov, and about a hundred sea otter hunters.[42] Captain Bailey described Unalaska that autumn as a fairly prosperous community with a population of 348. There were eight Americans: a deputy collector of customs, the employee of the U.S. Signal Service (Turner), and six agents and employees of the trading companies. "With the exception of the Tyone, or chief of the people, and a few designated as 'church workers,'" Bailey wrote,

> the population are all otter hunters, spending their time at the different hunting grounds extending from the Island of the Four Mountains in Seventy-two Pass, eastward as far as Sannak. Of late years a few of the people have been taken by the Alaska Commercial Company to the Seal Islands as laborers. . . . The greater part of the summer the place is almost depopulated of the male portion of the community, leaving only a few of the women and old men, who are supposed to be laying in a store of fish for the winter.

This was a situation Turner had found at Atka and would discover at Attu. A few women and children were hired to gather grass to dry for winter feed for the cattle kept by the company. The priest, the remarkable Innokentii Shaiashnikov, and two others had small gardens where they grew potatoes and turnips. The A.C. Co. "have also a small garden, but make no pretensions to raising anything but a few radishes and some lettuce, which, in the season, is only sufficient for their Sunday dinner." Summer fish had been scarce and the salmon runs were small. "Herring, however, have been plentiful," wrote Bailey,

> and if the people have the good fortune to get a whale or two they will be well supplied for the winter, as they depend more or less on the catch of whales to make food plenty during the six months of winter. Lately their friends at the Seal Islands have sent them some seal meat and blubber, and I understand that the fur company brings considerable quantities of it to Ounalaska for distribution among the people of the different stations.[43]

Turner expected trouble with the company, as he confided to Ridgway, but he felt it was unavoidable. "If I do not find *brains* in one Company I must seek them in the other, and, in so doing will only carry out my official orders. I try and not meddle with the business of either Company, hence, I have to be neutral and visit the Opposition [Western Fur and Trading Company] once in a great while."[44] His first year in the Aleutians had not been pleasant. "It was an exceptionally boisterous year," he wrote, "gale after gale rapidly succeeding the other."[45] The growing estrangement between Turner and Greenbaum soon reached a point of no return. On November 25, 1879, he wrote Baird a long letter explaining his circumstances.

> I had to grovel with Greenbaum to get passage back to Unalaska as he unhesitatingly assured me several times (in April 1879) that the vessel would not go beyond Kiska, when I subsequently learned she did go to Attou and that it was predetermined upon. For this I wrote him a very severe letter after I arrived here that resulted in my leaving their house fully determined on having nothing to do with such persons. I doubt whether the gentlemen of the home office of the A. C. Co. are aware how things go on in this country.
>
> Those persons dismissed from the employ and going down are afraid to enter complaints lest their own interest (i.e. that of receiving employment in another locality) be injured; hence

> these things are all disproved by the artful coloring given to the affair by the one against whom these complaints or charges be made.
>
> I have written a long letter to the President of the A. C. Co., together with copies of the letters that passed between Mr. Greenbaum and myself, explaining the present condition of affairs here. There is not a statement or assertion in those letters (excepting the one concerning the proposition made to me, and its nature excluded the presence of a third party) but that I can fully substantiate. Those here well know that I can prove my assertions hence they will work hard to injure me at Washington. I have received second-hand information that letters or word had been sent to Washington about me in the last winter, of a nature disposed to cast discredit on me. The amount of underhanded stratagems employed to control these people on the part of the agent of the A. C. Co. and their or his subordinates is wonderful. Any means through their religion, timidity or good-nature is brought to bear upon them.
>
> Then, let one show a sign of independence and he is quickly taught the manner of those men. . . . [He then relayed the episode of the man who had had his arm broken.]
>
> I am now living at the house of the Western Fur and Trading Company, among gentlemen, and by whom I will be well treated and I have every reason to believe that my interest will be furthered in every particular that I may desire.[16]

The Western Fur and Trading Company was an offshoot of the long-established California firm of Faulkner, Bell & Company. It had arrived in the fall of 1878 to offer the A.C. Co. its first serious competition. The captain of the U.S. Revenue Steamer *Richard Rush*, to quote him once again, described the firm in 1879: "The Western Fur and Trading Company has erected this year a fine store, with the necessary warehouses for the trade. It has provided quite an extensive stock of goods, and is competing with the former company. It has just started here, and has yet done but a small business." The new company survived until August 1883, when the A.C. Co. bought it out. The agent for the Western Fur and Trading Company in the Aleutians was Robert King. Ivan Petroff, who consulted him about Kodiak, wrote that King had been in the territory since 1868.[47] Turner thought King had "the best knowledge of Alaska of any man I have met, and besides, has done me many favors in a scientific line."[48]

Baird, no doubt, faced a serious dilemma. His friend and colleague W. H. Dall had expressed strong misgivings about the A.C. Co. in the early 1870s. He basically considered the firm an illegal monopoly and was convinced its employees had opened his private correspondence. Dall, however, had shown restraint. He had not, for example, complained in writing to the president of the company. Dall understood how Baird was forced to rely on the company for transportation for his fieldworkers and for the shipment of supplies and collections. Through the company, the Smithsonian had secured important ethnographic material, including the mummies removed from Kagamil Island in the Islands of Four Mountains. To alienate the firm would be a serious blow to further exploration and collecting.

Turner had arranged for his salary to be sent directly to his wife, Mary. She periodically wrote to Baird asking why the money was late. Occasionally, she forwarded her husband's letters to both Baird and Ridgway. In March 1880 she replied to a letter from the secretary:

> I was very sorry to hear that Lucien had got in to trouble up there. So that he will be recalled. he told me that the Agents were hard men to get along with, and he feared their [sic] would be trouble. he also said that he would do nothing against the Alaska Com. Co. as he thought a great deal of them as they had been so kind to him. I do hope Lucien is not to blame. I have written to him telling him what you wrote to me. If he is recalled will he be discharged or sent to another place please let me know all about the arrangements as I am very anxious about him, I should be very much mordified [sic] if he were discharged. I hope you will write to him and give him some advice. I would be so thankful to you.[49]

Baird answered that nothing definite had been decided about her husband, but that it was likely he would be recalled and sent to a different station. "They do not pretend to say whether he is to blame or not," he wrote, probably referring to the officers of the A.C. Co., "but as he depends upon the assistance of the Alaska Commercial Co. for the efficiency of his work, if that is withdrawn he cannot accomplish the mission for which he was sent there."[50]

In the meantime, Turner, who was oblivious that his recall was being seriously considered, prepared to depart for Attu. He had received a letter from the signal corps addressed to him there and consequently concluded that his request for transfer had been approved. "An opportunity" for transportation appeared in early June and he immediately sailed for the most distant of the Aleutian Islands.

Shortly after Turner left, Dall was again at Unalaska and in July visited Frederick Smith, formerly a member of the Western Union Telegraph Expedition, and now the deputy collector of customs. Smith was "at the same time acting in the interest of the Alaska Commercial Company as agent in the absence of Mr. Greenbaum."[51] He may have been the man Turner alluded to who broke the arm of the hunter who had dared to trade with the Western Fur and Trading Company.

A few days later Rudolph Neumann began his duties as general agent at Unalaska. He had worked at St. Michael from 1873 until his transfer to Unalaska.[52] He was related to major stockholders and officers of the company. Henry Neumann had worked at St. Michael since 1877. Neumann's family, like Greenbaum's, was Bavarian and he was conversant in Russian. A visitor in 1889 described him as well versed in the best literature of France and Germany. The library—"a pleasant sitting room" with an organ—was stocked by the company with more than three hundred books. Neumann's own rooms downstairs were "delightful." Reproductions of paintings by "great masters hung on the walls; one by Vereshagin, 'Blessing the Neva,' a watercolor, was exquisite and in this far-away once offspring of Russia seemed appropriate."[53]

Turner and Neumann had become acquainted at St. Michael when good relations existed between the company and himself. The company had supplied preserving alcohol for specimens and shipped collections to Washington.[54] Turner had asked Neumann to try an experiment with static electricity in the "great cold of winter" at St. Michael.[55] Edward Nelson had regretted Neumann's departure from St. Michael. On July 9, 1880, he wrote in his diary, "The Str. *St. Paul* left for the Seal Is. Mr. R. Neumann goes to Unalaska as Agent there so I loose my most obliging and efficient friend who has done everything in his power to aid me." The two men would continue to correspond after Nelson left Alaska.[56] Unfortunately, by the time

Fig. 10. Attu, 1880. Sketch by L. M. Turner. *L. Wayne Turner Collection.*

Neumann arrived at Unalaska, the rupture between Turner and the A.C. Co. had finalized. Turner was firmly aligned with the Western Fur and Trading Company.

Attu

The name of the vessel that took Turner to the west is unknown. From his data on birds, it appears he stopped at Chernofski and Atka before reaching Attu. Few vessels ventured that far out into the chain. The company's steamer *Dora* arrived October 17. Between then and May 11, no ship visited the island. Turner's last letter from Baird had been received in April 1880. He would not hear from the secretary for a year. As is clear from the *Descriptive Catalogue*, he spent considerable time in the company of Aleuts. In the *Catalogue* he explained how he secured many artifacts. They were "procured mostly from the point of land to the left of the entrance to Chichagof Harbor. The locality is about one hundred yards from the 'Tower of Pisa.' For many years this spot has been the principal place for growing potatoes. The implements were brought to the surface as the natives were cultivating the ground preparatory to planting."[57] A second site was alluded to in a marginal note in the initial catalog indicating items were found at sites on both sides of the harbor.

Turner's eleven months on Attu were punctuated by crises. There was the violent gale in October. The village was hit by a number of strong earthquakes. And in November the A.C. Co. attempted to have him assassinated. Turner made this accusation in September 1881, but it has not been detailed or substantiated.[58] The published abstract of his daily journal gives no clue as to what happened. No incident was mentioned in a letter he wrote to Baird from Attu on May 14, 1881, near the end of his stay.

Despite the exceptionally severe weather (according to locals, the February weather had not been so bad for several years[59]) Turner managed to explore part of the island on foot. He had three charts of the Near Islands drawn for him by one or more Attuans. When he sent them to Dall, he vouched for the accuracy of that portion of Attu over which he had hiked. If the trails drawn on the map with accompanying elevations are any indication, he must have spent considerable time exploring the island.

In September a walrus was killed by men from the village. This animal rarely ventures into the Aleutians. During February, several attempts were made by hunters to cross the strait to the Semichi Islands to hunt sea otters. One party of nineteen men returned in early April with only six skins. Formerly they had secured over one hundred. They did, however, bring news that sea urchins were once again plentiful after an absence of some years. This was a sign that the sea otter population would correspondingly increase.

In March Turner had a painful attack of "gravel." He passed two stones, "out a horrible channel in me," and began a slow recovery. On a morning in mid-May, he was at his window when he saw the schooner *Czar* enter the harbor.[60] His attention was diverted by the arrival of a rare visitor.

> I saw a bird just beneath the window on the ground, not more than seven feet from my eyes. At the first glance I supposed the bird to be *Plectrophenax nivalis* [the snow bunting]. A moment sufficed to convince me that it was not. I ran to get my gun; and, as I opened the door, of the entry-way, to get out, the door opened directly on the bird, which, with a chirp precisely like that of *Budytes flavus leucostriatus* [Siberian/Alaska yellow wagtail], flew off to a distance of 75 yards and alighted. I approached as nearly as I dared and fired at it, but failed to obtain it, as the gun was loaded with No. 3 shot. It flew off beyond the hills and was not seen again. The bustle and preparation for departure prevented me from following the bird.[61]

Fig. 11. Attu Village, c. 1874. Drawing by Henry W. Elliott, "The Village and Harbor of Attoo" in *Our Arctic Province*, opposite page 179). The Chapel of the Dormition of the Mother of God is on the left side of a small stream. The A.C. Co. trading post together with the government building are near the flagpole. The "barabara" church continued to be used until a wood-framed chapel was built in 1932.

Turner tentatively identified his visitor as a Swinhoe's or white wagtail, blown in from Kamchatka or Siberia. After the ship anchored and mail was brought ashore, Turner read a letter from Baird notifying him that he was relieved of duty and should return to Unalaska. Turner replied immediately, expressing pleasure over his accomplishments. "I am highly elated with my work at Attou," he wrote. "I think the observations will show some peculiarities not suspected in meteorology and also in ethnological lines." His termination, he felt, occurred in part because the letters he had written to Baird had been "detained unnecessarily." That is, the A.C. Co. had not forwarded them. Nevertheless, he prepared to depart. He had exhausted all his supplies and there was little in the village, where people had been "reduced to last extremities, as I am personally aware, because bad weather and stringency of A. C. Co. Their agent would not at times take American coin (silver) for flour just because the money came from the Western Fur and Trading Company."[62]

Turner left Attu in mid-May. The vessel stopped at Amchitka for a week or more, probably to deliver sea otter hunters.[63] A stop was also made at

Atka. He arrived at Unalaska on June 28 and turned over all government property to Sergeant Samuel Applegate of the signal corps. Applegate, unlike Turner and Nelson, was not enthralled with natural history. He worked for the corps for several years, perhaps until May 1886.[64] He occasionally corresponded with scientists about natural phenomena, made a few collections for the National Museum, and, after Ivan Petroff was fired from the census bureau, he wrote the description of the Aleutian region for the 1890 census. Applegate, however, had an overriding interest: he wanted to make money. After leaving the signal service, he became one of the most successful fur dealers in the Aleutians in the latter half of the century. Initially he transported sea otter hunters (mainly from Nikolski Village on Umnak Island) to various hunting grounds. As the sea otter population declined, he initiated blue fox farming. He built a fine home at Unalaska (locally dubbed "the birdcage" because of its ornate architecture), but he frequently wintered in California, to which place he eventually retired. Initially, however, he, too, confronted a hostile A.C. Company. "A friend of mine and of Applegate," wrote Turner from San Francisco on September 1, 1881, "just received a letter from Applegate in which he states that … the agents and others of the A. C. Company are so soon making things miserable for him. . . . He even now wants to come down home."[65]

As Turner left Alaska, his vessel stopped at several villages. At Belkofski in late July and at Kodiak in early August he noted flocks of snowbirds and heard the trilling warbles of abundant Alaska longspurs.[66]

The Years After Alaska

Turner arrived in Washington, D.C., on September 16. He began cataloging the artifacts he had shipped from the Aleutians.[67] W. B. Hazen requested a complete report on Alaska, and Turner asked Baird for working space at the Smithsonian. Baird's 1881 annual report noted the scope of Turner's collections (both at St. Michael and in the Aleutians):

> During the leisure hours at his disposition he collected for the National Museum one hundred and sixty species of birds—some of which were for the first time ascertained to occur within our limits, thirty species of fish, several species of mammals, nearly thirteen thousand specimens of insects, a good series of the

> land and marine shells, several thousand specimens of plants—embracing over two hundred species; and paid especial attention to collecting a complete series of implements and other articles of ethnological and archaeological character embracing over three thousand specimens, some of which were for the first time obtained. Much attention was given to the study of linguistics of the Unaleet and Malemutt Orarians, Nulato, Ingalet, and Unalashkan Aleuts. The vocabularies are comprehensive, containing not only a list of words, but much of etymologic value, stories, history, and other valuable information concerning these people, of whom little was previously known.[68]

Over the next few months Turner concentrated on the report that became *Contributions to the Natural History of Alaska.* On April 25, 1882, he signed the letter of transmittal, a sort of preface, and this indicates that he considered the work finished. In May he left the States again and spent the next two years at Ungava Bay in northern Québec, where he made important collections and observations. Before he left he wrote to his son Jesse giving him fatherly advice and encouraging him to collect birds.[69] Late in the year his wife gave birth to a daughter who lived only a short time. Although Mary Turner pasted newspaper articles about her husband into a scrapbook, nearly a decade of separation effectively ended their marriage. An eventual divorce was followed by her remarriage in 1898.

In September 1882 Turner wrote Ridgway that he hoped his report had been published, although, he said, "I fear someone else will do all he can to prevent it." The allusion was probably to Edward Nelson, who was preparing his own report on St. Michael. Twice Turner cautioned Ridgway to not allow Nelson to have access to his manuscript. When he learned of Nelson's ill health, however, he expressed sympathy. In April 1883 he wrote his friend that Baird was now saying the Smithsonian, rather than the signal service, would try to publish his report.

Turner returned to Washington for the winter of 1884–85 to organize his new collections and to write up the results of his investigations. He first focused on polishing the natural history material from Alaska, now scheduled for publication in 1886. He then turned to his Canadian research. Both Franz Boas and John Murdoch benefited from conversations with Turner about this time.[70] The Canadian work was finished by

Fig. 12. Mary Turner with sons Eugene S., eight years old, and Jesse J., fourteen years old. Taken at Mt. Carmel, Illinois, 1886. *L. Wayne Turner Collection.*

late August 1886, at which time he pressed the Smithsonian to hire him to write a complete Alaskan ethnography. "The results of my ethnological studies in Alaska, where I spent over seven years have never been written up by me; and the collections are being scattered and falsely labeled because there is, as yet nothing of a reliable nature yet published concerning them," he wrote to Baird on August 26, 1886. "It is a sad matter for me to contemplate giving up my labors in scientific subjects after having spent ten years in the Arctic regions and devoting all my energies to it among men who had no care for those not a fur trader."[71] He goes on to say that one third of *Contributions to the Natural History of Alaska* has been set in type and that the Labrador report was ready for the reviewing committee.

Six days later he again wrote to Baird, explaining that he would need four years to write a complete ethnological report on Alaska. If he confined the report to his own investigations, it could be done in two years. His financial situation had grown desperate and he needed a way to support his family. With no offer coming from Baird, he was forced to return to laying bricks. Out of practice from years in the north, he was unable to work quickly enough to stay employed. A letter to Baird in mid-September concluded in desperation: "I think that it is no more than just that I be reimbursed in full for all outlay made by myself in the Labrador and the Ungava districts and thus receive some kind of recognition for what I have done."[72] Finally in December Baird hired him for $900 to prepare a catalog of the artifacts he had sent or brought from Alaska. The *Descriptive Catalogue of Ethnological Specimens Collected by Lucien M. Turner in Alaska* was the result. At the end of the month Turner offered to sell the Smithsonian his private collection of 175 artifacts from Alaska and Canada for $725.[73]

J. W. Powell, director of the Bureau of Ethnology, noted in his report for 1886–87 that both Nelson and Turner were at work on Alaska material: Nelson on a report and Turner on a descriptive catalog. "When these two reports shall be completed," he wrote, "the amount of accurate information concerning the remarkable people to whom they relate will be materially increased."[74]

Turner continued at the Smithsonian until at least April 1887.[75] His hopes for a permanent position ended with two deaths that year. William B. Hazen, head of the U.S. Signal Service, died in January. Spencer Baird followed in August, and "Turner lost his strongest Smithsonian ally."[76] A year later a few Alaska artifacts collected by Turner were accessioned into Harvard's Peabody Museum.[77]

To those who followed Baird, Turner's limitations as a writer were perhaps more noticeable than his strengths. While recognizing the value of the information in the Ungava work, L. W. True expressed the reservation that "the manuscript will need careful editing throughout, on account of the faulty construction of sentences."[78] (This characteristic unfortunately also pervades the *Descriptive Catalogue.*) Although Turner presented portions of this material in papers for societies and journals in 1887 and 1888,

Fig. 13. L. M. Turner, c. 1886. *L. Wayne Turner Collection.* This shows Turner about the time he was completing the *Descriptive Catalogue* at the Smithsonian

the heavily edited complete work did not appear until 1894 in the *Eleventh Annual Report of the Bureau of Ethnology* (for 1889–90). *Ethnology of the Ungava District, Hudson Bay Territory* suggests what Aleutian scholarship has lost.

By the time this work was published Turner was living in the western United States and had turned to other pursuits. His arctic work had ceased. While holding various jobs in Indiana, Washington, and California, he continued collecting minerals and ethnological items. He sold specimens of western birds to Harvard University and the Smithsonian.[79] He effectively vanishes from the historical record. At the Smithsonian in 1894, G. B. Goode, director of the National Museum, declined to hire Turner to collect minerals. When directing that a "friendly letter" be written to him, he felt it necessary to remind his staff, "This is the *Labrador* Turner."[80]

By 1908 Turner was in San Francisco working as an engineer. On April 1, 1909, he checked himself into Lane Hospital suffering from emphysema and pleurisy. Seven days later he died. Unable to locate any relatives, city officials had his body removed and buried at Sunset Cemetery, a repository for paupers, the stillborn, derelicts, and the unclaimed dead. Eventually it became a public golf course and Turner's grave, along with the others, disappeared.

Turner's Place in Aleutian Ethnography

Although no ethnographic manuscripts, journals, or notes by Turner have been found, he elaborated the *Descriptive Catalogue of Ethnological Specimens Collected by Lucien M. Turner in Alaska* in the discursive style of nineteenth-century writers to include observations on Aleut life. The work is obviously a first draft. It lacks cohesion, wanders into lengthy asides, and ends just as it seems to be beginning. He included observations on Aleut society, past and present, and speculated about the origin and development of settlements in the islands. The reader is given glimpses of the naturalist himself exploring the islands and interacting with Aleut people. When supplemented with information tucked into the corners of his handful of published articles, the Aleut vocabulary, and the *Contributions to the Natural History of Alaska*, a fragmentary but important ethnography results.

When Turner appealed to Baird for funding in 1886, he may have been referring to works by Petroff and Elliott when he wrote, "It may be argued that I am not versed in the literature of the subject. I can only add that from what I have read I am pleased that I read no more on the subject." Bancroft's *History of Alaska* (substantially written by Petroff) and Elliott's *Our Arctic Province* had both appeared that year. Turner's *Contributions* also bears an 1886 publication date, but it may not have actually appeared until 1888.[81] Dall, Petroff, and Elliott have been the principle sources for information on late-nineteenth-century Aleuts. There are problems with all three.

William Healey Dall

Following publication of his *Alaska and Its Resources* in 1870, William Healey Dall (1845–1927) worked for the U.S. Coast Survey from 1871 to

1884. During this time he made four trips into the Aleutians. His first and most extensive stay was from September 23, 1871, to June 16, 1872. This was followed by briefer visits in 1873 (May to October), 1874, and 1880 (July to October). In San Francisco after his 1880 voyage, a reporter described him as "a gentleman of middle height, erect and slender, with bright, intellectual countenance aglow with nervous energy."[82] The reporter managed to elicit a rare glimpse of Dall's love for the Aleutians in a remark about wildflowers. "The Aleutian Islands abound with them," Dall said, "and when the wind is right the perfume can be noticed two or three miles off at sea." Dall was cautious and systematic in his approach, appropriate for someone mapping islands and producing charts on which sailors would depend. He became honorary curator of mollusks for the U.S. National Museum in 1880, and in 1884 he joined the U.S. Geological Survey as a paleontologist. His last visit to the chain was in 1895.

Dall's intellectual curiosity had a nineteenth-century inclusiveness, and he left his published mark across a plethora of fields in popular periodicals and scientific journals. His major Alaskan works included the early book *Alaska and Its Resources* (1870), and two lengthy reports: the curiously titled *On the Remains of Later Prehistoric Man Obtained from Caves in the Catherina Archipelago, Alaska Territory, and Especially from the Caves of the Aleutian Islands* (1878) and *On Masks, Labrets, and Certain Aboriginal Customs* (1884).

Dall has been accused of being too summary in his harsh judgments against Orthodox priests and Russian fur hunters and administrators.[83] However, he lauded much that had happened during the Russian period and gave particular praise to Father Ivan Veniaminov. He thought the Russian-American Company's "strict regulation of resident traders" and the establishment of churches and schools improved conditions for Aleuts under a policy that was "humane and wise." He referred to original Aleuts as "active, sprightly, and fond of dances and festivals . . . of immense endurance, indefatigable in the chase and inimitable in the grace, ease, and dexterity with which they managed their frail canoes." Comparing those earlier people with contemporary Aleuts, he mentioned "the iron endurance which their descendents still retain" and "the present artistic and indispensable *bidarka*."

On his return to San Francisco following his second visit to Unalaska, he gave a presentation on his archaeological discoveries to the California

Academy of Sciences, and later he enlarged the talk for an article published in 1874. In both he blamed the arrival of Americans for the acceleration of a decline among the Aleuts which, he said, had begun during the Russian period. Whereas the published article named no names, in his talk he was reported to have "deplored in indignant terms the neglect of the Government, or the Alaska Commercial Company, to provide the people with educational facilities, to the absence of which their decline is attributable."[84] The article he published stated that Aleuts "are everywhere at the complete mercy of the traders" and that "where anything has been done for their welfare, it has been prompted by evidently interested motives, and a desire to obtain a more complete control over them." Not only did Aleuts not have educational opportunities, they were "without the means of appeal to any court of justice, or any method of obtaining the protection of the laws." All of which, he concluded, was "the most serious and inexcusable blot existing on the character of the Government of the United States."[85] In 1879 he was asked to comment on a proposed bill for the appointment of justices of the peace and constables in Alaska. His primary recommendation was that any laws that were to be applied to the territory should be translated into Russian and published in bilingual editions of sufficient quantity for widespread distribution.[86]

Dall's ethnographic work was limited by his perception that interviews with contemporary Aleuts were of little value. His attempts to discover how masks were used, for example, yielded scant information. "With the present generation almost all that remains of the knowledge of these things will absolutely pass away," he wrote. "After some years pretty close intercourse a few hints have been dropped, or a few explanations vouchsafed, from time to time, but even then an inquiry would cause an immediate relapse into a wilful [sic] and stony ignorance in regard to anything of the sort."[87] A similar reticence had been attributed to Aleuts fifty years earlier by Litke following conversations with Veniaminov at Unalaska in 1827.[88] Veniaminov, however, had persevered with his inquiries. Although Dall wrote that in 1871 he had received "many details in regard to localities and customs"[89] regarding burial practices from Innokentii Shaiashnikov, he generally relied on earlier published sources. One of the "few explanations" he recorded was the use of "a little ball of bone half perforated." An elderly Aleut told him he had seen these "in his boyhood" used as a cushion at the tip of a bone lance or arrow so as not to damage the point when practicing at a target.[90]

Dall's work for the coast survey greatly improved early editions of the *Coast Pilot*. His study of tides and currents, for which he consulted Shaiashnikov, was especially important. Marcus Baker, who assisted Dall in the Aleutians, consulted Veniaminov's meteorological information at Dall's suggestion. "The original has enabled me," Baker wrote to Dall, "to detect further errors in the old pilot and to discover the trouble in many points hitherto obscure."[91] Dall contributed numerous place-names to the Aleutians. In 1871, on or near Unalaska Island, he named Expedition Island, Fish Rock (in Iliuliuk Harbor), Split Top Mountain, Arch Rock, and Spithead (near Dutch Harbor). Elsewhere he named another Arch Rock (near Sand Point) 1872, Archimandritof Rocks (in Kachemak Bay) 1880, Atkins Island (in Shumigans) 1887, Cape Bendel (Kupreanof Island) 1877, Bendel Island (Shumigans), Bluff Cape (near Belkofski) 1880, Mt. Davidson (Shumagins) 1872, Deer Island (Alaska Peninsula) 1882, Frosty Peak (Cold Bay) 1882, Herendeen Island (near Port Moller) 1874, Bay of Islands (Adak) 1873, St. Catherine Cove (northeast shore of Unimak) 1882, Sand Point (Popof Island) 1872, and Sandman Reefs (south of Belkofski) 1880. In a rare show of humor he named a dangerous submerged rock west of Sannak after the Unalaska A.C. Co. agent Captain Ernest Hennig, whom he did not trust.

Henry W. Elliott

Throughout much of his career, Henry W. Elliott (1846–1930) was embroiled in controversies surrounding fur seals. He grew from a passionate young investigator with a flair for drawing and painting into an aloof, self-assured expert over the entire territory. He first came to Alaska as a minor member of the Western Union Telegraph Expedition, where his travel was restricted to "the 'South East Strip; from Sitka down to Cape Fox."[92] Following the Alaska purchase he secured an appointment as assistant treasury agent for the Pribilof Islands. After a brief stay at Unalaska, he arrived on St. Paul Island in the late spring of 1872 as an assistant to Charles Bryant. From the beginning, however, he had his own ambitions. As he wrote to Dall, he planned to "collect as much material for a monograph of the Seal Islands as I can."[93]

In July 1872 he married Alexandra Milovidov, a member of a distinguished St. Paul family. "She is exceedingly quick and ambitious of learning," he informed Dall. "She is my voucher of no uncertain signature for the Russian language, which I now begin to use quite freely."[94] Charles Bryant commented favorably on Alexandra in a letter to Dall. "She is a very beautiful young lady, with fine health, of a very amicable temperament," he wrote before adding, "all that can be said unfavorable is that she has no education and cannot speak our language and he will have to devote a lot of time in educating her."[95] Elliott incorrectly called his wife "the daughter of the late Russian Governor of this island." He continued to refer to her as Russian and not as Aleut.

Near the end of his first stay in the Pribilofs, Elliott wrote that his monograph on the islands "will be rough for Scammon, Bryant, and others but it cannot be helped." These men, he said, had published glaringly incorrect information about the seals. Elliott was soon convinced to join forces with H. H. McIntyre, for a brief period a treasury agent but soon superintendent of the islands for the A.C. Company, and John M. Morton to have Bryant replaced with Samuel Falconer.[96] "Elliott has been made a complete fool of," wrote Dall, giving his friend the benefit of the doubt, "by playing upon his vanity and is doubtless perfectly honest in his statements." He referred to McIntyre as "that prince of scoundrels" and said Morton received $5,000 a year for doing nothing because his father, Senator Oliver Morton of Indiana, had helped the company get its original lease.[97] Dall defended Bryant against Elliott. Bryant himself continued his friendship toward the young artist and "was not sorry to see him," after Elliott paid him a visit on the East Coast. "As you know I always told you," Bryant wrote to Dall, "he was to some extent blinded by his vanity and will yet live to see it."[98] The contents of Elliott's report became known to Spencer Baird at the Smithsonian before its publication, and he urged Dall to write a formal rebuttal. "I look forward with anticipation of much enjoyment, to the criticism that I presume you will make on Elliott's Report," he wrote to Dall. "It will of course be your duty to set the whole matter in its true light."[99] Elliott had quoted a letter from Dall and consequently he felt justified in replying. He leveled his criticisms in letters to the *Boston Daily Advertiser* in July and to the *Nation* in September. He wrote that Elliott had seen only one-and-a-half percent of the territory over which he had made pronouncements and that his conclusions had been, in effect, fed to him by employees of the A.C. Company. The report was filled with "multitudinous errors and misconceptions." Elliott replied that there were but two factions in Alaska: those for the A.C. Company and those "bitterly opposed to it. To this opposition Mr. Dall belonged then, as he does now. If I sided with him I was right; if not, then wrong." Dall then accused Elliott of carrying their disagreement "into the region of purely personal controversy" and refused further discussion.[100]

Elliott maintained his ties to the Smithsonian, but Baird was clearly allied with Dall. "I always knew our lively Henry was mendacious," he wrote Dall after learning that Elliott had criticized the way the institution was caring for Dall's scientific collections, "but did not suppose he could manage to get quite so far from the truth. . . . It will give me great pleasure to choke Henry, for telling such lies & I shall take occasion to free my mind to him quite fully."[101] In later years, Dall wrote of Elliott's maps made during the early 1870s—maps made with a pocket compass and a few other supplies given to him by Dall—that "as an absolute fact they were very inaccurate as might be expected."[102] What friendship had existed was at an end.

Elliott returned to the Pribilof Islands a number of times throughout his career, notably in 1874, 1876, 1890, and 1913. Morris argued that there was no 1879 visit, the only evidence for which are a few watercolors bearing that date and which were most likely made from 1874 sketches.[103] Indeed, in *Our Arctic Province* (1886) where Elliott listed his personal observations on the islands, he referred only to visits in 1872–74 and 1876.[104] He repeated this in testimony before Congress in 1888.[105] Elliott's major writings were *A Report Upon the Condition of Affairs in the Territory of Alaska* (1875), *The Seal Islands of Alaska* (1881), and *Our Arctic Province: Alaska and the Seal Islands* (1886). Elliott is remembered as an ardent defender of the fur seals and one of the earliest conservationists. His watercolors of Alaska and the Pacific Northwest captured the landscape of a vanished era.[106] When asked his profession on March 17, 1876, by the Committee of Ways and Means investigating the Alaska Commercial Company, he said, "I am an artist."[107]

Ivan Petroff

Ivan Petroff (1842–1896) is notorious for fabricating documents that wreaked havoc in Alaskan history for decades. Somehow a man who may or may not have immigrated from Russia,[108] who had deserted at least twice from the U.S. Army, who had pretended to be "a correspondent covering the Russo-Turkish War of 1878 until it came to light that he was taking his information from the *New York Times*,"[109]—somehow this man arrived in Alaska as a treasury agent on Kodiak Island. He prepared the monumental but necessarily flawed report on Alaska for the Tenth Census, for which he visited the Aleutians from August 2 to October 9, 1878. Elliott gave himself credit for getting Petroff hired by the census department after he had met him "in the loft of Bancroft's book store" in August 1876. "He was a tall, spare blond with a low voice," wrote Elliott, "and very subdued in speaking and action; a quiet, retiring man about 35 years old then. . . . He was entirely devoid of imagination, or initiation of any sort."[110] Imagination, however, proved Petroff's signal personality trait.

Dall was among the first to recognize Petroff's disdain for facts. He had been forewarned by Petroff himself, who wrote to him in 1879 that he had once been a journalist and "one cannot handle or touch newspapers and escape quite fancy free—there is a dangerous fascination about the business."[111] *Alaska and Its Resources* had carried a "misprint" stating that Bogoslof Volcano, a few miles north of Umnak Island, had emerged from the sea in 1806 rather than in 1796 as Veniaminov had written.[112] Dall claimed that Petroff absorbed the misprint and proceeded to invent an eyewitness to the eruption. "An agent of the census by the name of Petroff," wrote Dall in 1884, "believing apparently that a little imagination would enliven his statistics, and misled by this erroneous date, gives in his report an account of an eye-witness of the phenomenon, 'born in 1797,' and 'who was one of the individuals who first noted' it, and with such terror 'that his trembling knees could scarcely carry him back to report!'"[113]

Nothing about Petroff or his writings, especially his duplicity, is ever straightforward. In *Population and Resources of Alaska*, the preliminary census report dated December 18, 1880, Petroff identified his informant as Peter Castromittin of Makushin Village, born in 1797.[114] Although Petroff alluded to the birth of Bogoslof he does not name the island but refers to Castromittin witnessing in 1806 "a new island . . . lifted bodily from the sea, 22 miles north of Oomnak Island." And then followed the astonishment and the trembling knees. Later, when Petroff fabricated the full testimony of Peter Kostromitin, he has him born at St. Paul in 1798 and moving to Biorka Village on Sedanka Island around 1818.[115] After that, during the 1824–1834 tenure of Veniaminov at Unalaska, Kostromitin (in Petroff's fantasy) witnessed the Bogoslof eruption. However, in the final *Report on the Population, Industries, and Resources of Alaska*, dated August 7, 1882, he jettisoned Kostromitin. In his place is "a Russian trader named Krukoff" who observes the birth of Bogoslof over three days beginning May 18, 1796.[116]

Kostromitin returned as an eyewitness to the birth of Bogoslof in Bancroft's *History of Alaska*, although the island is not named.[117] Both Ivan Krukoff and Peter Kostromitin were real people. Krukoff served the Russian-American Company at Unga and Unalaska and eventually settled in Nikolski, where he established a family.[118] Peter Kostromitin of Makushin Village is known to have died in 1888.[119]

Petroff's Kostromitin testimony, of such dubiousness as to render it useless, was a mere prelude. Petroff faked a first-person report from a promyshlennik named Tarakanov complete with an account of his capture by the Spanish in California.[120] He produced an entire journal, which he attributed to the martyred Father Iuvenilii.[121] Having manufactured these astounding fictions and having collected wonderful firsthand information, Petroff then used it all to write major portions of Bancroft's *History of Alaska*, a work that remained unchallenged for decades.

After stints as a fur trader on Kodiak Island from 1883 to 1888[122] and a newspaper editor in San Francisco, he was hired to collect data for the 1890 census and to translate Russian documents for the United States in its case against Great Britain in the 1890–1892 fur seal arbitration hearings in Paris. He collected much of the census data. The extent of his travel for this project has not been determined.[123] His translations were published, and it was soon revealed that, perhaps guided by the fictive Iuvenilii, Tarakanov, and Kostromitin, Petroff had interpolated statements and slanted his translations to booster the case of the United States. Although Elliott insisted Petroff could not have planned the falsification—"he was not bright enough himself, or daring enough to do it . . . if some one higher in official rank than himself had not suggested, or even directed it"[124]—Petroff confessed to "gross inaccuracies and interpolations, amounting to falsification."[125] He was fired by an embarrassed State Department and by the superintendent of the census. His name was expunged from the census although his ghostly hand can be seen from time to time in the finished work, especially in passages related to the Aleutian Islands. The American government ascribed his behavior to insanity and was quite content to have him disappear.[126] He plunged into oblivion, leaving various manuscripts to find their way into the Bancroft Library, where they lurk like so much quicksand for unsuspecting researchers.[127]

For all his shenanigans, Petroff had not only a respect for Aleut people but also an admiration for their abilities. His observations, fortunately or unfortunately, cannot be ignored offhand. His empathy was greater than Dall's or Elliott's, and he showed a genuine concern over conditions in the chain. He drew attention to the harmful effect that white men were having on sea otter hunting in the Unga/Belkofski area, whereas Elliott extolled the carefree and "entirely happy" white male fishermen and miners who had come to the area. In an 1880 interview with President Rutherford B. Hayes on behalf of the newly appointed Bishop Nestor of the Orthodox church (an interview reported but not yet confirmed), Petroff was said to have urged the establishment of schools among the Aleut and to have declared that they "are today less fitted to hold their own among their new countrymen than they were 13 years ago." He was reported to have told the president, "Should a full Territorial Government be bestowed upon Alaska this element of the population would be in danger of suffering neglect, because they are not fitted to take part in a Representative Government until fine educational facilities are extended to them, and the English language is introduced among them."[128] Petroff's warning would be realized in succeeding decades.

When published in 1886, both Elliott's *Our Arctic Province* and Bancroft's *History of Alaska* met unfavorable reviews by Dall. Bancroft's work appeared first. Dall's anonymous review in *Science* cautioned about the section covering the years prior to 1799 where "much of the material is of only approximate accuracy." The reviewer found the account of the Russian-American Company's tenure "sufficiently accurate" if lacking in analysis. It was more "materials for history, than history" itself. The period after 1867 was the weakest of all. Referring to the few years before the Alaska Commercial Company received the Pribilof Islands contract for sealing, the review stated, "The era of violent and unrestrained competition in this case, however, lasted only two or three years; while the monopoly which succeeded, though more confined in scope than that of the Russian company, does not differ in its essential characters, and is still in operation." It went on to say, as the criticism moderated, "This period, however, is so much nearer the historian, so many of the actors in it are still in the active pursuit of their business, and the passions and prejudices engendered by recent rivalry are still so hot, that historical impartiality is not to be expected."[129] Dall knew from the start that Petroff had written much of Bancroft's history as he had been in correspondence with him. As noted previously, he had been suspicious of the researcher's honesty as early as 1884.

A popular and frequently reprinted example of nineteenth-century travel literature, Elliott's *Our Arctic Province* has been regarded "as an Alaskan classic."[130] With its publication, Elliott's fame was firmly established. Dall, however, was not impressed. His anonymous review began, "This handsomely illustrated and printed volume is evidently intended for a popular audience. Little of its contents is new." (Elliott confirmed this opinion in a later issue of *Science*: "'Our arctic province' was not written for the eye or ear of scientific specialists."[131]) Dall was very familiar with Elliott's scientific work and government reports.

> The part of the work which is a re-arrangement of matter original with others is naturally less satisfactory than that on the Aleutian and Seal islands, where the author is at home in the scenes, he, for the most part, very fairly and accurately describes. . . . Apart from the biology of the fur-seals and birds of the Seal Islands, the natural history of the book is very shaky, and the anthropology almost a minus quantity. But it is hardly worth while to lay much stress on its deficiencies from a scientific stand-point, since it is hardly likely to be consulted for precise data of that sort. Its historical errors are less numerous but more important. To give a single instance, the author repeats the error of Petroff in Bancroft's "Alaska" by stating that in 1868 Messrs. Hutchinson and Morgan passed the season in exclusive control of the sealing on St. George and St. Paul islands. As a matter of fact, there were five or more competing companies.[132]

This last complaint was one that Dall frequently made.[133]

Parallel passages in *Our Arctic Province* and in Petroff's successive narratives for the 1880 census appear with disturbing regularity. Less obvious, but still present, are similarities between Petroff's reports and Elliott's 1875 *A Report Upon the Condition of Affairs in the Territory of Alaska*. Petroff's notoriety demands his statements find verification in other sources. Dall, in the review quoted above, found Elliott's Aleutian material the most satisfactory of any part of the book since Elliott was "at home in the scenes, he, for the most part, very fairly and accurately describes." But things are in a sorry state if much of what we get from an eyewitness are echoes and repetitions of Petroff. It is often as though the two works were written by the same hand. Elliott claimed he helped Petroff "shape up" his final report.[134] Either Petroff was the recipient of extensive ghostwriting by Elliott or Elliott later borrowed form, phrases, and substance from Petroff, whose work appeared five years before *Our Arctic Province.* Elliott occasionally referenced Petroff. For example, his allusion to a visit to Morzhovoi (Protassov) "by an agent of the Government in 1880" and the agent's "shocked" description clearly refers to Petroff."[135] At other times he wrote about events or conditions that occurred after Petroff's visit. One example is his discussion (however confused) of Bishop Nestor establishing his headquarters at Unalaska. In Petroff, this change of residence is only anticipated.[136] Elliott used Petroff's account of the latter's 1878 "centennial" visit to English Bay on Unalaska Island[137] to describe his own "stroll" to the bay "where Captain Cook anchored and refitted in 1778."[138] However romanticized and exaggerated Petroff's account was, he had actually visited that harbor although not on the date he later claimed.[139] Elliott's description, to anyone familiar with Beaver Inlet, is an obvious armchair fabrication.

Some of the parallel instances between these two writers are placed in Table 2, but here are three examples (with similarities indicated by italics). When Petroff described Attu he wrote in 1882: "The *extreme western settlement* of the United States, or of North America, is located on the island of Attoo. This was *the first land made and discovered by the Russians* as they navigated eastward from the Commander Islands, on the coast of Kamchatka."[140] In Elliott we find: "Attoo is the *extreme western town* which is or can be located on the North American continent. It is the *first land made and discovered by the Russians,* as they became acquainted with the Aleutian chain."[141] (In Petroff's preliminary 1880 report, the last phrase is identical to Elliott's.)

Describing general living conditions, Petroff wrote: "*As they live today, they are married and sustain the relation of husband and wife,* with families, more or less; *each family, as a rule, living in its own hut, or barrabara. They have long, long ago ceased to dress themselves in skins.*"[142] And in Elliott is found, "*As they live here to-day, they are married and sustain* very faithfully *the relation of husband and wife. Each family, as a rule, has its own hut or barrabora. They have long, long ago ceased to dress in skins.*"[143]

In the last example, discussing clothing, note the order of details with similar but not identical wording: 1) caps, 2) legacy of Russian uniforms, 3) plainness of dress, 4) kamleikas and baidarkas, and 5) goose-quill embroidery. First, Petroff:

> *[1]* Broad-crowned caps with a red band are still much in vogue among the male exquisites, evidently *[2]* a legacy of former times, when Russian uniforms were seen on these shores. As a rule, however, *[3]* the males dress soberly, with but little attention to display, color, or ornamentation, though they lavish some skill and taste in trimming their waterproof garments used in the case or in traveling; *[4]* as also the seams of the 'kamleikas,' the skin boots, and other waterproof covers, including those of their canoes and bidarkas, the latter being frequently embellished with tufts of gaily colored sea-bird feathers and delicate lines of *[5]* goose quill embroidery.[144]

And now, Elliott:

> *[1]*...they universally wear low-crowned, leather-peaked caps, to which they love to add a gay red-ribbon band, suggested most likely *[2]* by the recollection which they have of that gorgeous regalia of the Russian army and naval officers, who were wont to appear in full dress very often when among them in olden times.
>
> *[3]* The Aleutian men dress very plainly, young and old alike, little or no attention being given by them to details of color or ornamentation, as is the common usage and practice of most semi-civilized races; but they do lavish a great deal of care and skill in the decoration *[4]* of their antique 'kamlaykas,' 'tarbosars,' and their bidarkas: the seams of these garments and the boats are frequently embellished with gay tufts of gaily colored sea-bird feathers and lines of *[5]* goose-quill embroidery.[145]

Elliott was accused of plagiarizing from an obscure Canadian geological survey report for a chapter in *Our Arctic Province*. He successfully refuted these accusations.[146] Nevertheless, as a source for reliable ethnography, Elliott is as suspect as Petroff. That is, it is impossible to use the observations of one to confirm or refute statements from the other.

Table 2: Selected Parallels between Petroff and Elliott

Subject	Pages in **Petroff** (1880)	Pages in **Elliott** (1886)
Physical characteristics	9–10	163–164
Appearance of women	10	133–134
Use of shawls	11	165–166
Interior and furnishings of barabara	11–12	166–168
Soap	11	135
Diet (order of items)	12	168
Husband and wife relationship	12–13	169–170
Temperament	12–13	136–37
"Kvass" and "Hilarious dancing"	14–15	174–175
Attu	15–16	179–180
Atka	16–17	181–182
Transfer of remains of Atkan priest	17	182
Makushin	19	160–161
Akutan sea otter hunters (order of details)	16–17	181
Akun	21–22	154
Belkofski	22–23	119
Morzhovoi	23–24	121–122
Biorka	21	177

Dall may not have done much to encourage Turner's work, but, as far as I have discovered, he never expressed doubt about its accuracy or its ultimate value. The *Descriptive Catalogue* was an internal Smithsonian document. It was used by other authors, notably Otis T. Mason and Walter Hough, who wrote, "The latest information about the Aleutian Islanders is given in a manuscript by the careful explorer, Mr. Lucien M. Turner."[147]

Because of Turner's statement that the October 1880 storm at Attu had resulted in "all records written with ink [being] in most instances hopelessly ruined," it makes sense to ask what material he had with which to write an Aleutian ethnography. While at Fort Chimo on Ungava Bay in 1883, he wrote, "The notes etc. made on my Alaskan birds are, in part, through an inattention by me, here, and part in a box of private papers which were turned over to be kept for me at the Smithsonian. It would be impossible for me to direct you where to find them. If the matter could rest until I return next year I shall attend to it immediately on my return."[148] And in January 1886 he answered a request from Ridgway with the note, "In reply to your request of Jan. 25th I would state that the data of the Unalashkan collection can be given within a few days after I receive from you the original numbers of the specimens for which the data are desired."[149] All of this suggests he had extensive Aleutian notes. In addition, not all of his earlier ethnographic material had perished in the Attu storm. The 1878–79 Aleut-English vocabulary from Unalaska exists with a few ethnographic tidbits incorporated into definitions. Plants collected prior to the storm on Attu are in the U.S. National Herbarium, although, as Hultén noted, some were relabeled from memory.

Turner's ethnographical work in the Aleutians, however scattered, unfocused, and unfinished, remains unique and is set apart from the work of Dall, Elliott, and Petroff for three primary reasons. First, he alone made a concerted effort to learn Aleut and could, therefore, more or less communicate directly with the local population. (Although Elliott married Alexandra Milovidov of the Pribilof Islands, there is no indication he learned Aleut. Indeed, he referred to his wife as his authority in things Russian—not Aleut.) Turner, as detailed earlier, also began a study of Russian while in the Aleutians. When he came to write the *Descriptive Catalogue,* however, it is unknown whether he consulted Veniaminov's *Notes on the Islands of the Unalashka District* in the original or relied on Petroff's translations published in the census reports. He may have used both. He references Berkh's *A Chronological History of the Discovery of the Aleutian Islands* with the correct date of publication (1823) while Bancroft (Petroff), referring to the same event, gives the publication an erroneous 1820 date.[150] This suggests Turner may have had the Russian publication at hand.

Second, Turner spent more continuous time in the Aleutians than other researchers, living for extended periods in three primary Aleut communities in the eastern, central, and western islands. He interacted with Aleuts on a day-to-day basis, shared some of their difficulties, and felt at home enough to joke with them. This was a familiarity that might occasionally elicit information never offered to the more aloof Dall and Elliott. After the October storm, he had eight months remaining at Attu to record information. The extant observations from Attu, however fragmentary, must be considered unique and irreplaceable, because this was the most isolated and impoverished of Aleut communities, visited least and least studied.

And finally, the collections he made in the Aleutians surpass all others from the late nineteenth century. The items he shipped from the chain provide researchers and contemporary Unangan glimpses into an irrecoverable past. It is this collection that forms Turner's primary legacy. Continuing analysis of it will reveal new aspects about their culture. Turner's extant ethnographic notes are directly tied to his collections of natural history. A careful reading of them, as fragmentary and unpolished as the least of the stone implements he cataloged, will shed light on both the Aleuts near the end of the nineteenth century and those outsiders who lived among them. It is our misfortune that neither he nor anyone else ever wrote a cohesive and comprehensive ethnography that might have done for the latter half of the nineteenth century what Veniaminov's *Notes on the Islands of the Unalashka District* did for the earlier years of that century. The magnitude of this loss is seen with the realization that twenty-five years after 1886 the foundations of Aleut life had radically shifted. Skilled kayaking sea otter hunters had become land-bound fox farmers. Any hope of retrieving an ethnography for that earlier period was gone. We are left, as Turner himself wrote, with only glimpses of "people whose characters are set before us by their works and not by their words."

A Note on the Text

The *Descriptive Catalogue of Ethnological Specimens Collected by Lucien M. Turner in Alaska* is in the National Anthropological Archives, Smithsonian Institution, Manuscript 7197. It forms the core of this work. What appears to be an introduction to the Aleutian Islands is found about a third of the way into the original 220 pages. This edition begins with that section. The first seventy-two pages of the *Catalogue* is a partially annotated list of stone, bone, wood, and grass artifacts that Turner organized into series. Material from this has been integrated into the main text. Each paragraph in the text is followed either by bracketed page numbers from the *Descriptive Catalogue* or by identification from other sources. Paragraphs excerpted from works other than the *Descriptive Catalogue* are preceded by an asterisk. Editorial comments are bracketed. All section and chapter titles are mine. Works by Turner are identified as follows:

C = *Contributions to the Natural History of Alaska.* Results of investigations made chiefly in the Yukon District and the Aleutian Islands; conducted under the auspices of the Signal Service, United States Army, extending from May 1874 to August 1881 (Washington, DC: Government Printing Office, 1886).

E = "Ethnology of the Ungava District, Hudson Bay Territory." In *Eleventh Annual Report of the Bureau of Ethnology, 1889–90,* edited by J. W. Powell, pp. 159–350 (Washington, DC: Government Printing Office, 1894). (Reprinted 2002 by the Smithsonian Institution with a foreword by Robert Watt and an introduction by Stephen Loring as part of the Classics of Smithsonian Anthropology Series.)

N = "Notes on the Birds of the Nearer Islands, Alaska." *The Auk*, II, no. 2 (April 1885): 154–59.

R = "Review of Dr. H. Rink's Paper on the East Greenlanders." Extracted from the *American Naturalist*, August 1887, pp. 748–55.

V = *Alyut-English Vocabulary* (1878–79), National Anthropological Archives, Smithsonian Institution, Washington, DC, Manuscript 2505-c.

Turner's spellings of place-names have been retained despite inconsistencies (*Attoo* and *Attu*) with the exception that acute accent marks have been removed (Amchítka, Iliúliuk, Koróvinsky, Amák, Unímak, Unálga, Akután). These were not used in the *Catalogue* and their application in *Contributions* was not consistent. His occasional spellings for St. Michael and St. Mathew Island (St. Michael's, St. Mathew's Island) have also been kept.

The few ethnographic comments found in Turner's 1878–79 Aleut-English vocabulary have been incorporated into this edition. The short vocabulary he appended to the *Catalogue* has not been been included as Bergsland used the longer vocabulary in the *Aleut Dictionary: Unangam Tunudgusiis.*

An Aleutian Ethnography

1

General Description of the Aleutian Islands

Without a description of the physical features of the area under consideration it will be impossible to arrive at a proper conception of the geographical factors influencing the people whose characters are set before us by their works and not by their words. The Aleutian Islands form a vast chain, more or less disconnected, extending east and west from longitude about one hundred and sixty-three degrees west of Greenwich to longitude nearly one hundred and eighty-seven and a half west of Greenwich. The central portion of the chain decurving southerly and all of the islands embraced within the parallels of fifty-five and fifty-one and a half degrees north; so that the length of the entire chain from the western end of the mainland at Isanotsky (or "False") Pass to the western end of Cape Wrangell, the westernmost land of the United States, is slightly more than 1000 miles when following the trend of the chain. The north and south breadth of the area is scarcely more than two hundred miles. [73–74]

*The principal islands of the chain have their longer axis nearly in the same direction as that of the decurvature of the entire chain, the shorter axis lying to the eastward of north. The islands in the central part present a slight exception to these directions. [C:14]

*The peninsula of Aliaska is simply a continuation of the Alaskan Mountains, forming a comparatively long, narrow strip of land, extending nearly northeast and southwest. It is very mountainous, much broken into short ranges, usually several peaks on a wide base, or else isolated mountains often of great height, the portion of those over 2,800 feet high being destitute of vegetation. These mountains are quite abrupt on the southern side, and have numerous bays, coves, and arms of the sea thrust among them, even to their bases. The northern shore of the peninsula of Aliaska is a low, varied strip of land, a few miles to a few rods in width, the eastern end of the north side being generally wider and of less elevation, somewhat approaching the general characters of the tundras of the Yukon District. The Aleutian Islands are but an interrupted continuation of the Aliaskan Peninsula. [C:14]

An inspection of a map of Alaska will reveal the fact that the Aleutian Islands are simply a prolongation of the Rocky Mountains, bending to the westward and interrupted by precipitous breaks, of greater or less width in their trends, and finally continuing through the eastern portion of Asia. The general features of the chain are essentially the same, the principal differences consisting in the variable heights of the land, ranging from few feet above sea-level to towering mountain tops lifting their heads many thousand feet. The limit of perpetual snow is but little above 1800 feet and the summits of the higher peaks seldom change the white mantle that glistens in the few hours of absent clouds hovering around the loftier heights. [74–75]

The shores are mostly abrupt or precipitous, difficult of approach except where the deeply indented coast has preserved the falling masses of rock and stones rolled into shingle and boulders of all sizes by the constant lashings of the sea waves impelled by the relentless fury of an ever changing atmosphere producing violent storms of long duration that cause the very foundations of the mountain bases to tremble under the crushing impetuosity of the surging billows of an ever angry ocean. [75–76]

The geological characters of these islands have been repeatedly described by others and need not be referred to here. Each of the larger islands has the same extension as the entire chain or from east to west; the larger islands usually beginning or ending with islets of small size and often barren rock only. Many deep indentations extend into the larger islands often nearly cutting them in two, connected by low swales of but few feet above sea-level. The central portion of the islands are mountainous and of every possible diversity of surface; ravines of many hundred feet on either side slope toward the sea and through them course streams proportionate to the amount of snow melting and draining into the valley below. The central islands of the chain are somewhat less abrupt and precipitous on their shores than the eastern islands. The extreme height of the mountains somewhat less and so continuing to the westward where the water passages are wider and the sea less violent. [76–77]

*These islands are, generally speaking, very mountainous (among them several active volcanoes, some of them very high), their sides generally abrupt, containing innumerable indentations, such as deep bays and coves—these more abundant on the northern and eastern sides than on the southern and western. (Nearly all the anchorages, and the villages, with few exceptions, are on the north and east sides of the islands.) There is but little level ground on any of the islands, that little being formed at the entrance to the larger valleys flanked by high mountains on either side, from which descend innumerable small streams from the summits of the mountains crowned, in most instances, with eternal snows. These streams unite to form creeks of slight depth and width, having a short course before they reach the sea. Lakes of variable size are to be found on nearly all the islands, some of quite large area being situated on the higher hills. The hardness of the rocks and the slight degree by which they are held in solution, renders the water flowing over them remarkably pure and of excellence for drinking purposes. I much doubt if water from any part of the globe makes better tea. [C:14]

Vegetation covers the greater part of the lowlands and consists principally of annuals of many species. The arboreal or truly woody character of plant life is meager indeed, confined to a few species of *Salix*, rarely attaining a diameter of stem exceeding two or three inches and so distorted in growth that it is not possible to find a piece two feet in straight length. The alders, *Alnus*, seldom surpass the willows in size and these possess the same distorted character as those mentioned. *Vaccinium*, *Rubus* and *Empetrum* are the principal growths of bushes and these flourish on all favorable spots; the latter covering many acres in a single patch of vivid green and luxuriant growth. [77–78]

The greater portion of the vegetation of the Aleutian islands is below five-hundred feet from sea-level. Between 500 and 800 feet elevation the decrease is marked and at 1000 feet only the hardiest species grow. At 1200 to 1500 feet only the lichens and mosses with occasionally a flowering plant may be found. Above 1500 feet only the scantiest lichens cling tenaciously to the wind swept rocks. . . . But few spots are so favorably situated and contain enough fertile soil as to produce the hardier character of vegetables such as potatoes, radishes, turnips, lettuce and spinach. Turnips alone thrive well and the inability to procure a change of potatoes for seed causes those often replanted to deteriorate and become not only small but watery. [79, 81–82]

Luxuriant patches of grass, whose growth has excited the wonder and words of all who have seen them, flourish in favorable situations, but as these areas are quite restricted and the amount of rain falling at the time when such grasses are fit to be cut prevents the rearing of cattle and sheep on the islands to a greater extent than to supply an occasional beef and a limited flow of milk from the cows kept only by the trading company and the resident priest at Unalashka alone; even there necessitating hay and other food to be brought from San Francisco to sustain the starving creatures housed for fully six months in the year. The grasses are sufficiently nutritious to fatten the beef animals brought up in the spring and turned loose until the fall or when the weather of winter sets in for earnest. [82]

From the evidence before us we must conclude that no great change has occurred on the entire chain of islands, probably far less than has happened in the middle latitudes of the United States for there the treeless areas have been encroached upon until now the tree producing area is fully twice as great as it was in the beginning of the eighteenth century. Nothing can occur to effect a change in the primitive aspect of the Aleutian Islands. [83]

While there is little probability that the climate of this region has changed within the past five hundred years to any perceptible degree[,] the present atmospheric conditions may be taken as a general index of the past. The thermometer seldom ranges to zero on the eastern islands; very rarely below five degrees at Unalashka and slightly above that for the western islands where a minimum of eight degrees has not been recorded. The summer heat seldom going above seventy-eight degrees and then only for a few hours at a time; so that a mean temperature for the islands is not far from forty degrees. [79–80]

The preponderance of cloudy weather caused by the innumerable currents swashing through the passes, the warmer water from the Pacific commingling with the cold water of Bering Sea[,] causes the air to be filled with vapors surcharged and liable to precipitate at an elevation of only a few hundred feet. The proportion of cloudy weather is about eight-tenths and fair weather only fifteen-hundredths while clear days are rare indeed. The condensation of vapor or its dissipation frequently takes place from eight to ten in the evening so that the nights are more often clear than the days. The amount of precipitation varies on the different islands. The annual rainfall at Unalashka exceeds one-hundred feet [sic] while that at Attu is certainly not greater than fifty-five feet [sic] annually. [80–81][1]

The Near Islands

*The localities here included embrace the islands of Attoo, Agattoo, and Semechi. . . . Semechi is the smallest of the three, and lies about twenty-three miles to the southeast of Attoo. It is quite low on the southern side, where are found innumerable ponds and lakes, some of the latter being of considerable area. The low-grounds are covered with vegetation of various kinds, and the shallower ponds, in some instances, yield vegetable food in abundance for the great numbers of Ducks and Geese which breed there. On the northern side of the island the shore is precipitous, rising at several localities several hundred feet, and abounds in niches, ledges, and crevices where breed vast numbers of Puffins, Auks, Murres, and Guillemots, which find an abundance of food in the neighboring sea. [N:154–155][2]

*Agattoo Island forms the southwest portion of the group, and is of considerable size, being but slightly less than Attoo, and much larger than Semechi. The shores of this island are more elevated and abrupt, having many indentations, at the head of which small streams issue from the larger lakes. The general character of the surface is undulating, though much broken, being everywhere intersected by a network of ravines and valleys, separating hills and mountains, some of which latter are over 1600 feet in height. These valleys and the lower grounds contain many lakes, in which is found an abundance of fresh-water vegetation. High grasses and other plants crown the cliffs and occupy the tops of rocks, affording suitable nesting places for various Auks and Puffins. Thousands of Geese are also hatched here. Here too the Snowy Owl and two species of Hawks breed, the young of the water birds affording them abundant food. The only mammals occurring on either Semechi or Agattoo are marine species—the sea-otter, sea-lion, some three species of hair-seals. An occasional fur-seal may also be seen in the vicinity. [N:155]

*Attoo is the largest of the group, and has an east and west extension of nearly thirty-five miles, and a breadth of nearly fourteen miles. The shore is remarkably indented, often for several miles, forming bays and coves. The shores are mostly abrupt, with but little beach excepting in certain places on portions of the northern side and eastern end of the island, where several wide-mouthed valleys gradually rise toward the hillsides, which in most instances are very steep. Attoo is much more mountainous than either of the other islands of the group. The mountains are high, rising in a few instances above 2500 feet, and are accessible only by most fatiguing ascents, the approaches to the summits being steep and difficult. The mountain range extends length-wise through the island, with several spurs of irregular height shooting off at various angles from the main range. The valleys, some of which are quite broad, are traversed by streams, two of which, issuing from large lakes, are of great size. The sides of the hills and the valleys are plentifully clothed with vegetation, and many berries are to be found. In the fall of the year these are the favorite feeding-grounds of thousands of Geese, a few of which are hatched on Semechi but the greater part on Agattoo. The Geese, feeding on the ripening berries in late August, September, and October, rapidly fatten after their moult and become so heavy that I have known them to burst their skins in falling when shot on the wing. The high bluffs afford the Cormorants a safe breeding-place; the grassy ledges near the water form convenient nesting sites for Eiders; and in the recesses of the rocks Auks and Puffins abound. Here blue foxes (*Vulpes lagopus*) are found in numbers. The natives have very wisely restricted the foxes to this large island, otherwise they would not be able to procure the birds—Puffins and Guillemots—from whose skins they make a long garment for protection against the cold of winter. . . . [N:155–156]

*These islands possess a warmer climate than the eastern portions of the Aleutian Chain, the winter temperature never falling as low as zero. The lowest degree of cold recorded by me was 10.5° F., and this in the coldest season the natives could remember. The summer is often bright and warm; the maximum temperature reaching 76° F. Much cloudy weather occurs at times, but it is generally fair from July to October. Rain falls every month in the year, although March is known as the snow month. [See Chapter 17.] Fogs often continue for several days at a time, but seldom overhang the land; Semechi and Agattoo, however, are more foggy than Attoo. Rain often falls heavily, but only for brief intervals. Storms are often excessively severe, and during the winter are of frequent occurrence, the winds from the southwest and southeast being often very violent, causing a terrible sea to dash against the shores. [N:156]

2

Settlements in 1878

At the present time the distribution of the Aleut is confined alone to the following villages and nowhere else are they to be found. Unfortunately the loose application of the term Aleut, as applied by the Russians[,] has been employed in an abused manner by several American writers, who have had little opportunity to confirm their assertions. [216–217]

The westernmost people are those who dwell exclusively on the island of Attu and have no permanent settlement on any other island of the group. [217]

The next are the Atkhan Aleut who have a single village on the island of Atkha and no other outside, permanent village. [217]

The third are the Umnak Aleut who dwell on the island of that name. [217]

The fourth are the Unalashkans who dwell on that island and Borka [Sedanka Island] to the eastward but two miles. [217]

The fifth are the Akutan Aleut who dwell on the island of that name. The sixth are the Akun Aleut who dwell on the island of that name and are so intimately connected with the Akutan people that they may be considered as one people. [218]

The seventh are the Morzhovie Aleut dwelling on the western extremity of Aliaska and inside of Isanotsky (or "False") Pass. [218]

The eighth are the aggregations of Aleut dwelling on Sannakh Island. These are brought from all parts of the Aleut population and have here but few permanent dwellings being for the most part temporarily inhabited by sea-otter hunting parties. [218]

The next (or ninth) are those of Belkovsky dwelling on the mainland of the Peninsula of Aliaska. [218]

The tenth are the Aleut of Unga and Korovin Islands, mainly peopled from the Belkovsky Aleut and also include the Aleut of Protasof [Morzhovoi] settlement and Vosnessensky Island. The Belkovsky Aleut as here included with the Unga Aleut are the most eastern of those people and [who] have an east and west extension of nearly 1300 miles. [219]

The total population does not exceed more than 2500 souls. [219]

The eleventh subdivision include the Aleut of the Pribylof Islands. These latter are recruited as necessity requires from any position of the area inhabited by the Aleut. [219]

East of the 157th degree of longitude the Aleut do not dwell on the south side of the Aliaskan Peninsula; and, on the north side the eastern distribution does not extend farther than the 163d degree of longitude for permanent dwellings. To the east of the boundaries as thus defined comes an interspace beyond which are the true Mainland and Kadiak Innuit with which this paper has little to do. [219–220]

[A March 1878 census partially in Greenbaum's hand, compiled from material provided by Father Innokentii Shaiashnikov and omitting the Pribilof Islands, gives a total population of 2,049. The Tenth Census (1880) gives 1,997. When the population for the Pribilof Islands is added to each, the totals are close to Turner's estimate of not more than 2,500: 2,421 and 2,369. Greenbaum listed "church officials & families," "Creoles," "Aleuts," and "Widows and Orphans" separately, but all are combined in the following table. Non-natives were excluded from the census for the most part. The 1880 U.S. census listed "Creoles" and "Aleuts" separately, but they are combined here with the number of white residents excluded but indicated in parentheses.]

Table 3: Population of the Aleutian Islands, 1878, 1880

Village	1878 Greenbaum Census	1880 Census
Attu	98	106 (+1)
Atka	236	234 (+2)
Nikolski	107	125 (+2)
Chernofski	86	98 (+3)
Kashega	76	73 (+1)
Makushin	59	61 (+1)
Unalaska (Iliuliuk)	456	392 (+14)
Biorka	141	139 (+1)
Akutan	86	63 (+2)
Akun	38	54 (+1)
Avatanak	15	19
Belkofski	275	257 (+11)
Nikolaevskoe	31	43
Wosnesenski	20	21 (+1)
Unga	170	170 (+15)
Korovenski	35	44
Morzhovoi	120	98 (+2)
St. Paul	284	284 (+14)
St. George	88	88 (+4)
Total	**2,421**	**2,369**

Greenbaum census: A.C. Co. Records, 1868-1911, box 152, folder 1578, archives of the Arctic and Polar Regions Collection of the Elmer E. Rasmuson Library, University of Alaska Fairbanks. **1880 census:** Ivan Petroff, *A Report on the Population, Industries, and Resources of Alaska,* 47th Congress, 2d Session. House Misc. Doc., Vol. 13, No. 42, part 8. Serial 2136 (Washington, DC: Government Printing Office, 1884), 23.

3

Houses

The earliest inhabitants of those islands had no shelters constructed by the hand of man. The numerous caves afforded a protection from storm until the community became so great as to necessitate the removal of a portion of the people to another natural shelter until in time all of those places were occupied with a more or less numerous family. Rarity of attack from their enemies and safety of exposed shelters, probably constructed in resemblance to their cave dwellings, caused the latter to be erected in the immediate vicinity of their former abodes. The ocean currents cast wood upon the shores but seldom in such quantity and place as to render it available for building purposes. The supply being limited recourse was had to the next suitable material. The great ribs of the cast up whales, the living species abounding in the adjacent waters, were placed on end and the curvature of those bones admirably adapted them to form a hollow structure whose sides and interspaces needed to be filled in with sod or turf to complete the dwelling large enough for a community of a dozen souls. [93–94]

Social customs compelled a division of the household or else an enlargement of the structure. The latter appears to have been the general rule, doubtless provided by the welfare of the people and a measure of safety in case of attack for in the scattered places occupied by the people the alarm could not be given. From the conical form of shelter was evolved the square and later the oblong. Each of the latter having a square hole in the center of the roof to admit light and air[,] for fuel was too scarce to have a door at the side as was the case when the conical form was erected. [94–95]

The means of entering was by a notched log resting against the side of the hole next to the sea. This log was taken down at night and none was admitted whose voice was not known. The first act in the morning was to place the log in position for egress of the occupants of the dwelling. [95]

The size of the oblong structures was, in some locations, very great. The ruins yet visible on the more eastern islands indicating a length and breadth of domicile extending several hundred feet. They were subdivided into spaces occupied by different families so that the inhabitants of a single structure amounted to more than a hundred persons. [95–96]

These communal dwellings were successively added to as the necessities of room were required. Finally the central parts became a sort of work-shop wherein was prepared all manner of implements of the chase and war. [96]

But little wood was employed in the construction of the frame of these houses. The roof alone was partly of logs laid across on erect poles for their support, and from one of these supports to another was often the partition denoting the space for a family. [96]

A new structure was begun when the old one showed such signs of decay as to be beyond repair. The interior contained beds of gathered straw on which mats were spread for the people to sleep on. [96]

The eastern Aleut were noted for these large houses while their relatives to the westward erected smaller dwellings, rarely clustered and often widely separated. The general work-house, used also for the celebration of periodic festivals and beliefs, was of a moderate size but always of oblong form. There is no evidence that any form of tent was used by the ancient Aleut. [97]

The roofs of the huts are thatched every year or two in the fall of the year and great quantities of it is cut and dried to replace the old thatch which has been covered with sod for the past year. [166]

Stone Lamps

Among the excavated vessels found about the ancient village sites are those only which were employed as lamps formed of boulders and but slightly chipped out so that the quantity of oil contained in the cavity could amount to but a gill or even less; a quantity so small as to require frequent replenishing if a long continued flame was maintained. [187–188]

The wick could have been none other than some vegetable substance native to the islands, probably the moss universally used among the Innuit

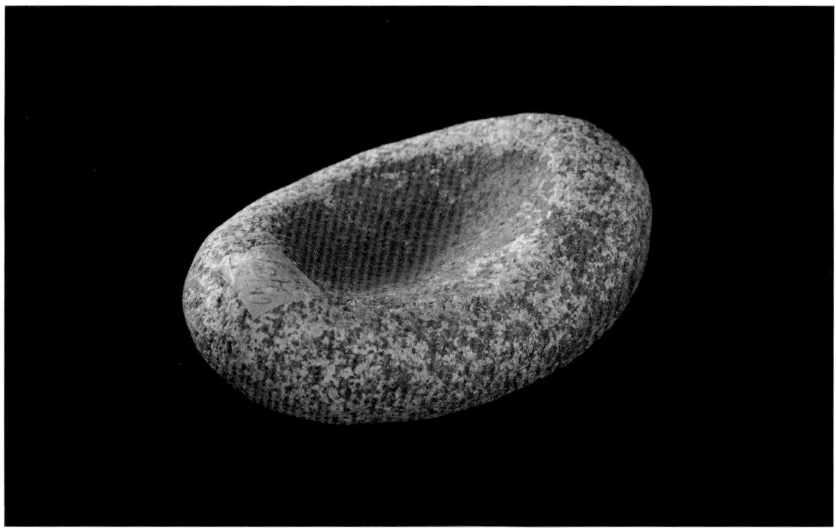

FIG. 14. Small stone lamp, Attu. *Department of Anthropology, Smithsonian Institution (NMNH A64701) (T401).* This is an example of the shallow stone lamps "but slightly chipped out" and which needed "frequent replenishing" of oil if used for long periods.

of the north. Such a flame would give but an insignificant heat, but a moderate degree of illumination is produced from it; sufficient light at least to dispel the gloom of the semi-subterranean huts or cavern walls enclosing the abodes of the pristine Aleut. [188]

The twenty-second series [in the list of artifacts] comprises a number of stone lamps. The rougher examples are formed from rounded stones picked from the beach and have on one side an excavation roughly chipped in. The character of the depression appears to vary with the form of the stone for where large enough the cavity is sad-iron shape but rounded behind, not angular. In other examples it is merely a depression with no definite form except somewhat circular. [26]

Reference will be made, in another connection, to the meaning attached to the size and signification of the different objects usually, but often erroneously, designated *lamps.* [26]

4

Boats

The frames of the boats required many months of labor to fit them in their respective places and especially was this the case with the bow and stern of the umiak, *ni ghil yakh*, which were bent or curved stems of wood and these so seldom were found on the beach that they were the most valued of cast up treasures from the sea. If the reports and statements of the modern Aleut are to be believed the *nighilyakh* of the present day is but a small affair in comparison with that of former times when the boat was capable of accommodating as many as thirty persons where that of the modern times will scarcely hold ten with any degree of comfort. [155–156]

*That the umiak is the original of the kaiak is proved by the tradition now existing among the people of Attu, the westernmost island of the Aleutian Chain, and where the writer lived for eleven months. [R:749]

On Attu Island it was related to me that the ancient Aleut had no such skin canoe as they have at present. That the old form of the kaiak was similar to that of the umiak (*nighilyakh*) and that the stem and stern was much upturned and the breadth much greater. There was no covering on the top, as obtains at present, but was open like the *nighilyak[h]*. It was merely a family boat in which the members of that group sat and paddled along the shore, never far from the beach, searching for such food as might be procured. Within this vessel the people dwelt during such time as the water was still and then performed all manner of work that the compass of the boat permitted. It was in fact a sort of floating dwelling. This was said to have been done before the people became enemies toward each other, caused by jealousy and divulged by a little white bird (the Snow-flake *Plectrophenax nivalis* [Snow Bunting]. It is a bear on the mainland and for his tattling becomes the enemy of mankind and teaches the remainder of the beasts to become fierce and wild) a little bird named *Ma thú gakh* by the Aleut, and *Snigiŕ* by the Russians, who have unwittingly transplanted the theme of the beautiful fairy tale of the Snow-maiden to the dreary wastes of Alaska. [156–157]

When ill-feeling and resentment came upon the people the chief man who was respected by all decided that the women and children should no longer accompany the men in their small boats. The ends of the boat were now covered and there was no necessity that they should be recurved to ward off the waves striking them. By degrees the entire top of the boat was covered and the position of the man was moved toward the center where there was left only sufficient room into which he could thrust his body. The width was narrowed in order to permit the use of his single-blade paddle and in time the double-blade paddle was employed. The chief then decreed that the kaiak, *iḱh akh* of the Aleut should be entered only by men and not by females. [158–159]

(It should be borne in mind that the two hatched bidarka or canoe is an innovation of the Russians and by the Aleut is termed *Úl yukh tá thakh*, while the three-hatched bidarka is named *Ul yúkh takh*, quite different words than applied to the single-hatched canoe solely employed before the advent of the Russians.) [159]

*The two-holed and the three-holed kaiaks are of Russian invention, and are used only in the sea-otter regions of Alaska or where the sea-otter formerly ranged. The construction of the two-holed kaiak was due to the Russian promishleniks, or, as there intended to mean, the leaders of a hunting-party, who had need for as many men and as few kaiaks as possible when waging war with the neighboring people. It was not a difficult stride to evolve a two-holed kaiak from that having one hole, and after that to create one with three holes in order to accommodate some high functionary who desired to travel in state while two men propelled the affair. [R:750]

*It was afterwards found that so many men had been killed that youths must be employed to take the place in the rear hole in order that the hunter could cast his dart at the sea-otter, now made doubly wary by the energetic pursuit of it from the increasing number of rival fur companies. As that creature was restricted to certain portions of Alaska, the use of the two-holed kaiak has never gone beyond those limits. The convenience of the three-holed kaiak has made it an accompaniment of the white trader wherever he has gone and been able to procure the skins with which to cover it. [R:750–751]

It will be observed that not until the *ikhakh* was developed did the people begin to make war upon each other. The umiak was yet retained as the family boat and its propulsion was effected chiefly by the women and boys. In the latter the women and children performed the same character of labor that had been formerly done in the family canoe or small, open boat. The large *nighilyakh* was then made smaller for family use or for parties of women who skirted the waters near the shore for food. During their idle moments they busied themselves in preparing articles from grass that grew along the water's edge. [159–160]

*Let it be as it may, the art of turning over the kaiak and the occupant righting himself is a diversion practiced only where the double-bladed paddle is in common use, and not by all the people using it as a means of propulsion. The Aleuts employ the double-bladed paddle exclusively, and the mainland Eskimo, with the Kadiak Innuit, employ the single blade to as far north as the upper portion of Norton Sound, where an occasional double paddle is used. [R:751]

[A model of a two-hatched kayak collected at Unalaska by Turner was described in Carl W. Mitman's *Catalogue of the Watercraft Collection in the United States National Museum* (1923, p. 210). Although this model has a sea otter attached, it is now missing the "spears, etc." which accompanied it at the time of the description.

"The bidarka is used by the natives of the Aleutian Islands for hunting the sea otter and other animals. It is a long, narrow, round bottom, keelless skin canoe; with nearly vertical sides; sharp cleft bow, rising from below in long easy curve; narrow, nearly square stern frame, beyond which the skin cover narrows to a thin, fin-like projection; hogback sheer; curved deck; figure seated in each of the manholes, with the waterproof skin garment, called kamlaykas[,] tied over the rims; seams of skin fringed with colored yarn, equipped with spears, etc.

"Dimensions of bidarka.—Length, 19 feet 6 inches; width, 30 inches; depth, 21 inches; paddle, 6 feet; spears of various lengths, from 4 feet to 6 feet 2 inches. Scale of model 1 inch equals 1 foot. Cat. No. 129,212 U.S.N.M."]

5

Clothing

The introduction of civilized garments has in the past twenty years revolutionized the manner of clothing the people of those islands so that it is only in the less frequented localities that they adhere to even a semblance of their former costumes. [199]

The clothing worn by the western Aleut consisted of a single garment made of the skins of birds or from the skin of the sea-otter; the latter was however worn only in extremely cold weather and when on land. The pattern was similar to that of a long gown extending quite to the ground. No other protection for the body was used. The feet were naked and when sitting in the canoe the feet were encased within the everted skins of the loon, goose and other large birds. There appears to have been no distinction in the dress of the two sexes. [139–140]

*These garments [bird-skin parkas] were used nearly exclusively during the Russian *régime*, and previous to the discovery of the islands they were the only garment worn by either sex. About forty skins are required for a single garment. [N:156]

*There is great difference in the length of the garments worn by the eastern and western Eskimo. . . . The one worn by the people of Hudson strait scarcely reaches to the hips of the wearer and is long enough only to tie around the hoop of the kaiak. The ones worn by the Eskimo of Northern sound, Alaska, falls to the knees, and those made by the Aleuts are so long that they interfere with the feet in walking. [E:222]

The bird-skin gown was prepared from the skins of the Puffin and Cormorant; thirty of the latter and forty of the former were required for the garment of a medium sized person. The head was not protected except by a band of sealskin to hold the long hair from waving in the wind and obscuring the sight of the person. [140]

The lower limbs were not incased in garments until after the occupation of the islands by the Russians. The upper body was protected by the long garment described on a former page. [210]

Gut Sewing

Another form of knife was used entirely for special purposes that did not require either a very sharp edge or great strength of material. The intestines and other viscera of the various large mammals were of great importance in the domestic affairs of the Aleut hut weather or shine [that is, in bad or good weather]. These intestines were taken from the beast and turned inside out to rid them of the matter contained therein. They were then washed through the water and then turned. A bone knife was employed to free the muscular coating and the fat from the walls of the intestine. When this was done a great care was exercised lest a rent or incision should be made. The gut was now distended with the breath and then fastened to a series of stakes set in the ground so that the whitish intestine should dry. When dry the affair was rolled up into a compact fold and laid away for a time until the women should have opportunity to convert the skins into such articles as waterproofs for the men to wear when out in their boats, bags and other receptacles for trinkets and valuables. [193–194]

The dry roll of intestine was loosened and then split along one of the creases formed by the act of folding. This process gave a strip of two to four inches wide and as long as two hundred feet, sufficient to make two waterproof (for an adult person) *kamláyka* in Russian and *Chi̊kh thakh* in Aleut. The older the mammal from which the material was taken[,] the poorer was the quality for many intestinal worms infest that tract and the points of attachment leave a roughened cicatrix that cannot be removed by scraping without injury to the intestaced fibres composing the coating. [194–195]

The thread used in uniting the edges of these strips was prepared from the sinew of the seals and cetaceans; the former was considered of better character than the latter on account of being less coarse fibres. [195]

The method of preparing the sinew for thread differs somewhat from that obtaining on the mainland. [196]

Fine shreds are stripped off the large piece by means of the thumb nail and two or more of the fibres are twisted by a process difficult to describe but consists in twisting each separate fibre and then laying it similar to the arrangement of the strands of a cord. The women are quite expert at it and in preparing the coarser and longer threads the strands are laid with rapidity. [196]

Whether this manner of preparing the sinew threads has been in vogue only since the introduction of metal needles is a matter of uncertainty. [196]

The number of bone needles found in the village sites, long since uninhabited, indicate no sign of eye or perforation for carrying the thread. [196]

[Among the cataloged artifacts were] designating needles or awls for piercing holes in skins or birds from which most of the garments were made. Since the cataloguing of the specimens was done in 1881 at the Nat. Mus. several of these objects have been lost. The bones of the cod and halibut were preferred on account of their toughness when dried. [58]

The articles of wear requiring to be sewed were joined by threads thrust through holes pierced into the material by means of bodkins fashioned from the wingbone of various birds. The bone from the wing of the bird being hollow and of strong nature well adapted it for such purpose. A portion of the side of the cylinder was broken off and then shaped something like a tooth-pick with a short, sharp point. The point perforated the material to be sewed and the rib bone of a fish was employed to make the hole of sufficient size to admit the thread which was thrust through by means of a notched bone of fish or bird. This pusher was quite small and the thread was larger than the barrel of the perforater so that when drawn through the diameter of the thread filled the opening. All the material[,] such as skin and intestine[,] was required to be dampened not only so that the piercer might more easily perforate it but also in order that when the stuff dried it would shrink and tend to prevent admission of rain and spray from the wave. [197–198]

[Among the cataloged artifacts were] a number of pieces of bone; usually, the humerus, of the goose, gull or auks abounding in the water of the vicinity. The bones have the lower (outer) end cut off and brought to a slanting point. They were used as piercers of skin for clothing or boat covers and such other objects that needed stitching by means of threads. [57]

In lieu of sinew a thin strip of seal intestine was often twisted to form a thread and for some purposes was better adapted than sinew but not so strong. In many of the seams, especially those of rain-coats and workbags of intestine, also bird skin garments, the employment of different colored threads ornamented the seams in an attractive manner. Vermilion paint,

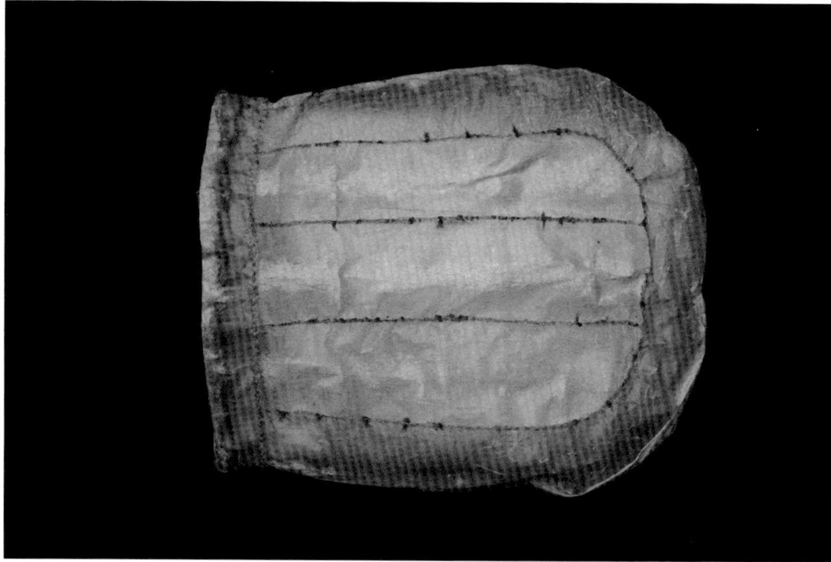

FIG. 15. Gut bag collected at Atka. *Department of Anthropology, Smithsonian Institution (NMNH E65279 3 of 4).* Another of the Atka gut bags. Note the transparency of the gut. The outer panel is a piece of gut that has been folded down the center and sewed to the three-panel sides with careful gathering at the corners.

hematite, the ink bag of the octopus and the root of a kind of grass or vine were employed to give different colors to the threads. The root was purely ornamental, having insufficient strength to support the strain of the bodily action of the wearer. [198–199]

Footwear

According to tradition the covering for the feet at first consisted of the skins of birds split down the back and the skin everted so that the feathers were worn next to the foot. Later grass socks, an article not now manufactured by the Aleut, were worn on the feet, and, finally the sealskin boot was fashioned reaching a perfection attained nowhere else among the Innuit. At the present day the Aleut boot is a strangely composite affair; the top or leg is formed of the gullet (or aesophagus) of the sealion, stretched over a wooden frame until it is expanded as much as its strength will allow. The uppers are of thick calf-skin leather, the soles are, preferably, of the scaly skin from the fore flippers of the sea-lions. The scales and semi-corneous exterior of that skin render that material peculiarly serviceable when walking upon water-washed rocks for it does not become slippery like the skin from other portions of the body of that creature. [199–201]

Preparation of Bird Skins

The manner of preparing the skins of mammals and birds for conversion into garments differs in no essential degree from that in vogue upon the mainland and probably has not changed in character with the migration of the people. [199]

As the manner of preparing the skins of birds for the long garment as worn to this day by the modern Attu Aleut has not been fully described[,] a few words concerning it will not be out of place although the capture of the birds is not differently undertaken then than now. [201]

When the men repair to the sea-otter hunting-grounds they take several women whose duty it shall be to attend to the capture of birds and the preliminary preparation of the skins for future use. [201–202]

The birds mostly sought are the Puffins, *Lunda cirrhata* and *Fratercula corniculata*, Guillemots[,] *Cepphus*, and Murres[,] *Uria*. [202]

*The natives [of Attu] have very wisely restricted the foxes to this large island [Attu], otherwise they would not be able to procure the birds—Puffins and Guillemots—from whose skins they make a long garment for protection against the cold of winter. [N:156]

The flesh is extracted from the skin by cutting off the wings and head of the bird and through those orifices the bones and meat is taken out in pieces. The skin is now everted and dried until wanted. Along in the fall the skins are taken from the place where they have been concealed for a couple of months and are looked over to discover any fatty, adherent matter. The next process is that of soaking the skins in a quantity of a liquid reserved for that purpose. After several days immersion the skins are removed and taken to a creek where they are placed in the water and trampled with the feet to remove the liquid used in tanning them. The skins are now dried by wringing and suspending where the air will have full access to them. When dry they are subjected to a chewing between the teeth which not only removes the oil and fat within the skin but also breaks the shafts or barrels of the quills that they may not iritate [sic] the body when in contact with it and also to prevent them from dropping out too rapidly. The process of chewing is very tedious and required great care so that when it is completed the skins (flesh side) are of a yellowish color. They are now ready to be cut into oblong squares, always slitting along the back. This gives a piece about seven inches wide and nine inches long. A sufficient number of these are sewed into strips and these added to each other until the length is built up from the bottom to the shoulders. The arms are separate pieces afterward sewed on. The construction to fit the shoulder and neck is effected by leaving out one or a part of a skin. The collar[,] sleeve and body seams are often ornamented with tufts of colored wool or plumes from other birds so that the flesh side worn outward often presents an ornate appearance with its fanciful decorations of those feathers and farther embellished with stripes of various colored pigments that renders one of the garments quite attractive when new. [202–204]

In former times other birds were killed that have now become either extinct or so scarce as to warrant their capture unprofitable. The Cormorants especially were excessively abundant and they served not only as an acceptable portion of the Aleut diet but their skins also were employed for conversion into a garment whose material is now supplied by the skins of other inferior birds. Portions of the skin and especially the head-plumes of those birds are used as ornaments on many of the objects fashioned at the present day. [205]

*When the native returns home with a sufficient number of birds for his own and family necessity, the labor of taking out the flesh begins. The beak is cut off just at the edge of the feathers, the meat, bones, and everything else inside the skin must come out at that hole. The wings are carefully drawn until the humerus can be dislocated from the body. The wing is then cut off. The skin is now turned inside out and the larger, adherent particles of flesh and fat are removed. The skins are then hung up to dry until the severe weather of winter compels the women to remain within doors. A certain liquid has been saved up for a considerable time until it acquires an intolerable odor. The skins are then soaked in this liquid until the oiliness and fatty parts are removed from the skins, and if the person is able to purchase soap the skins are then washed in a strong suds. If not washed in soapy water it matters little, as the greater part of the odor is removed by washing in some convenient creek until the person is tired, which occurs before long engaged. The skins are then hung up to dry. After that the skins are carefully scraped (No. 54 is the left jaw bone of

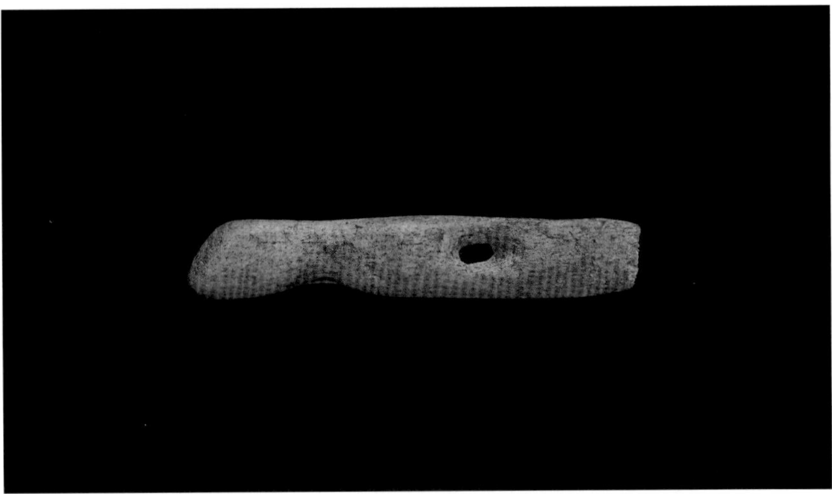

Fig. 16. Bone scraper used in preparing bird skins, Attu. *Department of Anthropology, Smithsonian Institution (NMNH A64934) (T634).*

some creature, evidently a bird. It is used to smooth the asperities of drying skins. [52]); and the tougher parts chewed between the teeth to make them pliable. An Aleut woman will go on a visit to a neighbor to have a *Chy peet*, or tea-party; in the intervals of drink and gossip a birdskin will be drawn from beneath the folds of her garment; and, she will then as complacently chew the skin as one of our country dames will draw out her knitting and pipe to while away the time. [C:118]

*The number of skins used for a *parka*, or long gown-like garment, with or without a hood, is variable, according to the size and height of the wearer. A common-sized man requires the skins for forty-five birds of the Puffin kind. The women and children require less. Forty-five skins are usually bundled together and rated as one parka. [C:118]

*The parka is worn with the feathers inside; and, when the garment is new, makes the wearer quite conspicuous. The skins are cut down the back, leaving a straight edge, to which another is sewed until the desired height of the garment is obtained. On the edge of this strip another strip is added. This will be heavy and inconvenient in sewing, so another pair of strips are sewed together until the desired height of the garment is obtained. The arm pieces are made separately, and are the last to be sewed on. The edges of the collar and sleeve are bound with cloth to prevent tearing. The flesh side of the skin is then ornamented with stripes of paint of various colors, such as vermilion, green, blue, or black. Before the introduction of dry paints the natives used various colored rocks, which they powdered up and mixed with blood of the raven or other land-bird, and applied it for ornamental purposes. A parka is expected to last for two years; but, in the soot-begrimed houses, it soon becomes a receptacle for all dirt. The parka may be washed in water occasionally; and, I believe this is only done when it becomes so infested with vermin that the owner is afraid to put it down for fear it will walk off. A washed parka of nearly two years old is a sorry-looking object. The long feathers are by that time mostly fallen off. A few patches of down and skin are about all that remain. [C:118]

*Before the advent of the Russians and the introduction of civilized clothing this parka was the only garment worn by the Aleuts, and is now quite extensively used by the Attu men and women. [C:118]

6

Weaving

During their idle moments they [the women] busied themselves in preparing articles from grass that grew along the water's edge. [160]

This grass was cut in the early days of August and the stalks immediately buried under a thin covering of sand on the shore so that the heat of the sun would wilt the blades gradually and slowly dry the juices from the grass and render them tough and light colored and not scorched and brittle as would be done if left to dry as hay. Great care was taken that the rain and wet should not come upon the grass to discolor it. In a few hours the grass was uncovered and quickly put into bundles and stored away in a dark, dry place until the time should arrive to prepare the blades for manufacture into such articles as mats[,] screens, baskets, bags and many other forms that the fancy could suggest and necessity require. The coarsest grasses with the stalks were employed as follows: Half a dozen stalks with their attached blades were selected and knotted at one end. A similar quantity of stalks were taken and they formed the beginning of the weft. A twist of the divided number of woof stalks secured the weft and another bunch was placed and twisted around by the woof stalks, similarly the operation was continued until a mat of dangling stalks were held by the single woof thread. At a distance some four inches below the first a second woof was twisted around the weft stalks. A third or fourth and perhaps a fifth was run until the mat attained a length of eight to ten feet and three or four feet wide. This mat was suspended about the inner walls of the hut to prevent the body or other objects from coming directly in contact with the damp earth-side of the huts. This character of matting was also employed as a cover for the mass of loose straw on which it was spread and then the skins upon the mat. A similar mat was also used for the doorway of the huts of certain kinds. [160–163]

FIG. 17. *Elymus mollis* growing at Unalaska, 2007.

FIG. 18. *Elymus mollis* harvested for weaving, 2007. The grass "cord" used to hold the bundle together was shown to the editor by Jennie (Prokopeuff) Krukoff, originally from Attu.

From this crude method of preparing the dry grasses evolved the finer grades of grass work from the coarse basket or sack in which was carried the slimy fish, sea-urchins, shellfish, or the flesh of mammals slain for food.

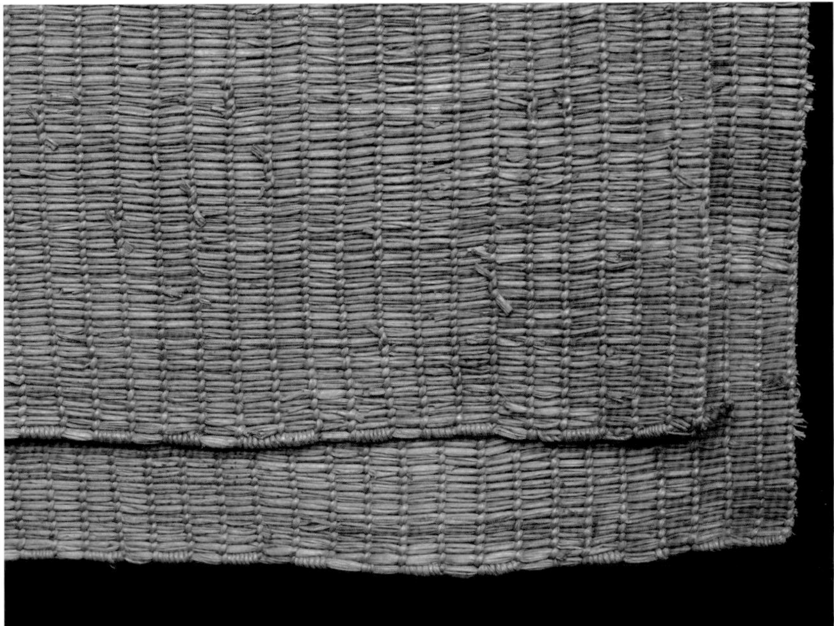

FIG. 19. Grass mat, Atka. *Department of Anthropology, Smithsonian Institution (NMNH E65283) (T323).* This detail of a large grass mat illustrates open plain twining. The back side of the mat dominates the photograph and is laid on top of the front side. Short ends of grass can be seen on the back, indicating where new weft and warp strands were added when old ones needed replacing. Note how the weft is wrapped around the end warp in the transition from one row to the next, and how the initial weft strands were bundled together with a sinew wrapping. Utilitarian mats declined in use after the introduction of wood-frame houses. They occasionally were used in chapels, however, as late as the 1930s.

The housewife tested her skill by preparing smaller receptacles from the better qualities of the grass blades and finally became proficient in weaving and plaiting grasses so that at the present day their handicraft is a marvel of beauty and example of the patience required to produce articles soft and of a texture nearly as fine as the silk of the French looms. [163–164]

The methods employed to attain this character of work are intricate and tedious to an extremity evincing in great manner the patience and painstaking necessary to produce the various objects made from the coarse grasses on the shores of the islands. [164]

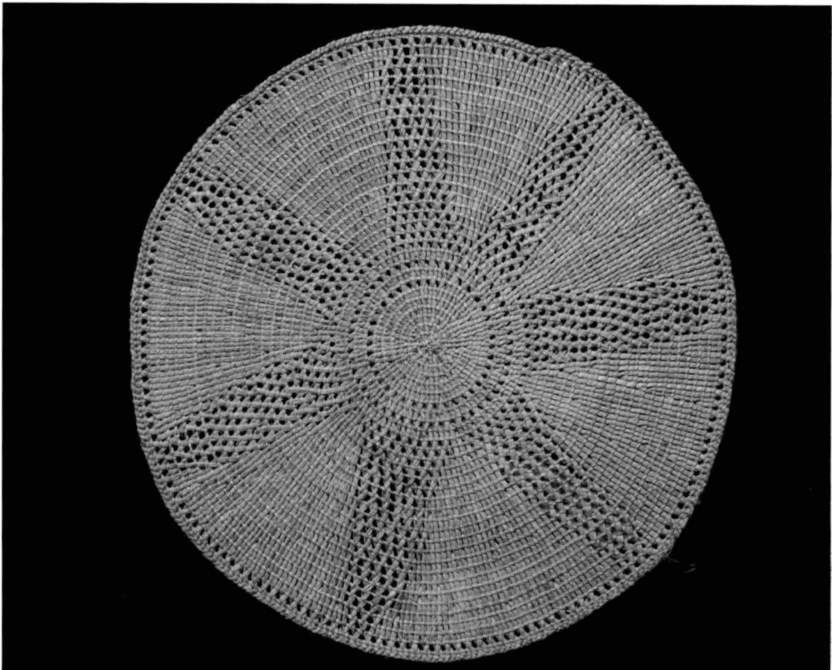

Fig. 20. Circular mat, Atka. *Department of Anthropology, Smithsonian Institution (NMNH E65219 2 of 2).* In this mat, the seven-rayed sunburst design was made using plain twining over vertical crossed warp. Note the different finishing rows in E65219 2 of 2 and E65237 (Plate 8).

An inspection of the multitude of objects belonging to the collection, included in this article, will reveal the fact that but few indeed are similar in patern [sic] and the method of weaving is nearly as diverse as the designs upon them. In order to enhance the beauty of these objects parti-colored tufts of woolen threads and silks are interwoven to increase the effect. [164]

In the more delicate grades of the work, such as imitations of the modern cigar-cases, card-cases and such like work, the blades of grass are too coarse for the purpose and but few of the blades are of sufficient strength when subdivided into minute threads to be used as weft and woof. The blade is subjected to a critical inspection and tested for strength. If satisfactory the thumb nail of the right hand is used as a means of dividing the blade into delicate threads scarcely coarser than a number 80 thread of cotton. [164–165]

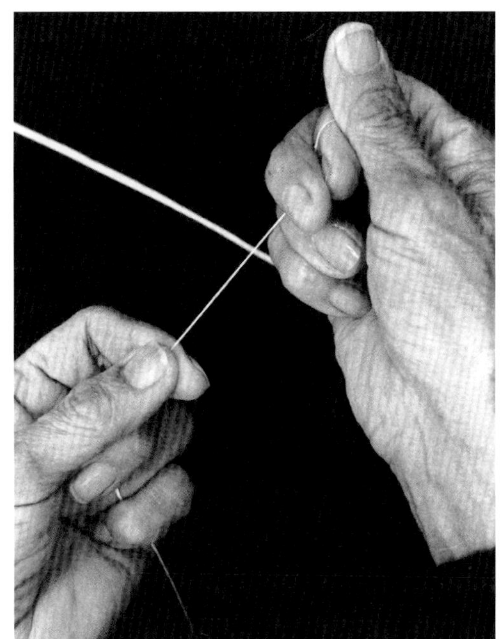

Fig. 21. A "delicate thread" of grass being tested for strength. *University of Alaska Museum of the North, photograph by Barry McWayne. Photograph #N70-464-15.* The hands of Anfesia Shapsnikoff (1900–1973) inspect the strength of a strand of split wild rye. Shapsnikoff's mother, Martha (Prokopeuff) Lazaroff, was born on Attu in 1881.

Several of these threads are laid crosswise in the palm of the hand and then tied with a thread that may be released when convenient. By a process of weaving[,] the circle of woof increases in size until the diameter of it is sufficient to cover the truncate end of a wooden cylinder. The ends of the threads are then turned up and the process continues around that stick, which serves as a guide for uniformity of the sides of the affair. [165]

When the old men and women, together with the younger members of the community, repair to their summer village to catch fish or dig the roots of the Sarana or Kamchatkan Lily, *Fritillaria*; or the Zholtia Koren, or Yellow-root, *Lupinus*[,] they employ much of their time in gathering the grasses that are to be converted into various articles of household use and convenience. Huge bundles of this grass are carried to the principal village where it is made into the various articles. [166]

FIG. 22. Two girls with their basketry, Attu. *Margaret Murie Collection, Alaska and Polar Regions Collections, Elmer E. Rasmuson Library, University of Alaska Fairbanks, Photo UAF-1990-3-5.* In this undated photograph, two girls stand at the entrance to a barabara. On the left is a bundle of wild rye prior to being separated into grades of grass. Between the girls is a basket bottom and two skeins of prepared and split grass. Each girl holds an unfinished basket that has been placed on a wooden cylinder to keep its shape.

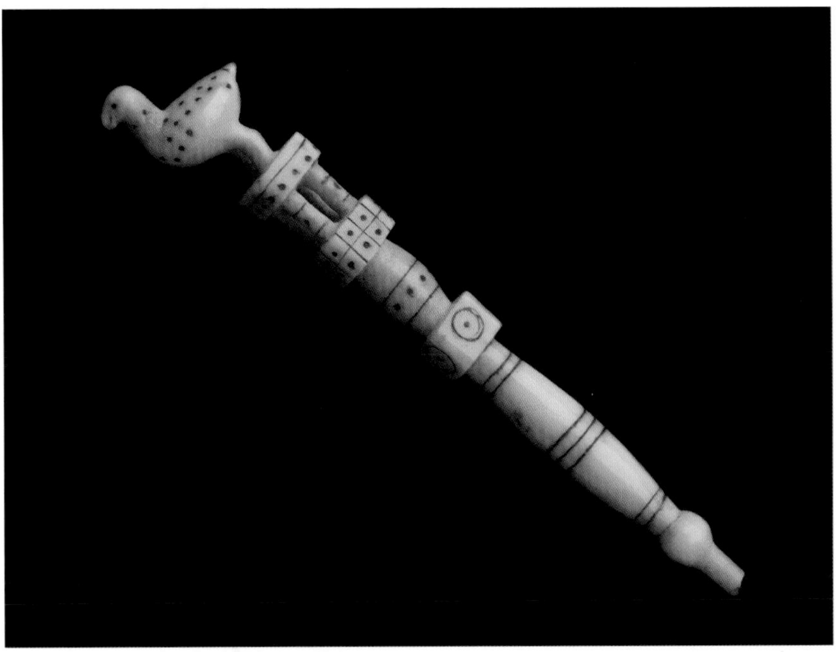

Plate 1. Miniature ivory staff. *Department of Anthropology, Smithsonian Institution (NMNH E35897).* This was among ivory items sent from Atka within two days of Turner's arrival. Its purpose and significance remain unknown, although the bird, dot, and circle motifs strongly suggest an Unangan origin.

Plate 2. Ivory bird with hooked beak. *Department of Anthropology, Smithsonian Institution (NMNH E35901).* Resembling an eagle, this carving with its repetitive dot motifs is similar to ones attached to Unangan bentwood hats. According to Nicholai Galaktionoff, the Unalaska people had a special relationship with eagles and could transform themselves into these birds. (Personal conversation with the editor, June 7, 2004.)

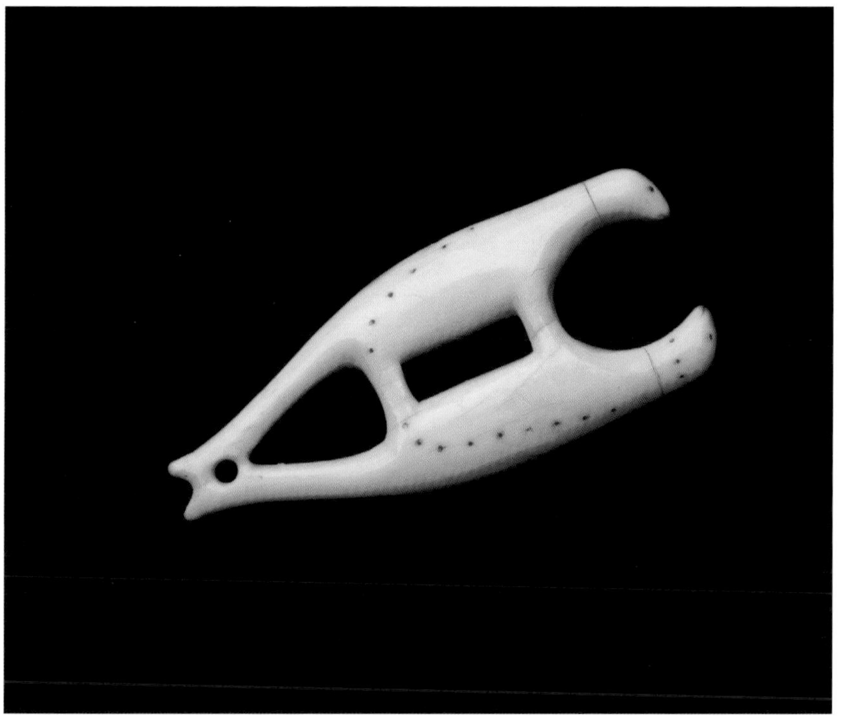

PLATE 3. Cleat in the shape of two sea otters joined face to face. *Department of Anthropology, Smithsonian Institution (NMNH E35902).* Lydia Black suggests this refers to the sea otter origin story in which an incestuous brother and sister were transformed into otters, one swimming east and one swimming west.

Plate 4. Model of two-man skin boat, Unalaska. *Department of Anthropology, Smithsonian Institution (NMNH E129215).* Note the sea otter spears with detachable points and the black and red club. The faces are carved with such realism that they might be portraits. The hands were frequently made from soft lead, which in this model has deteriorated. Women frequently helped men create models by sewing the clothing used by the hunters.

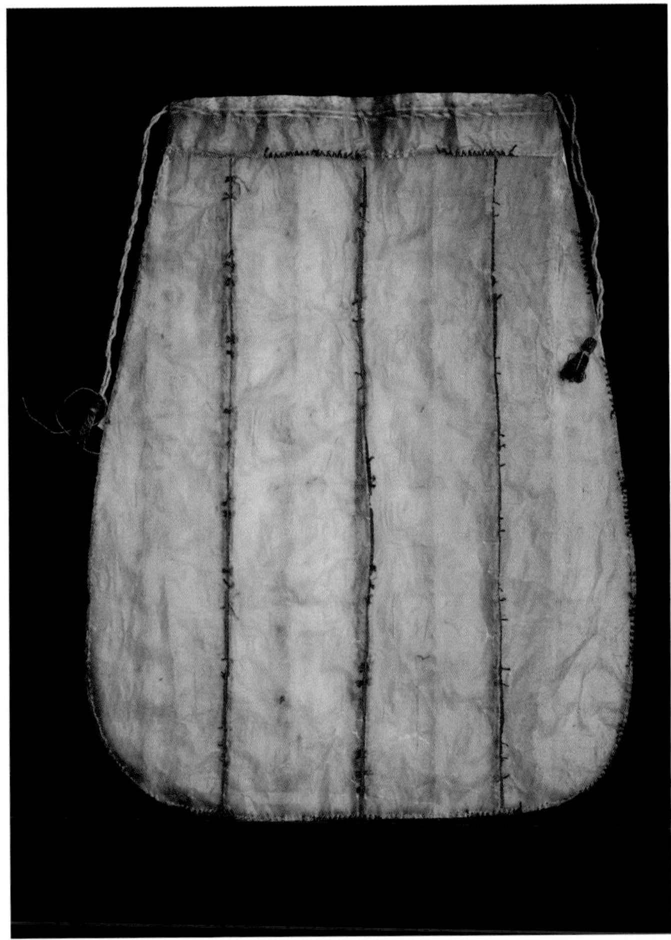

Plate 5. Gut bag collected at Atka. *Department of Anthropology, Smithsonian Institution (NMNH E65301).* In August 1879 Turner collected forty-four containers made from seal and sea lion intestine to demonstrate a range of sewing and decorative techniques. (See Appendix 2.) This bag, made by sewing together two separate four-panel sides, has seams reinforced with narrow strips of what is probably painted seal gut or bird esophagus. Tufts of brown thread have been used to decorate the panel seams. The same brown thread (and red thread, although much of this is missing) was used on the outer edges to overlay the running stitch with a type of blanket stitch.

Plate 6. Fish basket, Atka. *Department of Anthropology, Smithsonian Institution (NMNH E65297) (T337).* This utilitarian basket was woven with open plain twining and finished with a classic braid. The design was created using dyed gut or esophagus in false embroidery and plaiting. The bottom third shows traces of other design work that has deteriorated.

Plate 7. Covered basket, Atka. *Department of Anthropology, Smithsonian Institution (NMNH E65160).* This is one of several baskets Turner collected at Atka that illustrate a transition from utilitarian fish baskets to what, in the late nineteenth and early twentieth centuries, became known as the classical Unangan covered basket. In this example, the basket was woven with open plain twining similar to fish baskets. Designs were created by twining over crossed vertical warp, a technique known from mats and utilitarian baskets. The lid with its small knob and the repetition of designs from the side of the basket, however, became characteristics of later covered baskets.

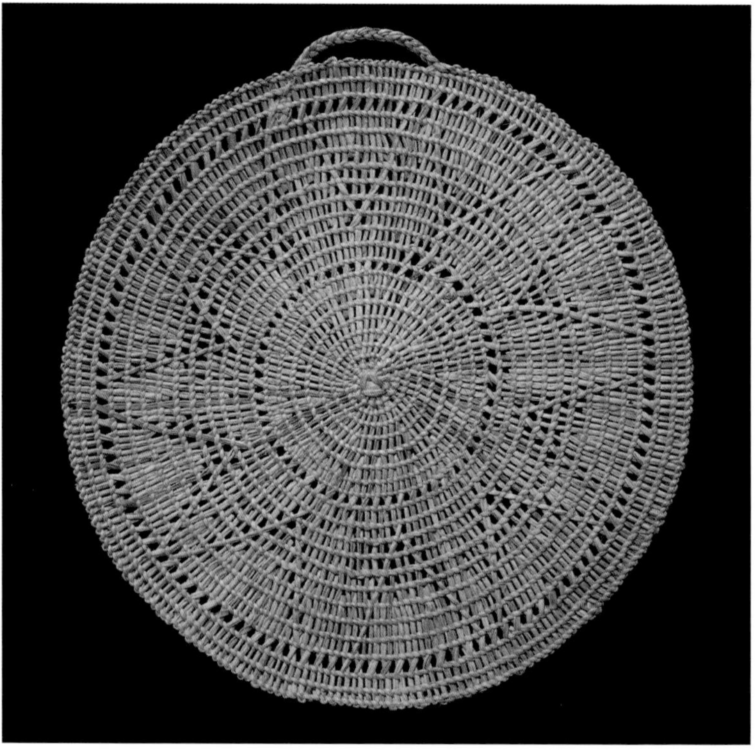

Plate 8. Circular mat, Atka. *Department of Anthropology, Smithsonian Institution (NMNH E65237).* Turner collected forty-three circular mats, each woven to show combinations of weaving techniques and design work. In this example, the ten-pointed sunburst design was made using plain twining over diverted warp. There are inner and outer circles of crossed warp. The outer row is finished with a braided loop attached with sinew. One challenge the weaver faced was to keep the design elements uniform while increasing the circumference of the mat through regular additions of warp strands.

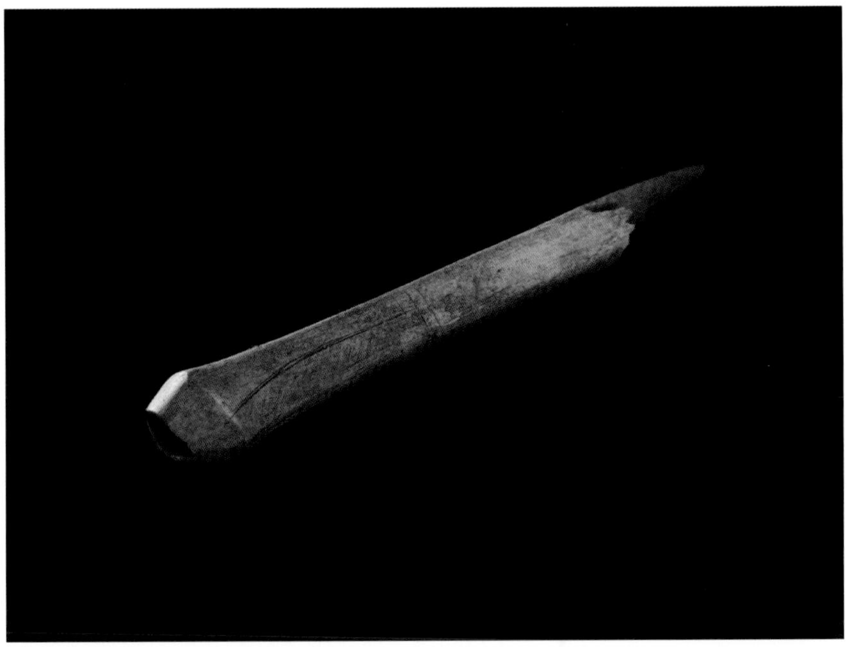

Plate 9. Bone spear head, Attu, 10.5 inches. *Department of Anthropology, Smithsonian Institution (NMNH A64977) (T677).* The spear point was inserted into the opening at the flared end of the spear head. The opening was lined with wood that would swell slightly to make a secure fit. The forked end of the spear head was lashed onto the wooden shaft. Note the faint traces in the center of design or ownership marks.

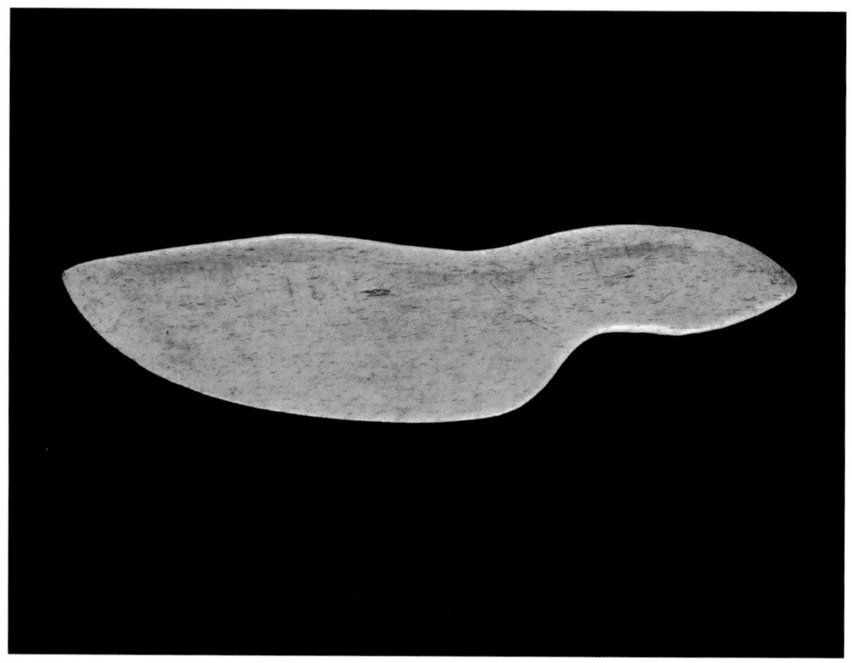

PLATE 10. Bone knife, Attu. *Department of Anthropology, Smithsonian Institution (NMNH A64307) (T07).* Turner wrote that this was "a better formed knife of bone." Whale bone, which is very dense, was often used as a substitute for ivory in making implements.

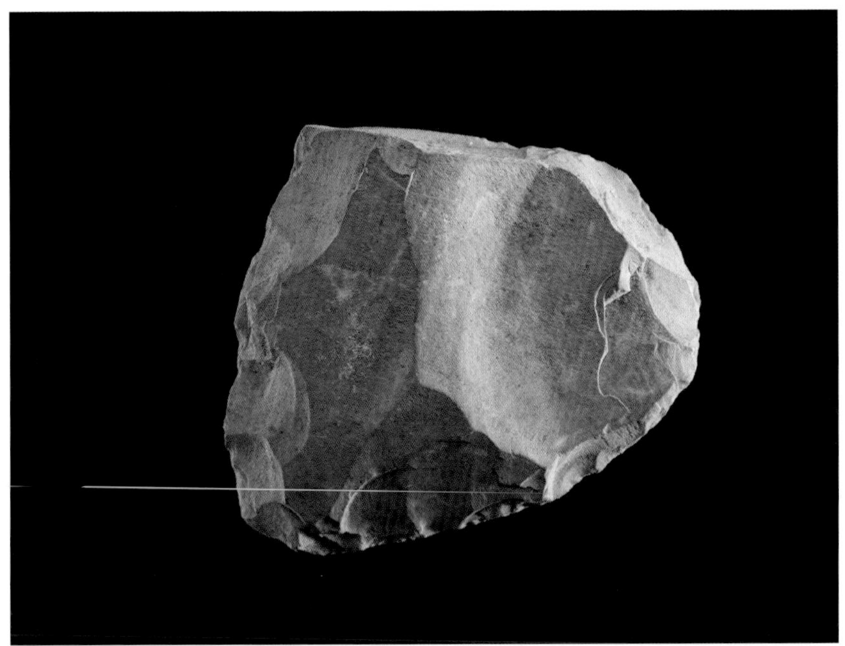

Plate 11. Stone tool, Attu. *Department of Anthropology, Smithsonian Institution (NMNH A64424) (T124).* Turner was shown how stone points were made using tools of particularly hard stone. He was surprised at the dexterity contemporary Unangan showed and wondered about the facility people must have had when they were "totally accustomed to that work." He described this stone as "one of the principal materials used in the fashioning of knives."

Plate 12. Stone knife, Attu. *Department of Anthropology, Smithsonian Institution (NMNH A64569) (T269).* Turner described this knife as one used to "sever the larger pieces of blubber and flesh" from a whale.

Plate 13. Killing stone, Attu. *Department of Anthropology, Smithsonian Institution (NMNH A64717) (T417).* Used in hand-to-hand combat, this weapon testifies to the fierceness of Unangan warriors.

PLATE 14. Large stone lamp, Attu. *Department of Anthropology, Smithsonian Institution (NMNH A64705) (T405).* This type of large lamp was given by young women of the village to the daughter of the chief upon her marriage to show approval and to enable her to continue "the fire that was to welcome her husband to his home."

Plate 15. Two sea otters on land, Attu. *Department of Anthropology, Smithsonian Institution (NMNH E65143 and E65144) (T843 and T844).* Turner wrote that these were carved from wood by a fourteen-year-old boy. They are examples of how carefully the young were taught to observe the natural world.

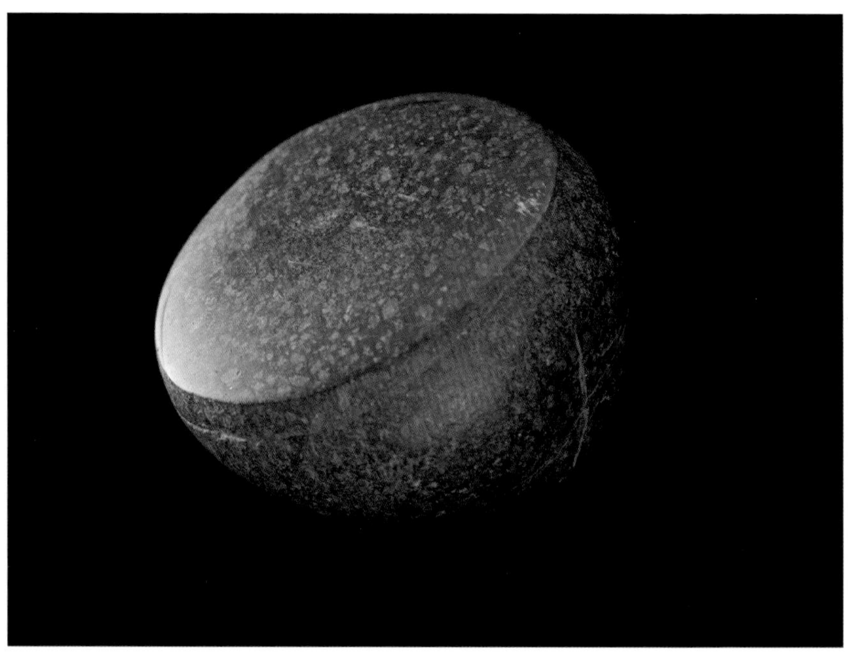

Plate 16. Stone muller, Attu. *Department of Anthropology, Smithsonian Institution (NMNH A64700) (T400).* This muller was used like a pestle for grinding "various hard or soft substances" into pigments. Note the traces of color adhering to the sides of the stone.

7

Fire Making

The methods of procuring fire were of three kinds: first the use of a stone containing quartz and pyrytes struck against another of similar kind or even a small stone from the beach. Sulphur was procured from the numerous volcanoes along the Aleutian Chain and a small quantity of this was powdered and sprinkled upon a mass of down from the breast of sea-birds. The sparks from the stone ignited the sulphur and feathers which quickly caught on some finely shredded blades of grass or beaten stalks of wild parsnip. This method of procuring fire obtains among the islands west of Unalashka even to this day. [181–182]

It was one [sic: once] my opportunity to visit the summer village on the eastern end of Atkha opposite Amlia Island where the natives (old men[,] women and the young people[)] fished during the summer while the men hunters had gone on the summer cruise for sea-otters. The dwellings there are simply dome shaped structures of less than ten feet diameter and only five feet high. The bare ground constituted the floor and the only means of egress was a small hole in the side of the sod wall that formed the affair. Half a dozen people could sit huddled in one of those huts and a dozen made the space so small that room was not to be thought of. I had been inquiring into the manner of making fire in ancient times and an old woman was explaining the method when I interrupted her with the remark that it was not credible. She turned and in a moment produced the material and created such a stench of burning feathers and sulphur fumes as to nearly overpower the crowd within the structure. In a moment I requested her to repeat the operation. She did so and at that instant I sprang for the doorway and pretended to become wedged in the passage. It was an awful minute for those within, half-suffocated by the fumes, screamed with all their might and pulled at me to admit some fresh air. I had the fun and then got such a good-humored tongue-lashing as only provoked Aleut women can give while two or three old men grinned their satisfaction and approval of the women's scolding. [182–184]

The second method . . . [employs] a wooden spindle of hardwood whirling in a conical cavity, one side of which is cut off to permit the dust from the atrition [sic] to fall into a small slot or trough, where the collected powder held the latent heat until the heap took fire from it. Tinder produced from willow catkins and powdered charcoal ignited from this and then increased to a coal, which flamed from the breath and then set fire to coarser material. [184–185]

The twenty-ninth series consists of two bone implements. Each is a rounded piece excavated with conical shape into the cavity of which a spindle for fire making purposes or for boring holes has been inserted. The bearing shows great amount of use for the sides are half charred by the heat from the friction of the spindle end. The bone is evidently a portion of the head of some cetacean. No. 80 [A64380] is the one described. No. 79 [A64379] is a similar affair having a well worn and deeper cavity polished by use until the interior is smooth as worked ivory. [34]

[Among the cataloged artifacts were] four pieces, A, B, C & D, to form the parts of fire-making apparatus still employed by the natives of Attu when on a hunting-party and their supply of matches gives out. The entire affair is somewhat cumbrous, consisting of fire-board, spindle, thong and hand-rest. Two persons are needed to work the affair, one to pull the thong while the other holds the hand-rest that supports the spindle. A moment only is required to produce fire by this method. It will be observed that the spindle is of harder wood than the fire-board, for if they were of the same kind of wood the friction would not wear off the fine dust from the cavity of the fire-board which collects and the latent heat in the dust-heap finally produces fire. [61]

At the present day flint and steel or the wooden spindle are employed when matches are not to be had. Also a piece of tinder is held at the mouth of a gun and a light charge of loose powder fired from the barrel ignites the stuff and fire may be obtained in that manner. [185]

In lieu of wood the trailing stems of *Empetrum nigrum* are employed as fuel. The hillsides and tops of the lower hills are covered with dense mats of this growth and furnishes an abundance of this character of fuel. The women gather, by pulling, great bundles which are transported on

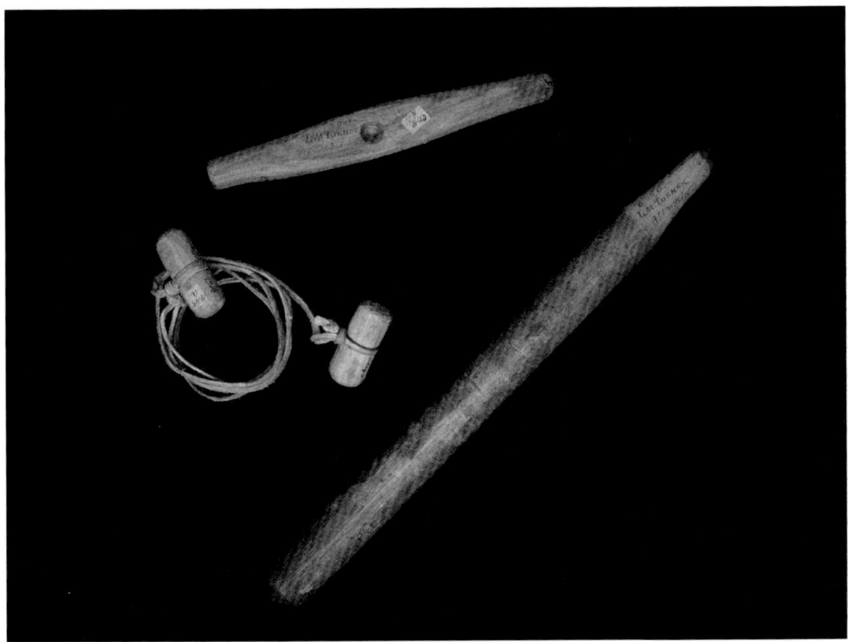

Fig. 23. Unangan fire drill, Attu. *Department of Anthropology, Smithsonian Institution (NMNH E65145) (T845).*

Fig. 24. A drawing of the same fire drill pieces assembled, based on the illustration in the original accession book.

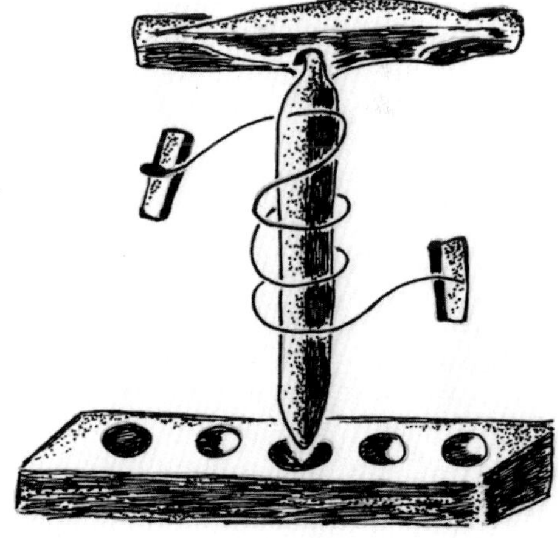

their backs to the dwellings and there, if a dry day, it is spread out to dry and in the course of a few hours is regathered and stored in one corner of the anteroom where the cooking is done. A small wisp is lighted and held under the vessel containing the water to be boiled or the food to be cooked. [185–186]

Grass stalks are employed in the same manner as the heather vines; and, one not familiar with keeping a blaze from such material will experience quite a degree of difficulty in the labor; not so with an Aleut woman, who will, in a few minutes, cause a pot of water to boil for tea. [186]

8

Hunting—General Considerations

One of the first considerations is what means the ancient Aleut had to support life. That there was an abundance of food to be obtained from the waters there can be no doubt for even with the surprizingly [sic] large population found on those islands at the time of their discovery near the middle of the eighteenth century we are informed that various whales, sealions, seals, birds of many kinds and fishes were to be found in the adjacent waters and occurring in such multitudes that with the necessities of so many people to be supplied the creatures had not yet been persecuted with such vigor as to render them very shy at the approach of man. The inference is plain that from such large resources to be drawn from with little exertion the mental scale of these people could be developed to a greater degree than though [i.e., than *if*] compelled to devote all his energy to the capture of food. Hence that the Aleut should possess greater intellectual development, his language obtain a more nearly perfect grammatical structure and his system of numeration be more thorough is not to be wondered at among all of the natural advantages surrounding him. That there were great diversities of intellectual and physical capabilities among these people would be no more strange than when compared with people greatly in advance of them at the present day. [99–100]

The character and quantity of food obtained by any people has a greatly controlling influence upon their development. That the Aleut had abundant opportunity to procure the following kinds of food at various seasons dependent oftentimes upon the weather and that during favorable circumstances he was not restricted as was his mainland neighbors by ice covering the shores of the sea for months at a time and from which he drew most of his supplies. [100–101]

That there was an abundance of other food to be had in earlier times none, who have considered the beasts, birds and fishes of those islands, will attempt to deny. That there was a plenty at certain places, far more than at others, can not be doubted. [107] At certain seasons the weather was so severe as to prevent the people from issuing from their huts and during that time they were reduced to starvation. [140]

The twenty-fifth series embraces two objects whose functions are that of spoons or ladles. Number 99 [A64399, missing] is a spoon of modern form cut from a piece of horn. No. 655 [A64955] is a fragment of cocoa-nut shell rounded and nearly three inches in diameter. It has two holes pierced to enable it to be lashed to a handle. [29] The various currents flowing past the Nearer Group of Islands often bring these nuts to the shore and the Aleuts procure them from the beach, often so fresh as to yet retain the coriaceous envelope surrounding the fibrous covering of the shell. The fresher specimens are, probably, thrown overboard by the whalers proceeding to the Arctic or Okotsk Sea from Honolula. [29]

Fig. 25. Spoon. This drawing of A64399 was based on the illustration in the original accession book. Turner wrote it was "cut from a piece of horn" while the accession record said it was a "Spoon made of Baleen."

I am not aware there is any locality on any of the Aleutian Islands that produces either clay or steatite for the manufacture of vessels in which to cook their food. Even at the present day much of the food is eaten raw either imperfectly dried in the moist atmosphere or else eaten just as it comes from the field or water. Certain portions of the *salmoniblae* such as the glutinous substance from the bones of the head and bases of the fins is often the means of assembling a number of those people who dispose of great quantities of that matter. The quantity of shellfish eaten is surprising and is always devoured in a raw state, excepting, perhaps, the tough clams and cockles found about the sandy tracts of the beach. [186–187]

Hunting Implements

The hunting-weapons form the most intelligent index to the character of the ancient Aleuts but when their history is written it will be found to differ from the accounts previously given. [48]

The means employed in the capture of quadrupeds and fishes, so far as those means were not perishable, are treated of in the preceding pages [i.e., in the cataloged list incorporated into this text]. The general form of all of those implements agrees, when compared with other material from the different islands, in every essential regard and the same stages of progress appear to mark the successive degrees of progress among the people from one end of the chain to the other. It does not stop there but links itself with the workmanship of the mainland in such manner as to be inseparable from the mainland Innuit. [107–108]

The transition from a rude flake of stone to the perfected arrow heads, attached to the finely finished shaft of wood, vaned with feathers to insure accuracy of flight, is not an easy step. The tree limb that suggested the bow, serving by its elasticity to straighten the tense thong that restrained it, was not less crude than the stone flake that formed the head of the shaft impelled by the released bowstring. [1]

The arrow first used was not the polished shaft of hard wood now employed, passing smoothly over the hand that grasps the bow near the middle. The head of the first arrows used were found to splint[er] and become blunted against the hide of the creature rendered at each pursuit more wary and less easily approached by previous attacks when clubs, spears and javelins were successively employed to dispatch the beast destined to furnish food and raiment for primitive man. [1]

From the flake of irregular outline the form of a triangle or leaf shape was gradually adopted and found to be most effective. However much the after portions of the arrow point may have been modified to adapt itself to the shaft or for particular purposes, including special forms for certain kinds of game and for individual or personal shapes to indicate ownership and finally in the social organization of the tribe such forms became the family and later the distinctive form of the community or tribe which may be traced with a degree approaching certainty, the point or anterior portion of the leaf-shaped implement has been modified only by length, breadth and thickness. [1–2]

From the various forms of arrow heads it is not difficult to believe that the crude flakes and the irregularly outlined foliate forms of stone set in the forward end of the arrow shaft as loose pieces were intended to become detached from the shaft and remain within the body of the object at which they were cast. [2]

Accurate setting of those pieces became necessary for when they were placed within the notched or split shaft they either deflected the course of the arrow or else split the shaft so that each time the arrow was sent against the object the shaft was rendered useless. Later a wrapping of sinew or thong prevented splitting and then suggested the neck of the arrow head [from] which[,] when chipped to accommodate its lashings[,] evolved the "ears" of the arrow-head. The neck and ears are the parts of the implement most distinctive and however much divergent they may be it is not difficult to conceive that the arrow-head is simply a highly specialized form of the stone head for the spear and javelin wielded by the strength of the arm. [2–3]

The stick or club used to administer a blow took final form in the spear and later into the javelin or dart which by its comparative lightness could be cast at a distance. The bow was developed and its missile is simply a form of javelin adapted to the use of that instrument. With the discovery of the bow the effect upon man and his surroundings were greatly changed. By its employment objects might be secured that otherwise were unobtainable. For large creatures the heavy spear held within the hand was yet reserved for close attack while the lighter javelin was used for provoking attack or for securing that within the limits of the individual's strength to cast it. [3]

For the capture of aquatic creatures the occupant of the water craft found the bow and arrow ill adapted to use on the water, for to approach unobserved he must of necessity be so near the surface as to render the manipulation of that weapon quite impossible lest it be so short as to be ineffective. Then the hand or throwing-board was devised and adopted to cast the dart farther than could possibly be done by the unaided hand; so that it is not difficult to perceive that the bow and arrow are devices employed on land and its representative used on the water. [3–4]

[The following paragraph comes from an unpaginated loose page in the manuscript.] As time passed on and those birds, beasts and fishes became shy at the approach of man he was compelled to devise instruments that would take the place of the distance between man and his prey. The simple shaft of wood was provided with stone or bone point sharpened for incision and the strong arm gave power for penetration. Again did distance work disadvantage and now comes the attachment of a thong by which the barbed spear-head was made to hold the slightly wounded creature until a death-thrust could be given. Later the point was made so as to uncouple and the disconnected parts effect not only the wounding but also a restraint upon the movements of the victim whose struggles to escape only aided its speedy death.

The objects classed as arrow heads may be conveniently separated into three divisions, including perfect heads, parts represented by fragments of central portions, and basal and anterior pieces more or less perfect. [4] [Turner's catalog actually has four divisions for arrowheads, series 1–4. Describing one perfect point (T796, A65096) he alludes to the practice of hunters carrying reserve points: "Characters are evident that would indicate a rude attempt at polishing or smoothing which may, however, be purely accidental or due to wear in the pouch carrying the reserve points in cases of emergency." (6)]

Lance or Spear Points

The fifth lot [series] comprises twelve (12) pieces more or less perfect in form and very evidently intended as lance heads for securing such creatures as seals, sea-otters and sea-lions. While the size indicates use for such large game the size of the spear-heads presents many variations from a roughly flaked, irregularly outlined head to the more nearly perfect ones resembling . . . dagger-blade shapes. . . . [9]

Those pieces having the basal portion represented unbroken indicate that the preference of form for the base of the stem was rounded and thinned; evidently that when the stricken object should escape from the attack that the point should withdraw from the shaft and remain within the body of the victim. This is supported by the fact that all the implements of stone intended to produce death of the creatures sought for food have, in their perfected condition of workmanship, that form and no other. Those of earlier construction, as is indicated plainly in the series collected, evince the transition from the stem with thickened square, or truncate, base to the thinned and rounded base having edges as sharp as the sides anterior to the barbs. There was an object gained by this method of procedure and will be referred to in another connection. [9–10]

[Series six represents broken spear points. Series seven consists of four large unfinished points, similar to arrowheads. Turner speculates that they may have been hastily manufactured when the supply of better tools ran out during an "unexpected abundance of game."] Number 837 [A65137] is worthy of remark for the reason that it is fashioned from a friable character of flint striated with minute veins of what appears to be quartz of nearly white color. The fracture of the flint is lustrous black, a character not evident in any of the remainder of the objects secured. The brittleness of the material may, in a manner, account for the crudity of form. [11]

It is not possible to describe each individual example of point intended to penetrate the flesh of the creatures affording food for the people of the Nearer Islands. So many forms are represented in the collection that they are readily divisible into seven classes, each showing a regular progression from the rudest character to a near approach to the next class and so on until the highest type is reached, containing a polished slate point set in a finely wrought bone or ivory shaft barbed on one side[,] usually a doubly dentate barb or series of one, two or three sets. [41]

The first class . . . are merely rounded pieces of bone of variable lengths and diameter, pointed and arranged with a beveled end to attach to a wooden shaft lashed by means of a thong.[1] This class may be characterized as thrusting weapons of the dagger or pierce type. Some are so small as to indicate having been the points only of larger parts now separated from them. [41]

The second class contains three flat pieces of bone, pointed and without barbs. Each of these show the posterior end notched for lashing to the wooden shaft that gave length to the implement. The barb is not yet developed and shows conclusively that these points were not intended to remain within the wound but [were] withdrawn after the blow was given. [42]

The third class more nearly resembles the first in general form but differs in the instruments[,] each having a more or less notched barb and sharp point for penetration and laceration for the barb is not so well defined as to suggest the possibility of having been retained within the stricken creature. Various shapes manifest themselves in this class, for here we begin to have the sharp edge developed on one side, the side where the barb is notched. The position of the barb is near[er] the point [than] to near the stem. [43]

The fourth class includes those pieces of bone, used as lance-heads, which have a flat form, sharp point and a well-developed barb. Usually, however, the barb is one, two, three or, rarely, four, set on the side. The barbs are deeply cut and were, when finished, sharp-pointed but now weather-worn. They were intended for lashing to shafts of wood and for retention within the creature struck. [44]

The fifth class indicates great progress to have been made in the construction of barbed implements attached to shafts for thrusting ... Each indicates the manner of attachment to the shaft, and of the methods employed there are two very evident and totally dissimilar. [45]

The first was merely a shaving of the stem to a thin edge and the shaft similarly treated. A neck or [indecipherable word] on the stem served to prevent the slipping of the lashing that held the shaft and point. The second consisted in trimming each side thin so as to fit into a cleft in the anterior or forward end of the wooden shaft. This was certainly a later device and from it doubtless sprung the idea of the coupling-joint now used. [45]

Each of the spear heads here included have barbs on each side. There are one[,] two[,] three or four barbs on each side. The form of the barb is different in the various examples, each appearing to be the result of the individual's preference. [45–46]

[One of the "better spear-heads" (T545), (A64845)] is quite well carved out and evinces a considerable degree of skill accompanied with an attempt at ornamentation. [46]

The sixth class represents a finer degree of skill in construction and continued to the present day. No. 773 [A65073] is a peculiar shape for insertion into a socket of the shaft or the bone-head of the shaft. The anterior end of the spear-head has a straight groove cut in for the reception of a stone point. This object is water worn and has sand tightly fixed in the groove. [46–47]

The remaining four examples of this class have one or two sets of barbs on one side only. A slot is cut in the forward end for the reception of a leaf-shaped metal (copper) point riveted through the bone jaws of the bone point. The stern end is flat and sets in a socket, evidently to become detached but held to the spear shaft by means of a stout thong passing through the eyelet. . . . No. 557 [E64857] is the only one made of walrus ivory. It has a point formed of the same material as the body. Two sets of bidented-barbs on one side, socket end and hole for thong characterize this implement, which is evidently of make within historic times. [47–48]

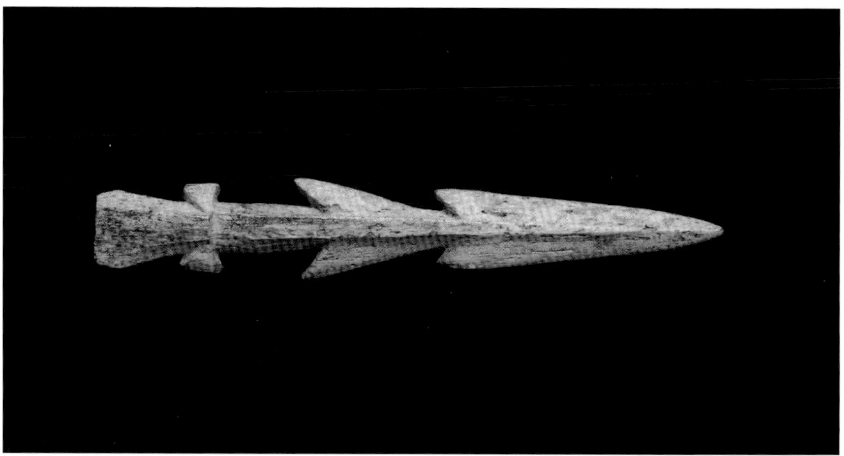

Fig. 26. Bone spear point, Attu. *Department of Anthropology, Smithsonian Institution (NMNH A64845) (T545).*

The thirty-fifth series embraces the seventh class of spear points. These are properly bone shafts to which the spear-head is affixed either loosely or firmly. The head shaft consisting of a long piece of bone, eight to twelve inches in length, and either fitted to be inserted within a socket on the end of the spear shaft or else the end itself has a cavity into which a point from the wooden shaft was inserted. These two, Nos. 548 [A64848] and 556 [A64856], implements indicate the transition from the affixed spear point to the detachable shaft. [49]

The thirty-sixth series embraces two large spear heads inseparable from the main shaft of wood. The size of these objects is quite large, number 677 [A64977] being ten and a half inches long, slotted at the rear end for the reception of the cuneate end of the main shaft, attached by means of a stout thong and prevented from loss by a thong run through an eyelet in the bone stem. The anterior end is expanded, tapering rapidly in front and having a deep cavity for the reception of the spear point, which was detachable. Ornamentation is here shown by the line incised into the length and circumference of the bone. [50]

The next implement is of ivory and is cylindrical, slightly more than seven inches long and more than an inch in diameter. The anterior end is swollen, or ringed, a conical cavity for a detachable point. The posterior end is wedge shaped for insertion into the V-shaped slot of the main shaft. A hole drilled through the ivory head held, by means of thongs, the head from loss. Ivory was a rare commodity previous to the coming of the Russians which lends color to the inference that this implement is of manufacture since historic times. This example is numbered 637 [A64937]. [50–51]

Knives

Among the most important instruments of stone used by the ancient Aleut were the larger kinds of knives of various shapes and sizes the former for individual preference and the latter for the various operations they were to perform. Certain kinds of stone were better adapted to be fashioned into implements that had not only a sharp but a serrated edge that, doubtless, contributed greatly in severing the tougher ligaments of the whale and larger seals. [191]

The nineteenth series of objects are cutters or knives for flaying mammals or dividing fish and cutting the parts into convenient size. None of these implements are made from flint or its varieties. The only material used in their construction is slate, shale and sandstone; some of the specimens exhibit a considerable degree of skill in their shaping to the present condition; and many of them indicate a long continued use as is evidenced, not only by the degree of smoothness but also from the well marked appearance of repeated grindings or rubbings to create anew the cutting edge that performs the function for which these blades were fashioned. [20]

There are three principal forms into which this (19th) series may be subdivided; each according to the shape; and, somewhat to the function performed in special operations. [20]

The first subdivision includes all those implements that have a reniform shape, somewhat resembling an irregularly outlined slice, taken longitudinally from a kidney, or convex on the lower or cutting edge and concave, or irregular, on the edge held by the handle or grasp. Some of the typical implements of this subdivision have the grasp or concave edge quite as sharply edged as the lower. No. 222 [A64522] is a perfect [example]. . . . It has been rubbed to sharpness which yet remains as fresh as when it left the hand of the last person many scores of years agone. The surfaces are rough and pitted. The opposite edge quite sharp and on one side is a distinct keel, not, however, the result of the artificer's skill. [20–21]

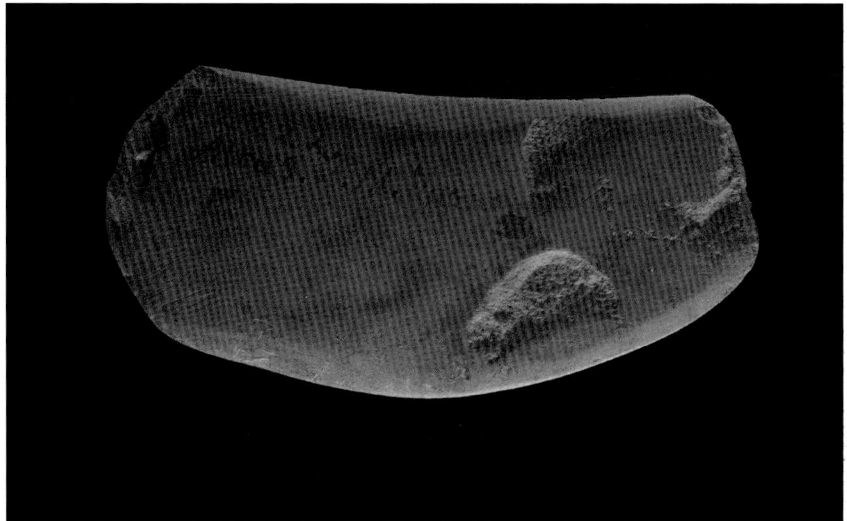

FIG. 27. Stone knife, Attu. *Department of Anthropology, Smithsonian Institution (NMNH A64522) (T222).* Turner described this stone tool as a "perfect" example of a knife with two sharp edges (the concave and convex sides) that was used for general cutting.

Some of these implements were hafted with wood which has decayed and left no trace of the particular form fitted for the hand to grasp. The cutting edge was but rarely straight-lined for even a portion of its length; a gentle curve for its greater length and an abrupt or upturned curve at either end, mostly however at the heel of the blade, or that portion held next to the body of the operator. The outline was simply that of the modern leather-workers "round-knife" or such as the furrier employs in cutting the various pelts into garments for wear. [191–192]

The second subdivision represents specimens which have three cutting edges. They are oblong nearly square implements, more or less irregularly outlined. They are intended as flensing or blubber knives to separate the fat from the attached muscle of the body of cetaceans and other large mammals by the lower or narrow edge incising while a stroke back and forth caused the front and rear edges successively to sever the attachments loosely holding the blubber to the flesh. After the creature was thus flayed, the same character of instrument was used to separate the blubber from the skin. No. 218 [A64518] is a type of this kind. [21]

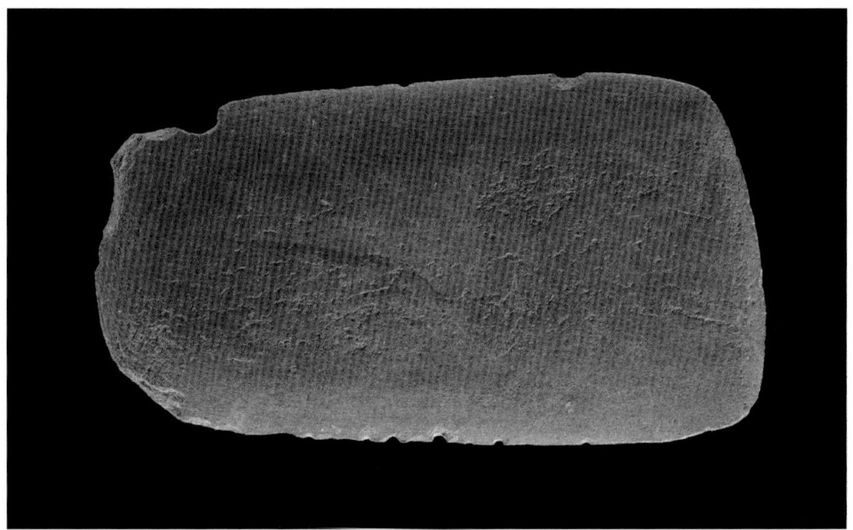

Fig. 28. Slate knife, Attu. *Department of Anthropology, Smithsonian Institution (NMNH A64518) (T218).* Turner described this knife as having three cutting edges. It was used both to separate fat from muscle in whales or other large mammals and to separate blubber from the skin.

The third subdivision comprises a peculiarly shaped knife having the sides somewhat curved inwardly and forming an apex. All the side edges of this character of implement are sharp and used for cutting. I can conceive of no special function to be performed by this form unless that of separating the intercostals muscles and for insertion into the smaller cavities having fleshy attachments. [21]

The thick skin of the large creatures obtained by the natives of those islands certainly required great skill to be cut by such imperfect edges as appear on the stone implements obtained from the village sites. An inspection of the freshly chipped edge will reveal a degree of sharpness that, coupled with a perfect knowledge of the manner of employment to the best advantage, would alone acquire, in the hands of those experienced in the use of such crude implements, a sufficient proficiency to sever any integument or cartilage necessary to the dismemberment of the beast, bird or fish. [193]

The manner of using the curved blade or edge was that of the operator pushing the knife from her with the rounded heel toward or from the person as the case might be. [193]

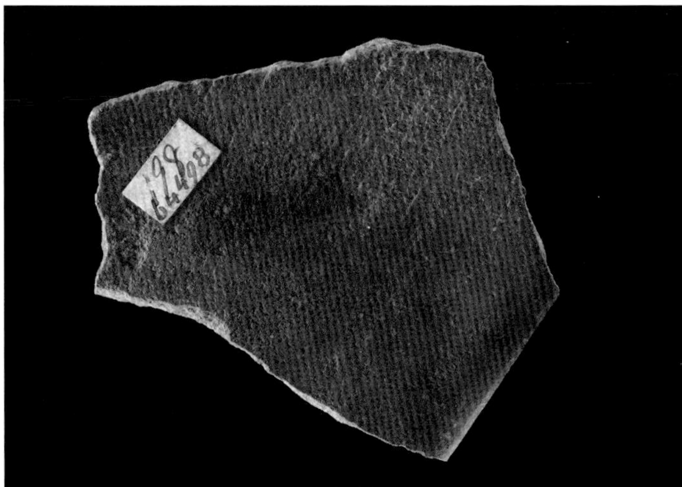

Fig. 29. Stone knife, Attu. *Department of Anthropology, Smithsonian Institution (NMNH A64498) (T198).* This knife had five usable sides. Both this and A64971 were examples of "cutters of flesh and for removing the pelts from the various creatures obtained for food and other purposes."

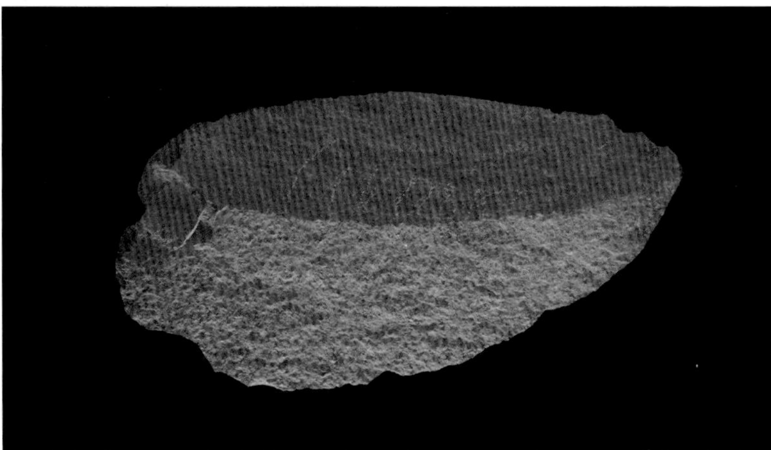

Fig. 30. Stone knife, Amchitka. *Department of Anthropology, Smithsonian Institution (NMNH A64971) (T671).* Although quite different in appearance from A64498, this knife was also used for both removing skins and for general cutting. This was collected at Amchitka, where Turner stopped briefly on his return to Unalaska from Attu in 1881.

The twentieth series embraces five knives fashioned from the bones of whale or seal. . . . Number 7 is a better formed knife of bone, having a curved edge rising to a point formed by the sloping back. The posterior half of back slopes so as to form a convenient depression for the hand grasp with thc short handle supported by not more than two fingers below. [23]

Tool Production

In the preparation of all articles of wood[,] sharp-edged flakes of stone were used to bring the wood to the required shape. [152] . . . It is more convenient to break a readily cleaveable stone that when so split will possess an edge sharper than human ingenuity may prepare, from and with such crude material, than to chip an edge that is none the less readily broken. For that reason all of the selected chips and flakes from the rough material used in fashioning implements are preserved as rasps, blades and shaves for dressing the shafts of spears, hafts of hand weapons and utensils, frames and paddles of the kaiak and umiak. [17]

Wedges of bone were inserted in clefts in the log and by blows the wedge was forced to split the wood which was again riven to the proper size and then trimmed with stone adzes and scrapers of stone. [152]

The adzes were hafted with a piece of wood serving for a handle to which the stone blade was securely affixed by means of stout thongs of sealskin. The flakes of stone used as shavers or scrapers were mostly inserted in the cleft of a stick, usually about half way and on each side of the flake the stick was lightly bound. The instrument was then used in the manner of a spoke-shave. It was seldom that a dull-edged implement of this kind was again sharpened for a new chip was broken off with a sharper edge than could be produced by the chipping process which left a serrated edge. Only the permanently hafted implements were re-edged. Often a piece of rough stone was employed to smooth the surface of a flat surface, and it was a matter of surprise to me to witness a modern Aleut perform that operation in so short a time that I could readily appreciate the facility with which one totally accustomed to that work could shape stone or wood at will. [153–154]

Upon inquiry I was shown the manner by which the flint and other stone implements were fashioned, and was told that a variety of other tools were required but that a notched piece of bone or ivory was employed much in the manner that a glazier chips a piece of glass and that the rough stone was first broken with a maul or stone and that the asperities were removed with a blunt pointed stone or bone instrument. [154] Number 124 [A64424] is a greenish gray stone of hard texture well adapted to receive a sharp edge and is one of the principal materials used in the fashioning of knives. . . . [11]

Stone and bone drills were used as perforaters of wood and ivory. [154–155]

[In series 28 Turner identified three pieces of bone "as material from which to fashion the various instruments and parts of spears and other weapons and utensils." No. 402 (A64702) was "the petrous portion of the ear of a whale." No. 404 (A64704, missing) was "a portion of the head bone of some cetacean." No. 781 (A65081), he was informed, was a bone from a sea cow. In series 32 he listed No. 600 (A64900) as "a piece of bone reserved for the fashioning of some important implement of the chase or of household use."]

The articles of wood that required bending, such as the hoop for the hatch of the skin canoe, was shaped and then wrapped with the fronds of the broad-leafed seaweed and then laid upon a fire. The steam evolved was sufficient to soften the wood and permit it to be bent to the required form. [155]

The Aleut of former years had no metals with which even to tip the spear used in the chase. When the Russians fired the first gun that sounded on the shore the natives were horror stricken. All implements of metal were means of evil spirits working harm to all but the whites who feared not evil or death. The anchor of the frail boats, termed schooners and ships, that fell from the bow into the water was deemed a lure for the evil spirits of the lower depths to fasten upon and thus aid the whiteman in his diabolical endeavors upon the natives. Many years passed before a native touched an anchor, the largest piece of metal that the Aleut gazed upon, for fear the evil touch would be transmitted from the submarine spirits, with which their ancestors had long contended and but seldom mastered. [168–169]

In later years many of the bolts, bars and fastenings of the larger vessels, of the Russian merchants, were of copper, a metal that was quickly seized upon by the Aleut as it was easily worked and the native artisan had many opportunities of witnessing the transformation of a sheet of that metal into wondrous shapes by the craft of the Russian hand. [169]

It soon was employed to the exclusion of all other metals. Brass was, however, excepted for it had certain properties that rendered it available where copper was not suitable. Even at the present day the natives prefer spear tips of copper for the sea-otter darts first because it is easily worked and not liable to corrosion and [second] should it strike a bone it bends and does not break like iron or steel. Knives were highly valued as the first possessions of a native and to this day a blade of iron or steel that would appear insignificant and valueless to a whiteman may be made to perform offices that would weary one with less patience; so that now the use of metal has been substituted for that of stone and bone. [169–170]

Certain operations of the present day require a moderate amount of heat and then the ancient lamp of boulder is placed on the ground and a spoonful of oil poured into the shallow cavity. A piece of cloth or shreds of dry grass is laid in the oil and set fire to. Such a heat is employed for drying the paint of the paddles used with the canoes or on the spears cast at sea-otters. The pigments employed are of two kinds, one a softish stone, hematite, of reddish color powdered by grinding on a flat stone with a stone muller. This paint is then mixed with a little seal oil and thinned with the blood of a raven. It is applied, usually, with the finger-tips and the painted portion held over the flame to dry in the heat. The second pigment is the ink-bag of the Octopus (*Octopus punctatus* Gabb). The ink-sac is taken from the creature and dried for future use. When required it is quite hard and greatly resembles a conical stick of Indian-ink. It was powdered by atrition [sic] and mixed with a little water or else the surface is rubbed with oil and the thinned black paint applied to the part and this held over the flame to allow the paint to be absorbed into the pores of the wood. After that is done the hand is oiled and rubbed over the paint which now assumes a stove-polish color and is said to be non-retentive of the water which would otherwise cling to the wood. [188–190]

Several other pigments are employed for ornamental purpose but as they are purchased from the stores they belong more to the modern decorative art than to that of former times and will be referred to later on. [190]

9

Mammals

Whales

The quantity of driftwood cast upon the shores of those islands was probably sufficient for general purposes but not for building such structures as are to be found among the Innuit of the mainland. Its absence was supplied by the use of the bones, jaws, ribs and vertebra [sic] of the larger cetaceans abounding in the waters washing those islands. Remains of those bones are to be found in nearly all of the ancient village sites. I saw at Attu Island an immense slab, of bone about three inches thick, thirty inches wide and thirty-six inches long, that had been used as a closure for a doorway of a hut in the village to the left of the entrance to Chichagof Harbor. It was so large that I could scarcely credit it until it was carefully examined and found that it had been roughly chipped to that condition by means of an ax. In former years the Sperm Whale was plentiful about that island and this huge slab of bone had doubtless been taken from a portion of the head of one of the largest of that species. In the same locality there were, in 1881, yet standing several ribs of a whale, that were a part of the side of a half-underground dwelling occupied at the time of the advent of the Russians in 1745. There are but few caves on the shores of Attu, and these are mostly of such character as scarcely to be designated by such expression. [150–151]

Certain hunters were skilled in the capture of whales and others in the sea-otter hunts or pursuit of sea-lions and other seals. The smaller marine creatures belonged to the captors but the larger whales were divided among the entire population. [122]

The whale-killing was conducted under special regulations of the chase often cumbered by masses of offerings and propitiations, as that only certain hunters attained a great skill in spearing those creatures; and, to the hunter redounded great praise for his prowess, and offerings for his continued success. [122–123]

The whale struck by the hunter's spear was supposed to remain three days under water and then rise to the surface to be floated to some locality. The hunter did not announce in words that the whale had received a fatal blow but he observed certain ceremonies that intimated his success. At the end of that time he chose a companion and they went to search for the carcass. Each village was aware a whale was expected to be found and the finders did not touch it until the hunter had proved his prey and then gave permission for its division among the people. Some of the smaller cetaceans were eaten but only in small quantity for the fat acted beyond the control of the eater, passing through the person without restraint so that to this day an oil-spot elicits the remark that the one has been eating of its flesh, an expression denoting the extreme poverty of the partaker. [123–124]

As has been remarked on a previous page, the capture of the whale was surrounded by many ceremonies of peculiar character and as the importance of those hunters was valued by the communities, in which they dwelt, the captor of a whale was looked upon as a public benefactor and his vocation finally became shrouded in mystery made more difficult by the degree of renown attached to the killing of those creatures until a sect of hunters and their descendants were honored beyond all other procurers of food. Feasts and festivities were established in commemoration of the events of their lives and praises sung for them after their death. [170–171]

Ascents to the summits of the hills gave the eager watcher ample view of the spout of vapor that discovered the presence of the whale he desired to capture. In these lonesome vigils the imagination had full sway and [in] the superstitious native [—] who believed that in every blade of grass or leaf of other plant, every rock, wave[,] cloud or snowflake[,] bird or beast[,] was accompanied by its spirit of life followed by the spectre of death [—] gave rise to many weird imaginings and as they preyed upon the mind of the watcher enshrouding his frame with mysterious sounds, that were heard only in that stillness, to take visible forms and become fastened in the thought of the person until he believed only his fancy and not reality. Seldom did he inquire, belief was enough and from this the strange recitations related upon his return to the people were but repeated and believed until those beliefs became a part of their lives and history. [171–172]

Certain stones afforded flakes transformed by the hunter's hand into heads of the shaft he would lunge into the side of the whale and there remain until the very movement of the creature caused the muscles to be severed by contact with the broken spear-head thrust into it. Slate and flint were known to be better adapted for this purpose as their brittleness soon caused a break from the shaft that gave force and direction to it. [172]

As soon as the Russians came another character of material was employed as a substitute for the slate and flint heads of the shafts used in whaling. The white men brought their bottles and flasks of brandy and other liquids and from the glass of those bottles was fashioned a spear-head more deadly than a dozen of those from slate. [172]

The glass sides of the larger bottles were chipped with such facility and its strength and brittleness made such vessels greatly prized for the purpose. Even to this day the Aleut whale-hunter employs no other material for his spear-heads used in whaling conducted under a different method than formerly obtained. Then a man in his single canoe stealthily approached his victim and struck it. Now a boy (youth) accompanies him on the expedition. [172]

Certain ones of the whales were possessed of a particularly vindictive spirit and these sought to destroy the hunter and his craft the moment it came in view. Charms of most potent character were worn to ward off the attack of those whales (the genus Orca is mostly referred to here) and divert them from the course of the hunter. [176]

Tools Related to Whaling

The tenth series embraces three very large implements intended as heads of spears for securing larger species of whales. They indicate blades of not less than six inches long by two and a half inches wide. The point and sides are similar to those of series three and four. The edges are quite sharp and the entire surface smooth, but without polish. The numbers are 113 [A64413], 265 [A64565], and 229 [A64529]. [13]

The fourteenth series embraces two characters of implements intended to be hafted in order to be effective for the purpose of employment as flensers. Nos. 101 [A64401] and 111 [A64411] are implements, No. 101 of which has a long stem to be inserted in a shaft of wood of convenient length, to enable the person to give a back and forth stroke in separating the blubber from the muscle or fat from the skin of the cetacean or phocid secured by means of other weapons employed in their capture. The form of the spatulate end for cutting is similarly edged to that of the common spear or arrow

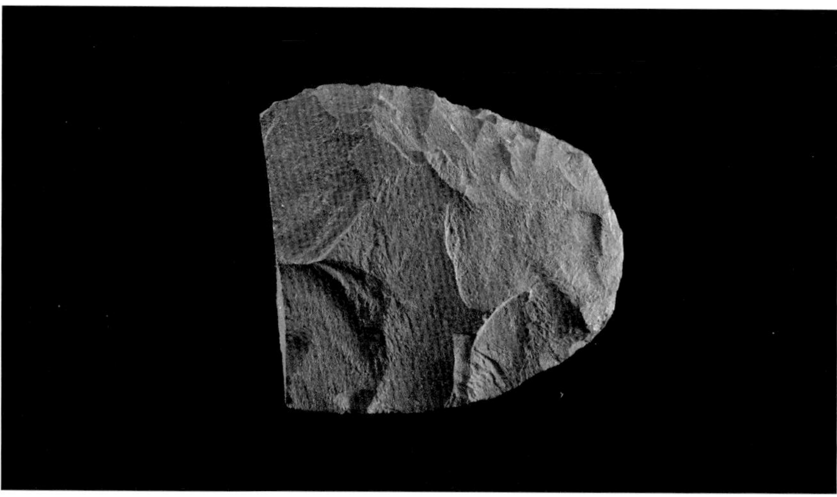

Fig. 31. Flensing blade, Attu. *Department of Anthropology, Smithsonian Institution (NMNH A64411) (T111).* This blade would have had a wooden handle. It was used to strip the skin or muscle from large sea mammals.

head, or in other words double edged when viewed from either side. The tip is rounded and penetrates while the sides cut length-wise. Numbers 263 [A64563] and 303 [A64603] are for hafting but lack the neck or stem. They were, doubtless used similarly to the metal blubber spades employed by white whalemen. [15–16]

The fifteenth series are the connecting links in the transition from the knife to the perfected spear-head of stone. These implements were held in the hand and served as knives to sever the larger pieces of blubber and flesh flensed from the body of the creatures serving for food of those people. Singularly enough[,] one of the stone knives is almost identical in form with one cut from the jaw-bone of a whale. These numbers, for the fifteenth series, are 269 [A64569] and 670 [64970]. [16]

Sea Cows

On the Near Group it is asserted that the Sea Cow, *Rytina gigas* Zimm., was at one time abundant about the shores of those islands. It was so harmless that this huge creature was considered as woman's game. (Whether this mammal or another species existed there can be determined only by exploration and excavation on Semichi where the bones are yet visible on the surface.[)] The living Attu people assert that the Sea Cow fed upon the seaweeds and that when hard storms came up the beasts would seek some quiet cove and lie just above the swash of the waves on the land. When their stomachs were full the creatures would cling to the rocks of a low reef and there doze in the sunshine. The Sea Cow was so little afraid of man that they scarcely noticed his approach and that the women would thrust a spear into the side while the beast gazed only in a stupid look upon the person. From the best information I am led to believe that the Sea Cow became extinct there at a later date than upon the Commander Islands. [179–180]

10

Birds

The women were expert in obtaining the various birds of the islands and as the means employed for their capture did not alarm the birds they had not the shyness that characterizes them at the present day. [205–206]

In the capture of the birds settling on the land various means were employed to entrap them. The birds whirling through the air were brought down by the bolas, described on a preceding page [see next section], slung amidst the outspread wings and necks of a flock of muttering geese that scarcely noticed the headlong fall of their companion entangled by the thongs to which the weight-stones were attached. The net of whalebone (baleen) strips interwoven with sinew strands set a few inches apart and then stood on end until it resembled a number of stalks of dried herbage. A string led from the net and when the geese assembled about the margin of a clear pool to preen their feathers newly protruding from the skin the net was drawn down without sound and the astonished captives found themselves in the meshes of a trap unsuspected. The goose-hunter flew to the scene and quickly wrenched the necks of the struggling birds. [206–207]

The cormorants were knocked from the rocks on which they sat. The eiders were noosed on the nest or clubbed while huddled in the lee of a rock during the pelting and surging of the surf into which fear made them hesitate to plunge. Nesting and other birds were obtained by many devices. There does not appear any pronged spear among the Aleut, ancient or modern, such as is employed by the mainland Innuit. [207]

*Among the Aleutian Islands the birds have forsaken the vicinity of the villages, and only by visiting the uninhabited islands can a complete series of specimens be obtained, as the people and foxes have driven the birds away. This is noteworthy from the fact that the natives of Attu speak of a large cormorant, which, from the description given by them, could have been none other than the greatly desired Pallas's cormorant (*Phalacrocorax perspicillatus* Pall.).[1] This bird is now not to be found, where but twenty years ago (when no fire-arms were used) it was quite abundant at Attu and among the other Nearer islands. [C:7]

The eggs of the myriads of birds that breed on those islands formed no inconsiderable part of the food of the people and during the season of egging all ages and sexes were engaged in securing the food that required no cooking to be of palatable character for the throat of one whose taste scarcely distinguished the difference between cooked or raw food. [207–208]

Bolas

The twenty-sixth series embraces five rounded stones none of which exceed the size of the egg of the barn-yard fowl. Numbers 412 [A64712], 416 [64716] and 414 [64714] have a groove cut entirely around or partially around the central portion either the longer or shorter axis of each stone. Numbers 673 [64973] and 415 [64715] are not grooved. [30]

Each of the stones of this series forms one of the three or four stones employed in the capture of birds whose flight is usually in flocks and never of the smaller birds. [30]

A string (leather thong) of about sixteen to eighteen inches long had one end securely tied around a stone of this character; three or four stones were thus prepared. The loose ends of the strings were knotted securely together leaving a distal length of ten to twelve inches from stone to central knot and when two stones were separated extremely the distance was twenty to twenty-four inches. The knotted end of the three or four cords was placed in the palm of the hand and the thongs arranged without interference. The stones were disposed on the hand and when a flock of muttering geese came low over the head of the person concealed at the top of the defile or the brow of the hill over which the unsuspecting birds flew the *bolas* was whirled among the birds and rarely failed to entangle one or more of the birds which fell fluttering at the feet of the person casting the stones and hastening to meet the fall of the bird. Many times I have witnessed the older women and men arrange the bolas and cast it at imaginary geese to illustrate the use of the stones so often designated as sinkers for nets. [30–31]

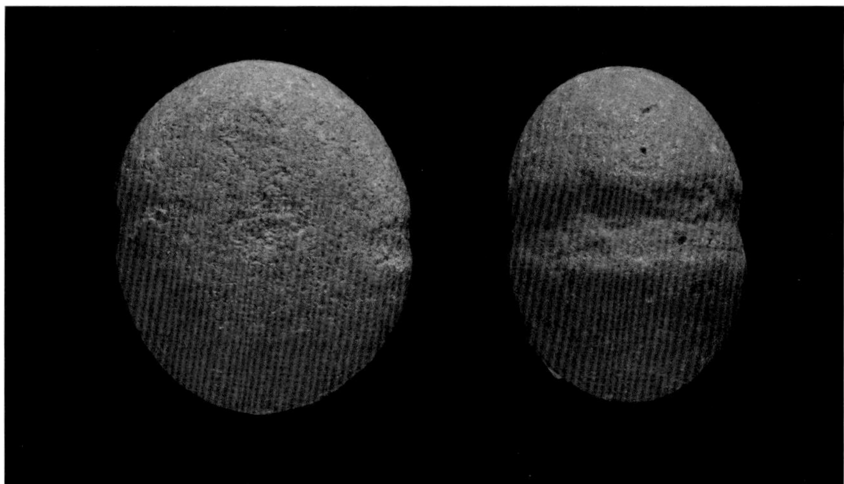

FIG. 32. Two stones used in a bola. *Department of Anthropology, Smithsonian Institution (NMNH A64712 and A64716) (T412 and T416).* Bolas had three or four stones, none larger than "the egg of the barn-yard fowl." The art of using a bola was demonstrated for Turner only by older residents.

*In the earliest times, and before the advent of the Russians, they used another means [*other than guns and nets*] to procure birds of all kinds, but especially geese and ducks. The beach was searched for three rounded stones of near equal weight and size, generally about one and one-half inches in diameter, though this differed with each individual's strength, the women also using lighter stones than those used by the men. [C:140–141]

*After the stones had been selected a groove was cut round the stone and deepened sufficiently to hold a strong thong of seal-skin about twelve inches long. Each stone was thus prepared with the thong securely tied to it. The three loose ends of the strings were then tied together, so that the distance between two outstretched stones was about twenty inches. The strings were then taken by the knotted ends and laid carefully in the palm of the hand. The stones that are attached to the other ends of the strings were carefully disposed on the coiled thongs in the hand. A flock of geese that came within distance would have this *bolas* thrown at them, and was certain to become entangled on the neck or wings of some goose, which fell to the earth and was immediately secured. The women were adepts [sic] at throwing these stones. An old woman told me that she had often secured two and occasionally three geese at a single throw. [C:141]

Notes on Specific Birds

[Turner's *Contributions* has extensive information on birds from both St. Michael and the Aleutian Islands. The following extracts, limited to the Aleutians, contain either ethnographic information or details about his stay in the islands. Modern common and scientific names are in brackets if they differ from those used by Turner.]

Horned Grebe

Colymbus auritus [*Podiceps auritus*]

*Among the Aleutian Islands it is to be found in the winter. I did not observe it there in the summer and at no time to the westward of Unalashka Island.... The native who brought me a specimen of this bird had no name for it, and declared it was the first he had seen. At Attu island I observed a Grebe, which I suspected was this species. It was so shy that near approach was impossible. [C:115]

Black-throated Loon

Urinator arcticus [*Gavia arctica*]

*These birds are to be found among the Aleutian Islands at any season of the year. At Amchitka Island a pair frequently were seen in the bay, during the month of June, but always just out of range for a shot. They would swim up and down the bay for half a mile and return by the same course. A native boy finally shot one of them, unknown to me until after he had plucked the feathers from the body. The Aleuts value the flesh very highly, but admit that it is tough. [C:116]

Red-throated Loon

Urinator lumme [*Gavia stellata*]

*Among the Aleutian Islands this species is quite abundant. It breeds in nearly all the islands of the chain. At Atkha several pairs were known to breed among the lakes of the highest hills. Several young of this bird were brought to me, while at Atkha in 1879, but want of time, when I received them, caused me to put them in an out-building. The next day I went to look for them, and found that the rats had carried them off during the night. [C:116]

*When the young birds are not yet able to accompany the parents the latter feed them on small fish fry from the sea. A pair which had nested a couple of miles back of the village at Nazan Bay, on Atkha Island, attracted my attention early every morning by their harsh, cackling notes as the parent flew toward the bay to obtain food. I endeavored to discover whence the parent came, and posted myself near the track it usually flew, but the intervening hills prevented me from detecting the locality. I could not but observe the regularity with which the morning visit was made to the bay. It never varied ten minutes from 8 o'clock a.m. [C:116–117]

*The flesh of this bird is considered palatable by many of the Aleuts and most of the people near Saint Michael's. [C:117]

*This species remains among the Aleutian Islands the entire year, but less in winter than in summer. [C:117]

Tufted Puffin

Lunda cirhata

*Among the Aleutian Islands, and on the south side of Aliaska, with adjacent islands, these Puffins are found in great numbers. Some of the islands afford better locations for breeding, and these are resorted to by incredible numbers of these birds. Their food consists of mollusks and other marine food, such as small fish. . . . [C:117]

*While the natives are on the summer hunt for sea-otters they improve the days unfavorable for that pursuit in visiting the breeding localities of the Tufted and Horned Puffins, to catch them for their skins. The hand is usually protected with a leathern glove of seal-skin, or else a coat sleeve is wrapped around on the hand. The bird makes little attempt to avoid capture, but holds by the beak to the person, and uses its feet to best advantage. The natives endeavor to catch the bird by the wing, as the claws are then used to retard the bird being withdrawn from its crevice or hole, and, besides, in the struggle, if the bird should be taken by the body the feathers might be pulled out. As soon as the bird is captured the native either breaks the small of the bird's back, or else bites it in the head. This latter method is preferred for killing all kinds of large birds, and is more practiced by the Aleuts, while the northern people break the back of the bird. [C:117]

[See the description of preparing puffin skins for garments in Chapter 5.]

Horned Puffin

Fratercula corniculata

*Later in that month [June 1878] I saw them in thousands near Amak Island, just north of the western end of the Peninsula of Aliaska. This is the beginning of the area of their greatest abundance. All the Aleutian Islands, with their adjacent islets, form an east and west extension of a continuous breeding ground of these birds for over a thousand miles in length. The Pribylof Group, Saint Mathew's Island and Saint Lawrence Island are also great breeding places of these Puffins. . . . [C:118–119]

*The skins of this bird are used to a great extent in making articles of clothing for some of the western Aleuts and some of the natives near the Yukon Delta and southward. [C:119]

Cassin's Auklet

Ptychoramphus aleuticus

*A specimen of this Auklet was obtained at Atkha Island, June 23, 1879. The bird was brought by a fisherman who lives at Old Harbor, on the northeast end of Atkha Island. He reported this species to be not abundant, yet common and breeding there. [C:119]

Crested Auklet

Simorhynchus cristatellus [*Aethia cristatella*]

*Among the Aleutian Islands this Auk is extremely abundant.... The note of this bird is a peculiar grunt of two or three syllables. It is impossible to represent the sound by any combination of letters. In former years when the Aleuts of one village or island made war on their neighbors the early morning notes of this bird indicated to the people the time of day for making an attack. [C:119–120]

Whiskered Auklet

Simorhynchus pygmaeus [*Aethia pygmaea*]

*Three specimens of this Auklet were obtained at Atkha Island, June 12, 1879. Two of them were adult males in the breeding plumage and one in the downy state. They were brought to me by a native, who had killed them near the base of Korovinsky volcano. They were reported to be common in that neighborhood. [C:120]

Fig. 33. Whiskered Auklet, *Simorhynchus pygmaeus.* Plate I. *Contributions to the Natural History of Alaska.* Courtesy, Rare Books & Manuscripts, Special Collections, Middlebury College Vermont. This illustration was made by Turner's boyhood friend, Robert Ridgway, who served as Curator of Birds at the Smithsonian from 1880 to 1929.

*I saw several individuals near the outer islet at the entrance to Nazan Bay, on Atkha Island. They were not recognized in any other part of the Aleutian Chain, excepting on the Nearer Group, where they were quite abundant. [C:120]

Least Auklet

Simorhynchus pusillus [*Aethia pusilla*]

*Many individuals of this Auklet were seen while I was on a sailing vessel travelling from one place to another among the Aleutian Islands. This species occurs along the entire chain, and as far east as Kadiak. . . . This bird does not come near the present settlements on the Aleutian Islands, while at Saint George's Island, of the Pribylof Group, it is wonderfully abundant almost in the village. They are very active while on the water, and disappear like a flash when they dive. Near Semichi and Atkha I observed quite a number of these little birds sitting on the water. [C:120]

Ancient Murrelet

Synthliboramphus antiquus

*A single specimen of this bird was obtained at Atkha Island, June 12, 1879. It was brought to me by a native, who had shot it at the base of Korovinsky volcano, on the northeast end of Atkha Island. Upon inquiry I was informed that these birds are plentiful in that locality, and breed in holes made in the turf, or sod, overhanging the brow of the cliffs. Among the Nearer Islands this Murrelet is abundant in summer, breeding, and is sparingly resident; rarely coming to Attu, but more plentiful on the western end of Semichi and the south side of Agattu. [C:120]

Kittlitz's Guillemot [Kittlitz's Murrelet]

Brachyramphus Kittlitzii [*Brachyramphus brevirostris*]

*A single specimen of Kittlitz's Guillemot was obtained April 24, 1879, at Iliuliuk village on Unalashka Island. It was the only one seen in that locality. The native who brought it to me asserted that this species is abundant throughout the year at Sannakh Island. They breed there, laying a single, pure white egg. The nest is placed among the roots of the large tussocks of grass on the edges of bluffs and cliff ledges. I observed several of these birds to the westward of Unalashka Island. They are not rare on Amchitka Island, and in the neighborhood of the Old Harbor, on Atkha Island. [C:120–121]

Fig. 34. Kittlitz's Guillemot (Kittlitz's Murrelet). Plate II. *Contributions to the Natural History of Alaska.* Courtesy, Rare Books & Manuscripts, Special Collections, Middlebury College Vermont. This is another illustration by Robert Ridgway and shows a typical Aleutian seascape.

Pallas's Murre [Thick-billed Murre]

Uria lomvia arra

*Along the entire Aleutian chain these birds are to be found. At Bogoslov Island millions of them breed every summer. I was in a boat within a few yards of that island in June, 1880, and passed within 300 yards of it in a vessel in June, 1881. A large colony of sea-lions breed here every year. Some of the crew fired rifle shots at some of the sea-lions, and when the sound of the report was reverberated against the bluff the air was filled with these birds. The entire surface of the island, from 100 feet from its base to its top, was made white with the breasts of these birds. The island is about 600 feet high, and conical, composed of disintegrating, angular pieces, constantly being detached, by action of the weather, from the mass which composes the island. When the birds flew from their nests small pieces of stone were thrown down, and these again started others, that on one occasion caused, by the great mass of fine rock falling on it, a huge rock to come bounding down its side right in the midst of one of the principal places where the sea-lions were lying. The large rock that fell was not less than twelve feet square, and weighed over a hundred tons. The thundering noise caused the hundreds of sea-lions to take to the water, and in their haste many were so injured as to be incapable of regaining their places when their alarm had subsided. The rock rolled on several, and mashed them flat. The birds took flight, and darkened the air with their numbers. [C:122]

Parasitic Jaeger

Stercorarius parasiticus

*This bird is a frequent visitor to the Aleutian Islands. I observed it at Atkha July 17, 1879, and again in June, 1880, at the same place. A few days after I saw one flying near the vessel while off Kiska Island. At the Semichi Islands it breeds abundantly, according to the assertions of the natives. I have seen the bird on several occasions near Chichagof Harbor, Attu Island, but it visits only this island from Agattu and Semichi. At Amchitka Island I saw several of these birds sitting on the hillocks and tussocks of grass. They were at this place exceedingly shy, and would under no circumstances permit me to approach within gunshot. [C:123]

Long-tailed Jaeger

Stercorarius longicaudus

*The Long-tailed Jaeger is rarely seen on the Eastern Aleutian Islands. I saw one at Sannakh Island in July, 1878. I saw a few at Atkha Island in 1879, and two at Attu Island in 1880. . . . Throughout the Territory of Alaska the Jaegers are known to the Russian-speaking population as *Ras bói nik*, a word meaning robber, thief. [C:124]

Red-legged Kittiwake

Rissa brevirostris

*The Aleutian Islands and the Pribylof Group are its home. On Akutan quite a number were observed on a high cliff near the village on that island. In the same year (1878) I saw a few at Sannakh. . . . [C:124]

Western Glaucous Gull [Glaucous-winged Gull]

Larus barrovianus Ridgw. [*Larus barrovianus*, Point Barrow Gull, was downgraded or lumped in 1895 with *Larus glaucus* into *Larus hyperboreus*, Glaucous Gull. *Larus glaucescens*, Glaucous-winged Gull, is the dominant gull in the Aleutians.]

*Among the Aleutian Islands these birds remain throughout the year, though in winter much less in number. They are compelled by severe periods of weather to come directly into the villages for food. I have frequently seen them sitting on the sod-covered houses of the natives. At these times I have seen them scarcely fly when approached. . . . The note of this bird is variable, in spring a harsh *kaoú*, which changes to a deep *honk* in a few weeks. When flying along the shore a prolonged, grunting croak is uttered. I have also observed that the Western Glaucus [sic] Gull changes its note during the winter, as at this time a note is uttered which is heard at no other season; and in the spring the note is not again heard. . . . The Aleuts have several names for it to indicate the special plumages as are shown by the age of the bird. The adult bird is called *Hlú kakh*, and is derived from the note of this species. [C:125]

Short-billed Gull

Larus brachyrhynchus [*Larus brachyrhynchus* was merged with *Larus canus,* Mew Gull, in 1910.]

*Among the Aleutian Islands these birds congregate in many thousands on the cliffs to breed. On the islands where I have been stationed natives also live. They and the foxes keep, to a great extent, these, and in fact nearly all other water birds, from breeding near the settlements. It is to the uninhabited islands that the majority of the birds resort, hence [I] did not obtain the eggs of this species. . . . The flesh is said to be very good; the Aleuts eat it either raw or cooked. [C:126]

Short-tailed Albatross

Diomedea albatrus

*Among the Aleutian Islands they are quite common, but generally far out at sea. They approach the land during dense fogs, and may then be found sitting on a small rock jutting from the water. I never could obtain a specimen in condition to save the skin, for the birds do not come near the settlements; and, when a native kills one he saves only the wings, from which to take the sinew for wrapping round his spear heads. At Attu I saw two specimens that were killed in the latter part of March, 1881. The wings had been cut off and the body partly plucked of feathers. This species passes the winter in this locality and may be found, during very severe weather, about the western end of the island of Attu. [C:128–129]

Fork-tailed Petrel [Fork-tailed Storm Petrel]

Oceanodroma furcata

*The Atkha people assert that these birds breed abundantly on the cliffs of Korovinsky volcano, on the northeast shoulder of Atkha Island. I have seen this species as far westward as Attu Island. At Atkha a native brought me a specimen of this bird, but it had been kept so long before an opportunity occurred to permit his return to the village that the bird was too far advanced in decomposition to allow the skin to be taken off. [C:129]

White-crested Cormorant [Double-crested Cormorant]

Phalacrocorax dilophus [*Phalacrocorax auritus*]

*The white plumes on the head of this Cormorant, in the breeding season, are used by the inhabitants of the Aleutian Chain to adorn the small sacks (used as work-bags) made by the Aleut women. The feathers of the neck are also used for the same purpose. [C:129]

Pelagic Cormorant

Phalacrocorax pelagicus

*In most localities of the Aleutian Islands this form is extremely numerous. . . . It is by far the most beautiful bird of Bering Sea. The plumage glitters with metallic reflections of blue, purple, and bronze. . . . The natives of all parts of the country use the flesh of this bird for food. Some of the Aleuts, especially those of Attu, prize the flesh more than any other bird. They formerly obtained many of these birds with a kind of net which was thrown over the birds when sitting on the shore rocks, being driven there by the severity of a storm so that the birds could not remain on the outer rocks without being washed off. In former years this bird was reported to be extremely abundant at Attu, but has greatly disappeared in the last fifteen years. Before the introduction of civilized clothing the skins of these birds were used for clothing. Fifteen of them were counted as a *parka* or long gown-like garment. [C:130]

American Merganser [Common Merganser]

Merganser americanus [*Mergus merganser*]

*A pair of these birds was seen in the possession of a native at Unalashka Island, January 17, 1879. He would not part with them on any consideration, as he supposed the good will of the person [Father Innokentii Shaiashnikov] to whom they were presented to be of more value than anything received from one outside the pale of his church. They were the only ones of this species seen in the country. [C:130–131]

Red-breasted Merganser

Merganser serrator [*Mergus serrator*]

*At Atkha it breeds in the small ponds on the high levels of the mountains. . . . The flesh of the Red-breasted Merganser is quite a delicacy among the Aleuts, who seem to prize it higher than the flesh of any Duck. . . . The Russian name is *Kro khál.* [131]

Mallard

Anas boschas [*Anas platyrhynchos*]

*The low land at the head of Captain's Harbor, on Unalashka Island, forms a winter feeding-ground for hundreds of these ducks. . . . During the fall and winter the flesh of this duck is excellent, being fat and tender. The Russian name of the duck is *Sé le sen.* [131]

Harlequin Duck

Histrionicus histrionicus (Linn.)

*The flesh of this duck is good, but somewhat fishy. The Aleuts have but little liking for its flesh, as they seldom shoot it when they have opportunity. The nest and eggs were not procured and the only nest I ever saw was near Iliuliuk village, on Unalashka Island. Two immense blocks of rock had become detached from the cliff above, and when they fell their edges formed a hollow place beneath. In under this I discovered a deserted nest, which the native who was with me asserted was that of a bird of this species. The form was similar to that of the nest of *C. hyemalis*, and in fact so closely resembled it that I persisted in it being of this bird until the native asked me if I did not know that the Old-squaw did not build in such places. [C:135]

Pacific Eider [Common Eider]

Somateria v-nigra [*Somateria mollissima*]

*Another peculiarity that was brought to my notice by a native was that these birds usually seek some slope where the Duck Hawk [peregrine falcon] has its nest on the high point forming one end of the slope. This was true in three instances that came under my observation. The Eiders were more numerous in such localities than otherwise. The natives always are glad when the Hawk comes screaming overhead as the canoe is being paddled along the shore, for they know the nest of the Hawk is near and that many nests of the Eider will be found close by. [C:136]

*The bird is very shy except when on land during boisterous weather. At that time the natives of the western islands of the Aleutian Chain used small hand-nets to throw over the birds as they sat stupidly on the shore. A bright night with a hard gale of wind was the best time to secure them. The birds then sat in a huddle and many are caught at one throw of the net. The natives assert that the common Hair Seals catch these birds when on the water and drag them under to play with them; hence, these birds are constantly on the alert for seals and take flight as soon as a seal is discovered near. [C:137]

Cackling Goose [Canada Goose]

Branta canadensis

*This date [by August 20] witnesses a few of the older young and adult males coming from the breeding-grounds on the Semechi Islands to the island of Attu. The geese have exhausted, by that time, the food supply of that place, and repair to Attu to feast on the berries of the *Vaccineum* that are rapidly ripening. Attu Island has a great many Blue Foxes (*V. lagopus*) on it; hence is resorted to only by adult birds. The birds arrive poor and lean, but by the 10th of September they abound in thousands, and are very fat at this time. The birds usually alight on the hillsides, and quickly strip the lower areas of the berries that have ripened earlier. Toward the evening the geese resort to the shallow pools (destitute of vegetation, with gravelly bottoms) on the sides of the mountains. After a certain holiday of the Greco-Russian Church in September, the natives know that the geese have become fat, and every one has prepared himself to hunt them. [C:139]

*Their miscellaneous assortment of guns—from the old-style Russian spill-out shotgun to the modern thin-barreled American or Belgian shotgun, that kicks as hard behind as it shoots ahead—is carefully dissected. A new tube perhaps is added, but of uncertain fixity of purpose, as it often flies out at times least expected. The breech-pin is taken out and carefully scoured and oiled. In the absence of screws a few thongs of sinew will secure the parts together, and, tightened by means of small wedges of wood, give solidity. It is a ludicrous sight to see an Aleut youth handle a gun of this description. He tries to hit a mark with a large number of shot and but little powder to give them force. He misses the mark, but consoles himself that the gun was fixed up to kill geese. But the younger ones of the youths rarely kill a goose, as they have not yet acquired the native cunning of the elders which enables them to secure more by this means than by relying on the good shooting qualities of their gun. [C:139]

*The adult natives take to their canoes and go some distance from the village to hunt for several days at a time. They sometimes take the women along to gather berries and roots for winter's use. The men take a small supply of salt to preserve the geese until their return. When a sufficient number is obtained they take them home and salt them in an old barrel. Should they not be successful, and remain out for a long time, the birds become very rank from lack of sufficient salt to preserve them. It makes but little difference to them if the goose is fresh or stale. I once remarked to a native that he was salting geese that were far advanced. He replied that they did not ask in winter, when food was scarce, whether food stinks or not. [C:139–140]

*The manner of shooting geese at Attu Island is different from that pursued in other localities. In the evening the geese repair to the shallow pools to preen their feathers and be secure from the attacks of foxes. These resorts leave unmistakable signs of the presence of geese of preceding nights. The native wanders over the hills until he finds a lake where "signs" are abundant. Every preparation is made for camping out a night or two. A pair of long boots, made of seal-skin and water-tight[,] are taken. A long sort of shirt (called a *kamlayka*), made of the intestine of the sea-lion, is used as a water-proof against rain and the wet of the rank vegetation of the low grounds. [C:140]

*A hut is generally to be found near the favorite night haunts of the geese. To this one journies in a canoe; and, on arriving the *chynik* (tea-kettle) is hung on the soon-kindled fire to boil, as the *chypeet* (tea-drinking) is a certain concomitant of all Alaskan jaunts, either of pleasure or of profit. The chypeet over, the approach of dusk is awaited. The hunters then seek the chosen ponds and secret themselves in a gully, or on the hillside near the place selected to watch the geese as they come in for the evening; for during the day the geese have been feeding on the smooth, sloping hillsides. [C:140]

*The hunter is careful to approach these lakes, lest he leave a foot-print or other sign of his presence, as the goose is ever on the alert for such traces and forsakes any lake that is suspected. They will in such cases hover round and round, endeavoring to discover danger, and when satisfied that the lake has been visited by man, or that he is present, their loud cries give warning to all the geese within hearing, as they quickly stream off and away to the head of the ravine from which they came. After such an occurrence the hunter would just as well go home, or seek some other locality, for no more geese will visit that lake until the next night. [C:140]

*A night on which the sky is partly clouded and a light wind is blowing is the best. If the air is calm, and the night bright, the still water reflects too strongly the outlines of the surrounding hills, making the water inky black and renders it impossible to distinguish a goose sitting on the water. [C:140]

*At the time the geese are expected, each person has selected his place and remains quiet. On the approach of the first flock for the night a low whistle from the hunter to his companion gives signal. A low *hŭnk, hŭnk* of the geese and a swirl of wings announce their approach. A straight dash, or a few circles round the pond, and they settle. [The hunters] shoot just as they alight and again as they rise. Sometimes they become so confused as to enable the holder of a breech-loader to get four shots at a single flock. The dead geese serve as decoys, and soon many are added to those already killed. The gentle wind slowly blows them ashore, while you are waiting for others. In a short time a sufficient number is obtained. At an appointed time another native comes from the hut to help bear home the geese. [C:140]

*Another method is still pursued at this place, but as it is being superseded by the use of the gun it will not be out of place to record it, as it is now adopted by the older men alone. A net is prepared in the following manner: Strips of whalebone about three feet in length are tied by cords at intervals of two inches apart, so that the length of the net may be thirty feet and three feet high. The net is placed edgewise on the margin of a pond frequented by geese in October. A stout cord is secured to the end of the net, and firmly fastened to a peg in the ground. The other end is secured in like manner. A long cord reaches from the middle and top of the net to the owner who sits a convenient distance off to be out of sight by the geese. On the approach of a flock of geese to the pond they are not alarmed at the net, as the strips of whalebone stand on end and resemble grass-stalks. They swim near the net; and, when sufficiently near, the cord held by the man is jerked by him and causes the net to be thrown on the geese. The interstices of the net entangles their heads, necks, and wings so they cannot fly. The hunter runs out to twist their necks and again sets his net for another flock. This method was employed almost entirely before the use of guns became general. [C:140]

*About the 1st of October the geese are so fat that they frequently burst the skin on their breast when shot and fall to the ground. During the summer the geese are not molested. The natives take many of the young and domesticate them. I have seen as many as fifty young ones at a time at Attu Island, owned by the natives, to whom the goslings become much attached, especially those who attend them. The goslings remain at large during the winter, but have to be fed during severe spells of weather. The house-tops being covered with sod, the excessive heat within causes the grass-roots to continually send out new blades of grass. The geese are constantly searching every house-top to find the tender blades. One man had a pair of adult geese which he assured me had been reared from goslings, and that they were then entering the sixth year of their captivity. These two geese did not breed the second year of their life, but that every year thereafter they had reared a brood of young, and brought them home as soon as hatched. The wings and half of the tail feathers had to be clipped every season to prevent them migrating. In the fall of 1880 this pair of geese went away and were gone so long that the man supposed they would not return. After some time they returned, and on catching them, to clip them, it was found that the male had a shot-hole through the web of one foot and a second hole in the other leg. This, doubtless, made the geese think "there is no place like home." This pair was killed later in the season. [C:141]

*As an illustration of the parental solicitude exhibited by these birds, I will relate that several years ago a heavy fall of snow occurred in the latter part of June at the islands of Agattu and Semichi, and covered the ground with more than three feet of snow. At that date the geese were incubating. The geese did not quit their nests, and were suffocated. The natives found scores of the birds sitting dead on their nests after the snow had melted. [C:141]

*After the 15th of November these geese leave the islands and are not to be seen until the following April. At Atkha the people rear a number of the goslings of this species. The young are obtained from the islets lying contiguous to the larger islands in that vicinity. [C:141]

Black Turnstone

Arenaria melanocephala

*They are reported to be plentiful on Unga Island and Sannakh Island. The sea-otter hunters[,] both native and white, detest this bird as it frequents the places most resorted to by marine mammals and is certain to give alarm to the otter or seal which the hunter is endeavoring to approach. . . . The natives of Unalashka, who go to Sannakh Island every year to hunt sea-otters, say that it does not occur at Unalashka and other islands west of the mainland. [C:150–151]

Black Oyster-catcher

Haematopus bachmani

*The Black Oyster-catcher is universally detested by both white and native hunters, as it frequents just those places most resorted to by seals and sea-otters, so that on the approach of a hunter to obtain those animals the bird is certain to give the alarm and cause the animal to disappear into the water. [C:151]

*I once procured a less than half-grown bird of this species. . . . The one I had was put in the house until an opportunity offered to preserve its skin. It always greeted the opening or shutting of the door with its deafening noise. At night it became lonely and attempted to sing a song. I got up from bed to quiet it, and succeeded only as long as I remained out of bed. Neither the bird nor I slept that night. By early dawn it migrated to another building from which it escaped when I unguardedly left the door open. [C:151]

*The Russian name of the bird is *Morskoi Ptookh*, or Sea Cock. The Aleutian name is *Hekh* at Unalashka and *Hegis* at Atka. At Attu the bird is only known by reputation, and is there called *Hekh*, from its note.

Rock Ptarmigan

Lagopus rupestris [*Lagopus mutus*]

*On some of the islands it is extremely abundant; among those may be mentioned Unalashka, Unimak, Akutan, and Akoon. It is resident where found; and, among the islands, rarely leaves its native island. At Akutan they are more abundant than elsewhere observed. They come even directly into the village, and may be seen or heard at any time on the hill-sides near by. . . . The flesh of this species is better than that of the Willow Ptarmigan and is much sought for as food. The best time to hunt this bird is early in the morning when the wind is calm and a moist snow is falling. The birds are then sluggish and dislike to rise to the hill-tops. [C:154]

Fig. 35. Turner's Ptarmigan, *Lagopus rupestris atkhensis* (Turner). Plate III. *Contributions to the Natural History of Alaska*. Courtesy, Rare Books & Manuscripts, Special Collections, Middlebury College Vermont. This illustration was a joint project of Robert Ridgway and his brother John L. Ridgway. The accuracy of the background suggests they had discussions with Turner about the inland terrain on Atka. Turner's ptarmigan is recognized as one of six variations of rock ptarmigan.

Turner's Ptarmigan [variation of the Rock Ptarmigan]
Lagopus rupestris atkhensis (Turner) [*Lagopus mutus atkhensis* Turner]

*When I first obtained these birds I was struck with the greater size and also with the shape of the bill and greater length of the claws when compared with the mainland bird. This bird frequents the lowlands and hills of the western islands of the Aleutian Chain. They are quite plentiful on Atkha, Amchitka, and Attu Islands. . . . The natives of Attu assert that this same species of Ptarmigan occurs on Agattu Island, and that it is quite numerous there, probably on account of the absences of foxes. [C:156]

American Rough-legged Hawk
Archibuteo lagopus sancti johannis [*Buteo lagopus*]

*An individual of this species was seen in captivity at Iliuliuk village, on Unalashka Island. I had just returned to the place from a sea voyage in July, 1878. The Hawk was a sorry looking object, having been shot through the wing. It eagerly devoured pieces of raw fish that were thrown to it. A Bald Eagle, also in captivity at the time, was its companion. The two birds got along well together. The Hawk was quite passive and rarely attempted to show a vicious disposition. [C:158]

Bald Eagle

Haliaeetus leucocephalus

*Among the Aleutian Islands it is plentiful. At Unalashka Island it breeds among the cliffs on the northern side of the island. They breed early in March. The young are frequently brought to the village of Iliuliuk, where they are kept for several weeks, or until some one maliciously kills them. Several adults were also seen there in captivity. They had been wounded and brought to the village. [C:158]

Peale's Falcon [Peregrine Falcon]

Falco peregrinus[2]

*At Attu Island I frequently saw one of these birds join the Ravens when the latter were performing their aerial gymnastics on the approach of a gale. The Hawk endeavored to imitate the Ravens, which paid but little attention to the antics of the intruder. At Attu this hawk is not common, though the natives assert that it is common enough at Agattu and the Semichi Islands. The natives told me that where this Hawk breeds there will be found the nests of Eiders. I could not believe it until a short stay at Amchitka Island forced me to recognize it as a fact, for, in each instance, the nests of Eiders were very abundant in each of the localities where the nest of this hawk was known to be. It is quite probable that the hawk selects the place with special reference to prospective young Eiders. [C:160]

Short-eared Owl

Asio accipitrinus [*Asio flammeus*]

*At Atkha Island I saw one of them as it flew from a patch of wild rye. It was the only one seen. At Attu I saw one, but missed killing it, as it was too far off for a large shot. The Aleuts have no good word for this bird. The women are afraid to touch it. [C:161]

Snowy Owl

Nyctea nyctea [*Nyctea scandiaca*]

*This Owl is not rare on some of the Aleutian Islands. A fine specimen was shot by Mr. Robert King, the agent of the Western Fur and Trading Company, at Iliuliuk village, Unalashka Island. The Owl had been observed for several nights on some of the buildings near the stable, doubtless watching a convenient opportunity to pounce on a pair of tame rabbits that lived under the stable. The bird was sitting on the flag-staff but a few yards in front of the dwelling of Mr. King, who immediately presented the bird to me. [C:163]

American Raven

Corvus corax sinuatus (Wagl.)

*The Raven seems to prefer the more thickly settled localities, and is more abundant near villages than in the less populated districts.... At Unalashka it is extremely numerous. I have counted over two hundred individuals at one time at that place. At Atkha and Attu Islands it is also very numerous. They are the scavengers of the villages. They have a great share of intelligence; though not shy they are extremely wary, and when they assemble round a pile of offal, left from cleaning fish, which some fisherman has just brought in, they are ever on the alert. It is scarcely possible to pick up a stone to throw at them without being seen, even though the distance off might make one think he has not been observed. When the person arrives at several rods from throwing distance, the Ravens take flight, to return as soon as the intruder is out of reach. [C:167]

*At Atkha the natives and others have many chickens. The Alaska Commercial Company had two roosters and several hens. One of these roosters, a veritable Turk, fought the younger rooster until the latter had, in some one of his battles, lost his right eye. The loss of this eye prevented him from guarding against the sudden attacks of the older rooster, which finally drove the younger to the outskirts of the flock or else to solitude. The younger roost[er] used to hang round some of the hens to divert them from the attentions of the older one, which finally gave him such a beating as to nearly kill him. The Ravens used to watch these affrays, and alight within a few yards to witness the fight, but always taking good care to keep out of reach of the old rooster. Out of revenge and a mixture of pure cursedness they would wait until the younger rooster was walking among the tall grass and sail directly over him, then drop down on the ground near him, uttering a loud *snwak*, which made the young rooster believe the old one had slipped up on him. I have seen this done over a score of times, and have seen the young rooster drop on the ground from fright. [C:167]

*On the approach of bad weather the Ravens retire to a high, bold precipice; and, over its top, or along its face, they go through the most astonishing, aerial evolutions, chasing each other for hours in and out, to the right and left, up and down. Their flight at such times is extremely varied with rapid beats of the wing or a short sail, a sudden halt, and turn completely over and fly back from where they started. They also turn over sidewise, generally to the right and under, coming up on the other side and continuing without halt. They frequently fly with one wing closed and the other straight up in the air. [C:167]

*The notes of the Raven are extremely varied to express surprise, danger, satisfaction, or nearly anything else, as they convey much by their note. A single male will sit on some slightly elevated knoll and with outstretched ruffled neck, he utters a note that sounds like that of a choking dog. Two will get close together in early spring and talk to each other for half an hour, uttering a series of *kuttle, kuttle, kuttle,* all the while. [C:168]

*When one has a piece of offal stolen from him he utters a *hwah.* On the wing they utter a short croak, at other times they utter *al lŭkh, al lŭkh*, which sounds like the Aleut word for *two.* The similarity of the sounds caused me to remark to a small boy, who was with me that a Raven, which had just flown by and uttered his *al lŭkh, al lŭkh*, had counted us correctly. The boy did not comprehend my remark until I informed him that there were but two of us and that the Raven said so as he flew by. The boy was some time laughing at the idea of a Raven counting us in the Atkhan dialect. [C:168]

*The Unalashkans call it *Ka lú kak*. The Attu Islanders call it *Kál gakh.* Throughout the entire Territory this bird is intimately connected with the myths and legends of the natives. They ascribe deeds of valor, heroism, sagacity, and deepest cunning to the Raven. [C:168]

Aleutian Song Sparrow

Melospiza cinerea [*Melospiza melodia*]

*The Aleutian Song Sparrow is a constant resident of the Aleutian Islands. . . . This Sparrow is not shy, as it frequently alights on the window-sill to search about the turf, piled against the houses, for food. I frequently threw out pieces of bread or cracker for these birds, and soon taught them to know where they could get something on days of bad weather; and those days come with sufficient frequency. [C:174–175]

*The house-top was a favorite place for them to alight early in the morning to sing. One bird delighted to sit on the wind-vane, while a gentle, unsteady wind would swing him round and back, evidently to his great delight, as he constantly uttered his song, which I have in vain tried to imitate, as it consisted of such rapid modulations that I could never catch it. They will at times sing part of their song and stop short, as though interrupted, look around for a few seconds, and begin where they left off. The song is usually sung in answer to that of a rival male. After being repeated many times one or the other of the males is certain to approach the other and again repeat his song. [C:175]

*The name of this Sparrow in the Attu language is *Chĭk ché ŭkh*, and refers to its note. [C:175]

[Turner provided local names for three additional birds:]

Green-winged Teal (*Anas carolinensis* Gmelin) [*Anas crecca*]: The Russian name of this species is *Chērók*. [C:133]

Old-squaw (*Clangula hyemalis* Linn.): The natives of Attu call this bird *A láng ŭk* from its note, which is repeated at short intervals. [C:134]

Northern Phalarope (*Phalaropus lobatus* Linn.) The Attu people call this bird *Chi′t khŭkh* and is derived from the note. [C:146]

11

Fish, Sea Urchins, and Cephalopods

Fishing Implements

Turner cataloged two fish hooks.] No. 756 [A65056, missing] is a portion of tooth cut into the form of a fish-hook having two barbs, one above the other. It is probable that the fish hook did not come into such perfect construction until the advent of the Russians. No. 755 [A65055] is a piece of tooth of unfinished workmanship, to serve as a fish hook. [55–56]

No. 321 [E65281] is a pair of tanned seal skin pantaloons or overalls worn by the fisherman in his kaiuk while fishing. This garment is nearly impervious to water and by its smoothness is readily cleansed from the slime of the fish coming in contact with the person sitting nearly immoveably [sic] in the vessel from which he fishes. [63]

[No.] 833 [A65133], water-worn stone with groove, used as net sinker. [No.] 392 [A64692], perforated flat stone used as a net sinker.

Notes on Specific Fish

[Modern common and scientific names are in brackets if they differ from those used by Turner.]

Three Spined Stickleback

Gasterosteus cataphractus [*Gasterosteus aculeatus aculeatus*]

*This species is quite common in the small streams which form the outlets of the lakes on the low grounds. They usually lie under the overhanging banks of the stream, and often will scarcely move when touched. The specimens taken by me were collected July 14, 1878, at Sannakh Island, the great sea-otter ground of Alaska. [C:87]

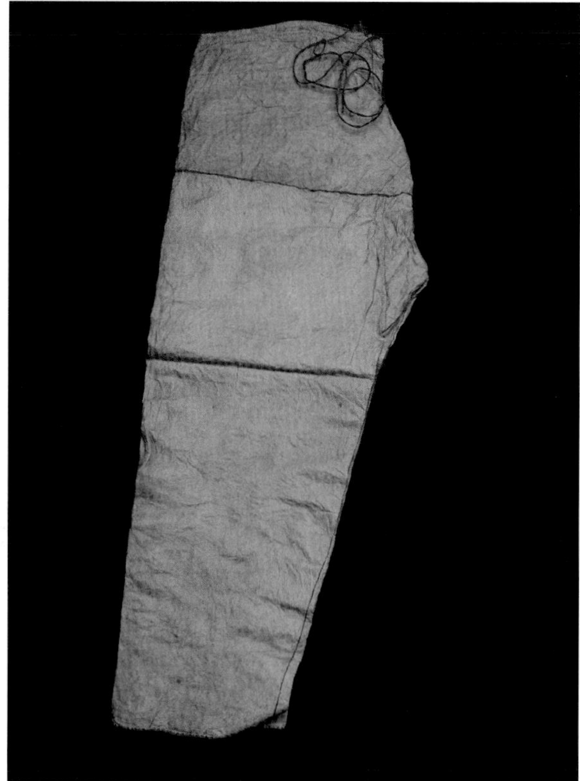

Fig. 36. Sealskin trousers, Atka. *Department of Anthropology, Smithsonian Institution (NMNH E65281) (T321).* These sealskin trousers, too fragile to open for photographing, were ideally suited to fishing from a skin boat. They were relatively waterproof and were easily cleaned of any slime from fish that were stowed inside the craft, where the fisherman's legs were immobile for long periods of time. It is significant that even in this piece of everyday clothing the Unangan seamstress found time and material to add a touch of color along the seams and at the cuffs.

Starry Flounder

Pleuronectes stellatus [*Platichthys stellatus*]

*Among the Aleutian Islands this species is extremely abundant and in some particular localities is the only fish to be found. The Aleuts care but

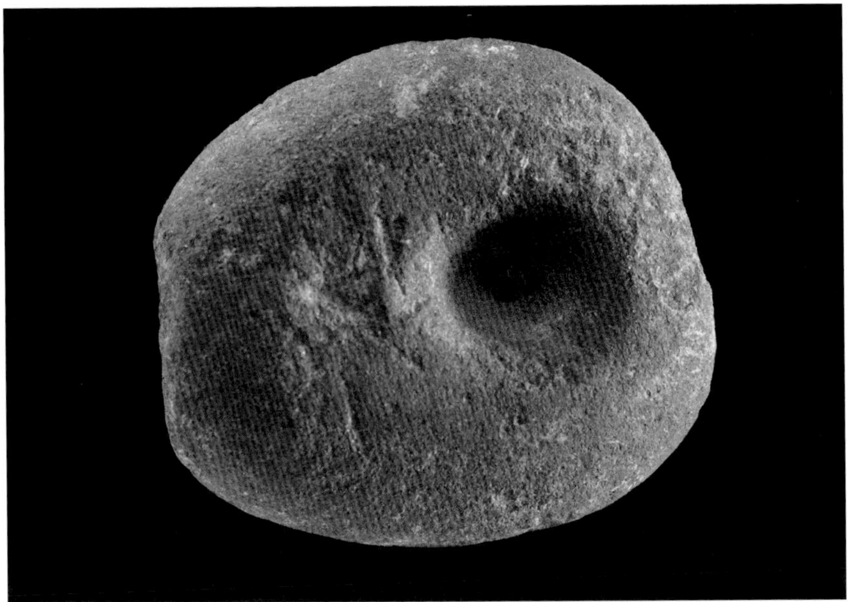

Fig. 37. Stone sinker, Attu. *Department of Anthropology, Smithsonian Institution (NMNH A64692) (T392).*

little for this fish, and will often throw them back in the water when caught. There is but little meat on them, and that is full of short, strong bones. The Russian name of the Flounder is *Kámbal.* The smaller ones are called *Kambalúshka.* [C:87–88]

Arctic Flounder

Pleuronectes glacialis [*Liopsetta glacialis*]

*During calm weather I have had opportunity to observe the habits of Flounders from the wharf at Saint Michael's and Unalashka. The fish towards evening usually come near the shore, especially when the tide is rising. The fish lie on the sandy bottom waiting for food to come in reach, or else by a quick movement of their fins throw the sand over their back so as to completely hide their body. . . . At Unalashka Island the Flounders attain a greater size than observed at Attu Island, and scarcely as large as some individuals seen at Saint Michael's. [C:88]

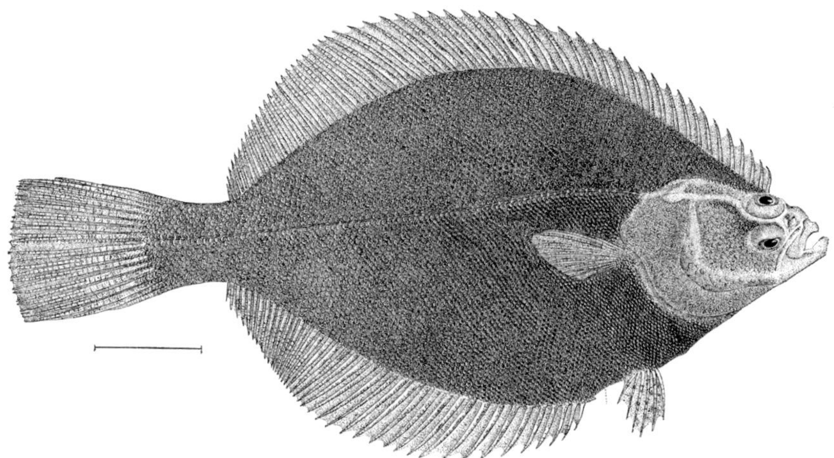

Fig. 38. Arctic Flounder, *Pleuronectes glacialis.* Plate 1. *Contributions to the Natural History of Alaska.*

Halibut

Hippoglossus vulgaris [*Hippoglossus stenolepis*]

*Among the Aleutian Islands it is a constant resident, and there attains an enormous size and weight. In some localities it has been caught weighing over 300 pounds. The larger individuals are extremely difficult to kill, and require a great amount of "playing" before being brought to the surface and there dispatched with a club ("*Kolotúshka*" of the Russian-speaking Aleut). The fish are often taken while fishing for cod and other fish. [C:88]

*The usual method pursued by the Aleut of the present day is to make a wooden hook that resembles a shoe with the sole detached, excepting at the heel, from the upper. Through the part which I have likened to the sole of the shoe is driven a strong spike, usually three or four inches in length, and set at an angle of about forty degrees from the sole, and directed inward. The upper part is then fastened so that the under surface will be about an inch and a half from the point of the spike. The bait is securely fastened to the lower part, and when the fish attempts to swallow the bait, the upper lip is pushed on the spike by the interference of the upper part of the hook, so that any attempt of the fish to withdraw from the hook is only to transfix the upper jaw more firmly on the spike. [C:88]

*This hook is usually set in the early morning, and is watched from the house or shore. An inflated stomach of a seal is usually attached to the line

Fig. 39. "Aleutes catching Halibut, Akootan Pass, Bering Sea." Drawing by Henry W. Elliott, *Our Arctic Province.*

as a float, and when it is seen to move, then it is known that a Halibut is at the bait. Other fish rarely attempt to take the bait, as the wooden parts of the hook move round so that they are frightened off. Occasionally a large cod may be taken that way, but only the persistent endeavors of the Halibut enable it to be taken by this means. [C:88–89]

*At Attu Island the Halibut attains a great size, but the larger ones are rarely taken. The Atkhan Aleuts secure large fish of this species. At Atkha two canoes usually go together so as to assist each other in case of necessity. When a large Halibut is taken the man gives a signal to his comrade, and begins to tire the fish out. The comrade approaches so as to be near when the fish is drawn to the surface, as they are so strong that they have frequently upset the canoe of the fisherman, who is nearly always drowned if alone. [C:89]

*When the fish is exhausted it is drawn to the surface and struck on the head with the club used by all the Aleut fishermen. The one who comes as assistant is the person who does the killing, while the other holds the line, ready to give play at the least movement of the fish. After the fish has been killed it is secured between the two canoes and taken to land. This method is pursued only for large fish; the smaller ones are managed by a single fisherman. [C:89]

*The fish usually lie in water of 20 to 100 fathoms. The larger fish in the deeper water. Their flesh is excellent, but dry, unless properly cooked. The best way is to roast a large piece of the belly with a little water and scraps of fat pork, to keep the fish from becoming too dry. If properly attended to it makes a feast fit for a king. The natives usually boil the fish, a not very choice way of preparing it. Large strips are cut up and hung on poles or lines to dry. It becomes very hard, and unless it is not eaten with sufficient fatty substances it is not healthy. [That is, it must be eaten with fatty substances.] The dried strips are usually put in the stomach of a sea-lion and kept for winter consumption. [C:89]

Codfish

Gadus morhua

*The Cod fisheries of Alaska are of great importance, the banks very extensive, and containing an abundance of fish for all purposes. The favorite localities are the Shumagin Islands, Cook's Inlet, and throughout the Aleutian Islands. North of Aliaska the best-known locality is about thirty miles northeast of Amak Island, and another of probably less importance lies thirty miles off shore from Capt Strogoto the mouth of Sulima River. Among the Aleutian Islands, especially on the north side, a hook can scarcely be thrown in the water without taking a Cod. One of the localities where the best fish are taken among the Aleutian Islands is off the north head of Unalashka. Another is at the entrance to Nazan Harbor (Atkha Island) and on the north side of Atkha Island. Of the northeast shoulder of Kiska Island, and in recent years of the northwest shoulder of Attu Island, they are abundant. [C:89]

*I have learned of nothing that would lead me to believe in large migrations of the Aleutian Cod. They retire to the deeper waters of the neighborhood on the approach of winter, and draw near the land in May. They are most abundant in July and September in some localities, and in others in February and March. The time of their greatest abundance at any particular locality varies according to circumstances that are not yet well understood. While at Amchitka Island in 1881 I saw the bones of Codfish of such size as to excite wonder, yet I was informed by natives that the Cod only comes on the north side of that island in July and never stay later than the first of September. Bones of immense size were extremely abundant on the soil around the ancient village sites. At Attu island the Codfish are very numerous at the present day. They attain immense size there. I saw one individual in February, 1881, that weighed just out of the water an even thirty pounds. The fish was fat and vigorous. It was caught in water of about twenty-five fathoms. The natives of Attu inform me that the Cod has not long been an inhabitant of the waters around that island. Its advent was near 1873. Previous to that time individuals had been obtained but rarely, and many of the men had not seen a Cod previous to that time. At Atkha Island the Cod also attains a great size. I have never seen a sickly fish at that place. In the entrance to the "Old Harbor" (*Starry Gaven*), on the north side, the old men repair in summer to catch the Cod to dry for winter. They assert that they are plentiful and of larger size than [at] any other locality near that island. [C:89–90]

*At Unalashka these fish are very abundant and here unhealthy fish are quite common, though on the outside of the northeast point of the island large, healthy fish are taken in greatest abundance. The supply among the Aleutian Islands being always equal to the demand made on them. The natives frequently sell the surplus fish to the company, which salts them to send to the Pribylof Islands for the use of the people there. Of course only large fish are bought. The price paid is five cents in trade or money for each fish in the fresh, cleaned state. The size of the runs of fish depends greatly on the season and depth of water from which they are obtained. The larger fish are obtained from the deeper water. The average weight of the fish among the Aleutian waters will be about twelve pounds. Individuals of 18 to 24 pounds are quite common, while the majority of the catch will be about fifteen to sixteen pounds. It is possible that the off-shore fish will average one or two pounds more than the shore fish. Myriads of small Cod are to be seen round the wharves at Unalashka during the latter part of September, and all of October. These bite readily at the hook. [C:90]

*A piece of other fish is generally used for bait for catching Cod. The Codfish is one of the principal food-fishes of the Aleuts. They frequently go out to the banks, some miles off shore, and in the course of a few hours return with their canoe loaded down to the water's edge with fine fish. They prepare great quantities of these fish for winter's use by drying them. Their manner of preparing them is as follows: The head is partly severed from the body at the throat, the gills are taken out, a slit along the belly and the entrails are removed, the backbone is cut on each side and either removed as far as the tail, which is left to hold the two sides together to allow them to be hung over a pole, or else it is left in and dried with the body. When fish are abundant this is rarely done. The sides are then cut transversely through the flesh to the skin and the body then hung up by the tail to dry. During rainy weather an old seal-skin is tied over the bunches of fish to keep them dry as possible. When the fish are sufficiently dry they are stored away for future use. The ravens have a fine time watching the stages of drying fish, for if there is anything which a raven loves it is a fish that an Aleut has hung up to dry. The natives of Attu will not permit cats to be kept on the island, because the cats, which they formerly had, ate or destroyed more fish in one night than an Aleut woman could hang up in a day. It would be interesting to know how many Cod are taken by the Aleuts west of Unimak Pass. If each fisherman reported daily to the "Tyone" the number taken, the amount could be given to the agent of the company there, and at the end of the year a very nearly approximate total could be given. [C:90]

Tomcod

Tilesia gracilis [*Microgadus proximus*]

*Natives of Unalashka speak of the fish as *Válh nya,* a name used by all the Russian-speaking people where this species occurs. . . . Among the Aleutian Islands I have seen this species only at Unalashka, and there only on two occasions and not half a dozen fish altogether. I do not believe that it occurs to the westward of that island, as all inquiries concerning it at Atkha and Attu elicited no information that led me to recognize this species as existing there. [C:91–92]

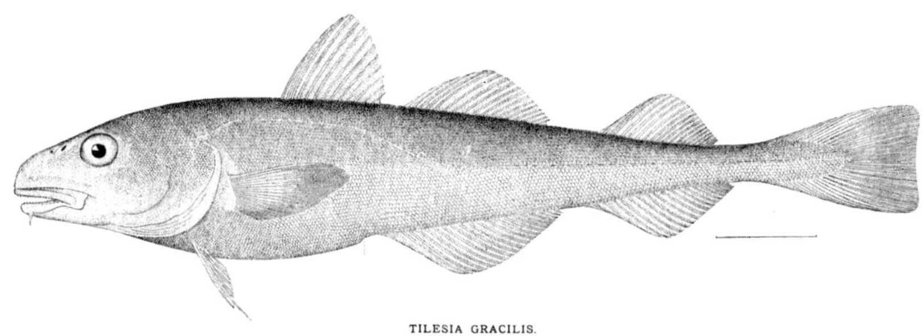

Fig. 40. Tomcod, *Tilesia gracilis.* Plate 3. *Contributions to the Natural History of Alaska.*

Poacher [Bering Poacher]

Agonidae *siphagonus barbatus* Steindachner [*Occella dodecaedron*]

*A single specimen of this species was picked up dead on the beach at Iliuliuk village, Unalashka Island, in August, 1878. It was the only specimen seen there. I could obtain no information concerning its habits, excepting that the natives asserted that it is "a seaweed fish," leading me to infer that it frequented the patches of *fuci* and other *algae*. It was shown to several persons at Attu Island. Those natives assured me that it is frequently found there. It is a small fish of only five and a half inches in length. It is not used for food. [C:94]

Alaska Sculpin

Cottus polyacanthocephalus [*Myoxocephalus polyacanthocephalus*]

*The Spiny-headed Sculpin is very abundant among all the Aleutian Islands. I am not aware that it occurs north of Aliaska on the American side. It does not differ in habits from the other species, and like them is used for food by the Aleuts and some of the whites. [C:95]

Irish Lord (Jordan's Cabezon) [Yellow Irish Lord]

Hemilepidotus jordani

*A single specimen of this species was taken in October at Unalashka. It is a common species, and occurs throughout the Aleutian Islands.... This fish is considered excellent food. It is not infested with parasites like other fishes of its kind. [C:95]

Rock Cod

Chiridae *Hexagrammus asper* Steller

*This fish is known to the English-speaking people of Saint Michael's and the Unalashkan districts as "Rock-cod," and to the Russian-speaking population as "*Terpóog*," a word meaning a rasp. [C:95]

*The "*Terpóog*" frequents the rocky ledges, points of land which extend into the water, and shallow coves. Those places where the various kinds of sea-weeds abound are the best resorts for this fish. When the tide is high they seek their food among the rocky reefs. The natives value their flesh very highly. The meat is quite firm and contains few bones; it has a peculiar greenish color, but soon becomes light in color after the death of the fish. The women do most of the fishing for these fish. Any kind of fresh meat is used for bait. Frequently the women will be taken by the men to some favorite locality and remain there to fish while the men continue the journey in search of wood cast up on the beach, or go out to sea to catch Cod or other fish. [C:95]

*During the winter time the foxes of the Aleutian Islands catch many of these "Rock-cod," as they are left in the shallow lagoons or rock crevices by the receding tides. The fox is quite expert in catching the fish. He will watch them for a long time until they wander into the shallower water, upon which the fox springs, even immersing his entire head to seize the fish. [C:95]

Rock Greenling

Hexagrammus superciliosus [*Hexagrammos lagocephalus*]

*This species does not differ in life habits from the other two. It is abundant throughout the Aleutian Islands. During the months of August, September, and part of October, the old men of the [sic] Attu take their wives and repair to some favorite haunt of these fish and while there they catch a supply, which is dried for winter use. The boys and girls go at low tides along the beach and with their hands search among the sea-weeds and rock crevices for these and other fish which are to be used as food. [C:96]

Mackerel [Atka Mackerel]

Pleurogrammus monopterygius

*When I arrived at Unalashka in 1878 I heard much talk about the "Mackerel." During the summer of that year I had an opportunity of conversing with those who frequented the western islands of the Chain where these fish were said to abound. Several persons referred to these fish as "Spanish Mackerel," others called them "Horse Mackerel" and "Alaskan Mackerel," and under several scientific names. They were served at the table on several occasions, and all who ate of them highly praised their good qualities and spoke of their great resemblance in taste to the Atlantic Mackerel. It was not until in May, 1879, that I had an opportunity of visiting the locality where they were said to be abundant. [C: 96]

*During the summer of 1879 I was at Atkha Island, and soon made inquiry concerning the fish. I was told that they make their appearance in the narrow pass between the islands of Atkha and Amlia about the 1st of

June; and, that the fish invariably come from the Pacific Ocean, which here mingles its waters with that of Bering Sea. [C:96]

*The first arrivals of fish are the males of largest size and beauty of color. They arrive a few days before and await the arrival of the females and immature males. By the 18th of June the fish have come in countless thousands. They arrange themselves with their heads toward the tide currents which rush violently through the pass. The flood tide sets in from the Pacific, while the ebb flows toward the Pacific, or, in other words, a southerly directed current for the ebb and a northerly directed current for the flood tide. The pass is very rocky, with numerous sunken rocks in the middle and on the eastern side. The western side of the pass has the deepest water and is three fathoms deep in the channel. On the north side of the pass numerous ledges of rocks, hidden rocks, kelp patches, and small islets of but few feet above the water's edge are to be found. It would be very difficult navigation for a vessel of over twenty tons to go through there with safety. The natives of the present day cross pretty well to the north side of the pass until they get under Amlia Island and then run near the shore of Amlia with their small *bidari* or open boats. [C:96]

*Among the sea weeds or kelp patches on a cloudy day of clear lower atmosphere the fish may be seen in the following order:

*The young males and immature females form a stratum of three or four fish deep and several feet wide, beneath these a second stratum of older males and females, whose roe is not yet developed, and will later, in the spawning season, take their place with those in the third stratum, which is composed of vigorous males and females. The latter are the most abundant. The female deposits her eggs on the kelp, though much of it must doubtless be lost by the swift currents washing it off. These males and females remain in this place until the spawning season is over, generally by the 20th of July. After which they gradually disperse and quickly find their way back to the Pacific. Many times I have seen huge Halibut (*Hippoglossus vulgaris*), lying like large flagstones beneath the lower stratum of fish, waiting for one to come within reach. Without moving a great distance I could see over a dozen Halibut at a time. I estimated the weight of some of the larger ones to be not less than three hundred and fifty pounds. [C:96–97]

*The natives of Atkha repair to this place and have several turf houses of small size built there. It is also a garden spot where a few vegetables, such as radishes, turnips, and a few potatoes are planted. To attend to their gardens and to be near the fishing-grounds the Aleuts of many places have built these summer villages and call them *Laýt nik*. Here assemble all the old men not able to hunt and the children and women of the hunters gone off on a summer's cruise for sea-otters. These lay in a store of dried and salted fish for their sons and friends. I made several visits to this place to learn the habits of the fish. [C:97]

*The natives obtain the greater number of the fish in the following manner. Each man has a two-holed bidarka (canoe). In it a small boy sits in the front hole while the old man sits in the rear hole. The man uses a pole of several feet in length (generally not less than 12 feet long), on which is firmly secured a hook of iron, having a flattened point with a sharp edge and a notch filed on the inner side to act as a barb. When the canoe arrives at the place the boy is ordered to seize hold of a strong frond of the Giant Kelp, which streams out sometimes for over a hundred feet, and among which the fish are most abundant. After coming thus to anchor, the man carefully thrusts the pole into the water, and if the fish are plentiful he will soon feel them surging against it. He now begins to jerk it up and down in the water to gig any fish that may come along. In a few seconds he brings one out. The work now becomes exciting, for scarcely has the pole been again thrust in the water than it is jerked into another fish. A man may thus, in a couple of hours, take two to three hundred fish. After the canoe is loaded it is taken to the shore, where the women slit open the back of the fish, take off the head, clean out the entrails, and with a cut on each side, the backbone is removed to the tail. The two sides of the fish are left hanging together by the tail. This is to enable the fish to be hung over a pole to dry. Often the men bring the fish directly to the principal village and clean them there, though this is done more often when the fish are to be salted. At the season between June 25th and July 25th the fish are extremely fat from the abundance of a small crustacean, which has previously come in myriads to the same places as these fish. The fish which are to be dried are usually taken about the 1st of August, as they are so fat before that time that I have seen the oil drip from the drying fish. They also, from the presence of the oil, become rancid in a short time, and are said not to keep so well. [C:97]

*At Attu Island I also had an excellent opportunity for studying the habits of these fish. At this place the fish are most abundant at the entrance to Chichagof Harbor on the northeast shoulder of the island. Several islets and many reefs are disposed nearly across the entrance to the harbor. Between these the tide currents run with great velocity. An abundance of large kelp patches is found in the vicinity. The fish arrive at Attu, from the southwestward, about the 24th of April, though this date varies according to the openness of the season. It is rarely later than the 1st of May. The fish come at first in a straggling manner, and their first appearance is made known by their being caught on hooks while the men are fishing for other kinds. The first comers are usually nearly adult males. They are not fat on arrival, but soon become so from the abundance of small crustaceans that fairly swarm among the patches of sea-weed by the 10th of May; and at which time the fish are tolerably numerous. By the 10th of June thousands of these fish can be seen in the shallow water (about one and a half to eight fathoms deep) below. The natives here take considerable quantities of these fish, and dry them for use at an early date. They rarely salt them, for reason that, they state, this fish makes the consumer thirsty. When they go to catch them they the [sic] visit the various localities known to be the haunts of these fish, and by looking beneath the mass of kelp fronds can see them if present; if not, the fish are off in the open water. They then watch every floating piece of detached sea-weed. It is constantly turning round and round like in an eddy of water. The fish are playing with it, and there will be found an abundance. The gaff is quickly thrust into the water, and one is soon struck and brought out. [C:97]

*I here had opportunity to come to the conclusion that these fish will bite readily at the hook. I saw them jump and struggle to get at the gaff and could feel them strike against it while it was in the water, and at times it was impossible to hold it in position, as the mass of moving fish carried it along with them. [C:97–98]

*Any kind of fresh fish may be used as bait on a small cod-hook for these fish. A piece of scarlet flannel tied above the hook is good to attract the fish, as they will then bite voraciously. With the hook a person can catch the fish as fast as [it is] put into the water. With the use of several hooks on one line several fish may be taken at once. With the gaff the fish are taken in great quantities, equal to all demands. The run lasts at Attu until July 25th, after which the fish are spent and slowly disappear from the waters. [C:98]

*These fish were not known at Attu previous to 1875. They came unexpectedly and were caught on hooks set for other fish. Since that time the people have had an abundance of them. From my own observations I am led to assert that 500 barrels of 200 pounds each can be procured at Attu in the season from June 1 to July 31. At the entrance to Chichagof Harbor is the only known locality at Attu where these fish resort. The natives assert that the coming of these fish was coincident with the disappearance of the sea-lion *Eumetopias stelleri* [*Eumetopias jubatus*]; and those natives maintain that the fish drove the sea-lions off. Just opposite to my own conclusion, for I think the fish come to those places where they will be least persecuted by the sea-lions. [C:98]

*These fish are also reported to be abundant at Kiska Island, between the islands of Atkha and Athakh [Adak]. Also between Unalga and Unalashka, and also in the passes between some of the Shumagin Islands. I saw a few individuals in Captain's Harbor, Unalashka Island, in the early part of July, 1881. This is the first instance of their occurrence in that locality. They were small in size, and of the size which constitutes the upper stratum as spoken of in regard to the disposition of the fish on the spawning grounds of Amlia Pass. [C:98]

*This fish could be easily taken in great quantities, especially at Amlia Pass and Attu. Some writers of Alaskan affairs have mentioned exorbitant prices paid for a barrel of salted fish of this kind. They can be prepared at a cost of two dollars per barrel for the fish at either Attu or Amlia. The cost of the barrel and salt, of course, is to be added. Only the necessary sheds for protecting the barrels from the weather would have to be erected. Native help could be procured at a cost of a dollar per day for a man, and fifty to seventy-five cents per day for the women, who can clean the fish as expertly as the men. [C:98]

*Ere many years these fish will command a highly remunerative price to those who will engage in the enterprise. Nothing has been done by either trading company in the matter of bringing these fish into a market. [C:98]

*In the beginning of this article I gave the various names used by the white people who have become acquainted with the fish only on reputation. The Russian-speaking people refer to them as *Soo dach kē´*, a diminutive form of *Soo dák*, meaning a *sangre* or *perch-pike*. The natives of Unalashka and Atkha Islands speak of them, in the Aleutian language, as *Ta mŭ´th ghēs*, while the Attu people call them *Tŭ´v ween*. At Atkha, on June 18, 1880, I had several specimens brought to me for the purposes of description. . . . [C:98]

Capelin

Microstomidae *Mallotus villosus* [*Mallotus villosus*]

*At Atkha Island in 1879 I had an opportunity to observe these fish as they came in to the sandy beach of Nazan Bay to spawn. The 21st of July of that year a boy brought a basket of these fish and asked me to buy them. I inquired where he had obtained them. He replied that they were abundant along the sandy beach not far from the village. I immediately went to the place and found that the waves of the preceding day had thrown millions of these fish on the beach. The number was increasing every time a wave was broken on the beach. . . . The natives assert that these fish deposit their spawn only in the places against which the waves will wash when the fish-fry are ready to be hatched. [C:102]

*The natives prepare great quantities of these fish by drying them in the air. They are not cleaned; a blade of strong grass is twisted between the gills and neck, which makes a rope of fish. These ropes will sometimes be many yards in length. [C:103]

*At Attu these fish are said to be very abundant every third year. This was also stated to be a fact at Atka. One thing is certain that they were very plentiful at Atkha in 1879, and not in 1880 or '81, and that they were not at Attu in 1880, and were reported to have been abundant in 1878. [C:103]

*The Gulls, Terns, Sea-lions, Killer-whales and Hair-seals have a great liking for these little fish. Thousands of Gulls and Terns were hovering over the schools of these fish at Atkha in 1879. At Unalashka Island these fish are said to be common at times, but I could get no definite information concerning them. The Russian-speaking people call them *Kō′ rūsh ke*. [C:103]

*I know of no fish which has a sweeter taste than this species. When fried to a rich brown color they are excellent. The head is all that is necessary to be removed, as the entrails contain nothing. [C:103]

Salmon Trout [Dolly Varden]

Salvelinus malma

*The natives of the Aleutian Islands make but little use of these fish, as they are taken most abundantly during the season when the salmon are plentiful. [C:104–105]

King or Chinook Salmon

Oncorhynchus chouicha [*Oncorhynchus tshawytscha*]

*Among the Aleutian Islands this species is not often obtained. It appears there to be a mere straggler, and among the eastern islands of the chain not more than a couple of dozens are taken in a year. I saw a fine female, which had spawned and had returned to the sea, taken at Unalashka, September 25, 1878. This individual weighed 38 pound, and was in excellent condition for the table. It was taken while seining for other species of salmon. [C:106]

*At Atkha Island this species is occasionally taken in the early spring, but not more than half a dozen are yearly procured. At Attu they are rarely seen. But one was taken in 1879, and one in 1880. Both were taken in the latter part of September. . . . The Russian-speaking people call this species *Chavícha,* a word derived from the Kamchadale language and applied to this or kindred species. . . . The Aleutian name of this salmon is *A mé ung.* [C:106–107]

Dog or Chum Salmon

Oncorhynchus keta

*This species was not observed among any of the Aleutian Islands. I was informed that it is taken in scanty numbers at irregular seasons at Unalashka and Attu. This fish remains sometimes in the rivers until the end of the year.... [C:107]

Sockeye or Red Salmon

Oncorhynchus nerka

*About the 1st of May the Aleuts of Attu Island prepare the weir (*zapór* of the Russians) which obstructs the passage of the fish to the lake. A level place in the bed of the creek is selected where the banks are so high that in times of very high water it will flow over the top of the weir before it will undermine the place where the upper log of the weir is secured in the bank. Each head of a family and the young men contribute so much material in the shape of stakes of the requisite length, generally about 9 feet long and 3 inches in width by 2 inches in the thickness. A long log is laid across the stream at a convenient height (about 5 feet above the bed of the stream). The stakes are then set slanting, with the lower end further upstream. Large rocks are used to hold the stakes in position and to allow the water from above to pass through. After this is done the bed of the creek below the weir is cleared of all loose stones, so as to allow the net or hand-seine to be used in catching the fish, which collect below and cannot pass beyond. [C:108]

*Early in the morning the people visit the locality; and, if sufficient fish have collected during the night, all the people at the place assemble, and those most expert in using the seine stand some distance below the weir. The young boys and girls have gone into the water some distance below, and with shouts and beating the water the fish seek the shelter near the weir. Those holding the seine then enter and soon have all the fish secured. They are thrown on the bank and cleaned. The fish are owned in common; any one who desires to work can do so, those not so desiring will of course be remembered, in winter, when the fish are to be distributed. After the fish are dried they are carried on the backs of the women and children to the principal village and stored, in October, in sea-lion stomachs for winter's food. The stomachs of these animals are very large, and when fresh are inflated with air and stretched as much as possible, sometimes having a capacity of over 35 gallons, or a little more than a barrel. These skins make a convenient receptacle for storing these fish, as they absorb just sufficient moisture to keep the contents in good condition and also prevent mold from spoiling them. When food is scarce, the chief or some other selected person divides the supply of fish, giving to each person a stated quantity, so that each will get an equal share. [C:108–109]

*The fall of snow of the preceding winter has much to do with the summer's catch of fish at Attu. The streams are short and shallow, so that if sufficient snow has not fallen during the winter to feed the streams with water during summer the fish will not enter the creeks. The supply of these fish laid by at Attu for the winter of 1880–'81 was not over 1,200, for during the preceding year but little snow had fallen and but little rain in July and August of 1880. This same species is also caught at that place by means of a small seine about 120 feet long, off the mouths of the small streams as the fish are waiting for a favorable tide to help carry them over the small bars at the mouth of the creek. When the wind is blowing on shore the fish keep at some distance, but when blowing from the land the fish come into shallow water. The net is carried out by means of two canoes lashed together, or else from a small, open skinboat called a *bidará*. Two men row the boat, gently drawn along the beach until the fish begin to show signs of being within the net. The boat is then rapidly taken to shore and the two ends slowly dragged out until the captured fish are drawn out. This manner of taking fish is practiced by all the Aleuts, while the traps across the streams are not used at all places on account of scarcity of wood. At Atkha and Unalashka seines or nets are mostly used. [C:109]

*The Aleuts in former times procured their fish in the same manner. At some places are traces of former superstitions concerning the fish streams. A man who was guilty of some crime against his fellows was not permitted to cross the stream during the fishing season. At Umnak island women at certain periods are not, even at the present time, allowed to participate in the labor of catching the fish, for fear of polluting the stream. . . . This species is called *Krásnaya rē'ba* in the Russian language, . . . and *A' nuk* by the Aleuts. [C:109]

Silver Salmon

Oncorhynchus kisutch

*They are quite plentiful among the Aleutian Islands. Here they are preserved by drying, salting, or drying for a few days, then salting very slightly and hanging in the smoke to finish drying. When prepared with care and smoked for several days with good hard wood (any other than spruce or cottonwood) they are fine eating. When fried these fish are very dry, and have a tendency to crumble to fine pieces while in the pan. The fibers of the meat do not hold together. This species is the last to arrive at the Aleutian Islands and remain until the snow covers the ground. . . . [C:109]

*The eggs of this species are collected by the youngsters and put into the skin of the fish after all the flesh has been removed. This is as carefully saved as is the ukali made by the adults. The Russian name of this species is *Kē'zooch*. The Aleuts call it *Ka ke' thakh*. [C:110]

Humpback or Pink Salmon

Oncorhynchus gorbuscha

*They are distinguishable at a glance by the arched back, which gives them the common name Hump-back or *Gōrbu'sha* in the Russian language. . . . The Aleuts give the name *Ath ga' yuk* to this salmon. [C:110]

*The relative values of the different species [of salmon] stand as follows, according to the opinion of those who have had opportunity to test the matter: first, the *chavícha* [king salmon], then *gorbuscha* [pink salmon], *kisutch* [silver salmon], *keta* [dog salmon], and *nerka* [red salmon].[1] [C:110]

*The natives have different opinions of their relative values. The Aleuts consider the cartilaginous nose and forehead of the *kisutch* to be the best food when fresh. I have seen the entire family seated on the parlor floor with a *kisutch* before each member, who was industriously stripping that portion off the head and devouring it. The heads make a rich soup which is highly praised by some of the white people. The belly of the *chavícha* is usually cut from the body of the large fish and salted as a separate piece. This is the finest of all salted fish. It is very fat and has a taste that once partaken of is rarely forgotten. When freshened and dressed with spices and vinegar it is a tempting dish. The Russians make a kind of pastry of salmon-bellies, rice, eggs and such other things as may be at hand. When prepared in good style it is very nice, but when it has a few shreds of Attu garlic in it it is better to let it alone if you expect to entertain friends during the next several days. [C:111]

Herring [Pacific Herring]

Clupeidae *clupea mirabilis* [*Clupea pallasii pallasii*]

*The natives use seines with meshes of two inches across for these fish and catch them by the ton. They are eviscerated and dried for food. Among the Aleutian Islands this species is wonderfully abundant. At Unalashka they are plentiful in the latter part of July and again in September, though

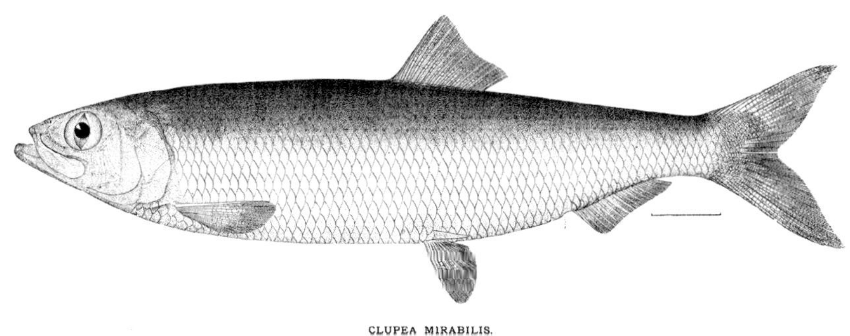

Fig. 41. Herring, *Clupea mirabilis*. Plate 14. *Contributions to the Natural History of Alaska.*

the second appearance of the fish is not always certain in this locality. The Aleuts of Unalashka catch thousands of these fish in seines. I knew one haul of a seine, about 75 feet long, to successfully land 3,600 of these fish at Immŭgné cove, near Iliuliuk village, on Unalashka Island. [C:111]

*At Atkha Island they are excessively abundant in Old Harbor, on the northeast side of the island. The Atkhan people preserve large numbers of these fish by drying them. I do not know that they occur at Attu; for during the two seasons that I was there, none put in an appearance, and as the natives did not speak of them I am led to conclude they do not visit that island. All along the south side of Aliaska and the Kadiak district these fish are plentiful. Their range is comprised between the southern coast of California and Bering's Strait. [C:111]

*The herring of the Aleutian Islands are larger than those of the Saint Michael's district and possess a decidedly superior flavor. The Russian name of this fish is *Selld*; . . . the Aleutian name for the herring is *U'l ngan*. [C:111]

Ray

Raiidae *Raia parmifera*

*The Aleuts look with disgust upon these fish. [C:111]

Sea Urchins

Certain localities afford countless myriads of a species of sea-urchins, *Strongylocentratus dröbachiensis*, Ag., which are essentially and principally the food of the sea otter, *Enhydris lutris*, DeKay, found also in those waters. [101]

The echinus seeks the shallower waters when gravid and the deeper water after discharge of their ova. In the deep water they are not sought for by the Aleut but when they appear in the shoal bays and coves they are searched for and during certain seasons ovaries are filled with eggs which are devoured by the people with evident relish, at times they form an important factor in the diet of the Aleut who repairs to the shoal waters and in the course of a few minutes will secure more than half a bushel of the spiny creatures. The females usually gather them at the present day simply that the males are usually otherwise engaged in some occupation pertaining to the sea-otter hunt or cod fishery. The women seek some grassy knoll and there sit with a flat stone nearby and a smaller hand-stone with which to crack the tests and remove the spines, the latter often being done by rubbing the shell against the side of the basket or sweeping it among the grass stalks on which they wipe their slimy fingers also. [101–102]

The contents of the shell amounts to a couple of tablespoonsful and as the Aleut stomach is capacious and not easily satisfied the number of echini that will be consumed at a single sitting by a modern Aleut is more than surprising. The heap of empty shells accumulating around them is not less than the size of the pile of filled shells before the golden repast was begun. The words of these gossips, for they love to tattle over a pile of the sea-urchin tests, are scarcely less than the pieces of shells between them. [102 –103]

In certain localities the accumulations of these tests and spines have excited the calculative faculty of writers who have spent more time in preparing a learned dissertation upon probabilities and surmises than upon observing the manner by which such accumulations may have been formed. The creature is capable of making only the slowest progress while in the water and when the individuals occur so abundantly as to cover the bottom of the entire bay or cove it is simply impossible to estimate the number. A storm driving in to the bay often throws up the entire number exposed to the action of the waves until the cast up shells are piled in winnows three or four feet deep and several yards wide with a length equal to that of the head of the bay or cove. The tests are composed of material that does not easily decay and soon becomes covered by the more luxuriant grasses preferring a dry or well drained subsoil such as these remains would create. Each year or two the shells would receive additions from the same source and in the course of time would form large beds covering acres in extent. Certain it is that storms do influence the number of these echini. In 1877 a severe storm destroyed nearly all of the sea-urchins on the islands of Semichi and Agattu. What was the result? The sea-otter, formerly abundant, forsook those haunts and up to 1881 only a few sea-otter had been taken since 1877, but the natives of Attu that spring (1881) were congratulating themselves on the abundance of the food of the sea-otter and the prospect of the return of that valuable mammal to their hunting-grounds. [103–105]

That no human remains are to be found among the accumulations of echinus tests is not so very startling when we consider that only healthy

Aleuts repair to the shore, gather and feast upon them. [105]

That no evidence of fire having been used amongst the deposits of sea-urchin shells is also not strange when we know that the echinus is not fit for food when cooked; and when the day is cold the baskets of food were taken to the half underground huts and devoured there; the shells were cast about the sod that formed the walls of the dwelling. [105–106]

That no weapons of any kind are not [sic] to be found among those deposits is not surprising but that they are to be found among the tests and debris surrounding the sites indicating house location is certainly not strange. Fancy a lot of men, women and children with grass baskets slung on their backs, weapons of hafted stone, spears, darts and other implements of the chase, searching the shallow water for creatures that have no means of defense and no more agility than a snail. Does the country boy arm himself with a butcher's cleaver when he enters the woods to search for the chestnuts contained within the hull which needs but a stout stick or a stone to break that the nut may roll out? [106–107]

Cephalopods

Octopus

Octopus punctatus [*Enteroctopus dofleini*]

*This creature is distributed in great abundance throughout the southern and eastern part of the coast line. It is not plentiful north of the Aleutian Islands, but among them is extremely plentiful. The natives assert that it was common in Unalashka previous to 1867, but an earthquake caused them to leave the neighborhood of Iliuliuk village. Of late years they are beginning to reappear. At this place they do not attain a very great size; seldom over three to five feet in expanse of arms. At the islands west of the islands of the Four Craters this species is found in great numbers, and in some localities attains a great size, some individuals being over 10 feet in expanse of outstretched arms. At Kiska Island the largest individuals occur, though but little larger than those of Attu. [C:113]

*They frequent the shallower parts of the flat-topped reefs of rocks and rocky shoals at the entrances to harbors and between islets. They are generally drawn up in a crevice of the rock, awaiting an unlucky fish to pass within reach, when the arms are thrown out with lightning like rapidity, and seizing the victim it is slowly drawn toward the body and devoured. The animal then remains very sluggish for some time. The natives also find them where the receding tide has left them in a crevice of the rocks. The animal is said at this time to be easily frightened and will run over the beach to the water with astonishing rapidity. The natives catch them with a hooked gaff, which is carefully placed under the animal when it is discovered in the shallow water. By a quick jerk the animal is withdrawn before the disks have an opportunity to grasp the surface of the rocks. The flesh is used as food, either in a raw condition or boiled. It is considered very fine eating. When going out on a fishing party the people are generally successful if a "Rak" (Russian name) is secured for bait. Fish of all kinds, which will bite at the hook, eagerly seize this food. Again, the fisherman often pulls up a fish and to it is attached an Octopus which has seized it as it was dragged near its retreat. It oftentimes seizes the bait of the fisherman and is brought to the surface. It is very difficult to manage a large individual, as the arms are pulling and thrashing in every direction. The native endeavors to seize the animal just behind the head, where a slight squeeze will instantly kill it. The women are very expert in this, and will frequently kill those of such size that the men will hesitate to struggle with. [C:113]

*The gall of this animal is dried and used as an article of paint for canoe-paddles, and ornamental stripes on their garments. The gall is of an India-ink color; has a lustrous fracture, and is prepared as a pigment by pounding, or grinding, it on a flat stone with a little water. It is applied with the hand and well rubbed in. After an hour or so the painted surface is carefully oiled with seal or other animal oil, and held over a fire to allow it to be absorbed. It then turns a dark slaty black, and is extremely durable. [C:113]

12

Plants

[Because, as noted in the introduction, Turner's list of plants contains errors, his identifications in this chapter have been correlated with those in Hultén's *Flora of Alaska and Neighboring Territories* (1968) and in Golodoff's *Wildflowers of Unalaska Island* (2003).]

Trees

There are many indications tending to the support of the supposition that the islands are slowly rising, as is evidenced by sites of habitations, now many feet above sea-level, that were formerly at the shore. Great roots of willow and alders are now to be found, at several hundred feet elevation, on hillsides where there is not at present either of those bushes growing; in fact nothing but scanty grasses. Anyone having visited the region cannot have failed to observe the slow process of decay of vegetable matter and also the slow growth of it inasmuch as affects the woody portions of the plants. [147–148]

As the land rose above the sea and the waters were restricted between the islands the warmer water of the south side may have been pushed farther from them by the heavier, colder water of the north side and the filling up (shoaling) of Bering Sea causing the water as a mass near the mainland to be more affected by the cold and formation of ice which each year works an imperceptible change yet in the course of time would be apparent. The precipitous character of the shores and the abundance of detritus falling would quickly obliterate the changes that may have been apparent. It is a subject that is speculative to a great degree but worthy of more earnest study. [148–149]

At the present time the willows and alders grow to a size of only few inches in diameter of stem and are fitted for no useful purposes on account of their distorted growth, thriving only in the deeper ravines along which course the cold streams from the hillsides. [149]

Willow

Salix pallasii var. *obcordata.* [Hultén: 353, *Salix barclayi*; Golodoff: 48–51]

*This species of willow attains the greatest size of any among the Aleutian Islands. The growth is exceedingly crooked, rarely straight for more than a foot, attaining a diameter of 2 to 3 inches, but often decayed within. In all the valleys and wider ravines this species is found in abundance. The roots form an intricate mass, often much exposed, and, with the crooked branches and trunks, form an impenetrable thicket of considerable area. When drift-wood is scarce the Aleuts grub up these shrubs (for they are not fit to be termed even an approach to trees), to be used as firewood. When the wood is well seasoned it produces a bright hot fire, making a much better heat than any of the drift-wood which is cast upon the beach. Veniaminof states that in former years the willows grew to such size in one of the ravines opening on the west side of Captain's Harbor at Unalashka Island that the Russians and Aleuts procured sufficient of these trunks to be used advantageously in making *bidaras* (open skin boats), and *bidarkas*

FIG. 42. Willow, *Salix barclayi*. Located in Unalaska Valley, 2007.

(skin-covered canoes). I visited the locality to find traces of such former growth and found the willows to be of but little better size than in other places near by. It is a fact that on the tops and high sides of some of the hills just beyond the present graveyard at Iliuliuk are to be found at the present day large roots of the willow exposed to the air and but little decayed. At those heights the willows do not at present grow, and no species of willow is now found growing near them. Those roots are of equal size of any that now grow in the ravines many hundred feet feet [sic] below. I may add that I have heard visitors to those places make the assertion that those roots are the roots of oaks. [C:75–76]

Other Trees

*Among the Aleutian Islands the only trees are the spruce from Sitka [*Picea sitchensis*, Hultén: 62], set out by the priest of the Unalashka district in 1832, on the island of Amaknak, a few hundred yards from the village of Iliuliuk, on Unalashka Island.[1] The trees grew, some died, and now but fourteen remain; the other eight were either broken down or died. They have not reproduced their kind, though an abundant crop of cones is produced. Alders and willows are the only large shrubs found on the Aleutian Islands. Their growth is scarcely superior to that of the same species at Saint Michael. Even though drift-wood is scarce and cord-wood is dear, the Aleuts prefer to burn a few wisps of grass or a bunch of *Empetrum* rather than go the same distance for the alder or willow. Though it is true that among these islands the *Empetrum* attain its rankest growth, the entire hillside is covered with it, and the grasses contend in height with the willows. [C:16]

The quantity of driftwood cast upon the shores of those islands was probably sufficient for general purposes but not for building such structures as are to be found among the Innuit of the mainland. Its absence was supplied by the use of the bones, jaws, ribs and vertebra [sic] of the larger cetaceans abounding in the waters washing those islands.... The principal uses to which wood was applied was the manufacture of shafts for the weapons, such as spears, darts, arrows, and for hafts of other implements, for frames of kaiak and umiak and paddles and oars for propelling them, requiring, of course, the better portions of the limited quantity of drift[wood]s washed to the shores. Each community held the right to all cast upon its limits and punishment was as certain for any infringement of that right as for the theft of food found within it. [150–152]

Plants and Berries

Of the annuals the variety is so great as to render a list of others than those entering into the food and domestic economy of the people impracticable in this connection. The list of food plants and berries is as follows: [78]

Adder's-tongue Family (*Ophioglossaceae*)

Moonwort

Botrychium lunaria. [Hultén: 40]

*At Attu they were found on the gravelly level at the head of Chichagof harbor, among the scanty grasses just a few rods west of where are the remains of the former houses of the natives who were taken to the Commander Islands. At Sarana Bay, on the northwest side of Attu, this fern grows in great profusion and attains a height of nine inches in the rich, warm, sandy soil which is at the head of the bay, among the rank grasses of that place, near the present houses which constitute the summer village of the Attu people. [C:81]

Grass Family (*Gramineae* or *Poaceae*)

Wild Rye

Elymus arenarius [Hultén: 193]

Manufactured grass work. [79]

Elymus mollis Trin.

Manufactured grass work. [79] [Hultén: 193 lists this as a subspecies of *Elymus arenarius.*]

Species of Poa, Bromus, Featuca, Triticum and Aira are cut, put in sheaves and used for thatching the huts or for strewing on the floor. [79]

Lily Family (*Liliaceae*)

Wild Garlic

Allium schoenoprasum [Hultén: 307, *Allium victorialis*]

Bulbs eaten. [79]

*A species of garlic occurs plentifully at Attu on the south side of the island. The natives dig it in the latter part of August, and use the bulbs for seasoning geese and other water-fowl. It is very strong, and when once eaten of is never forgotten. It does not, to my knowledge, occur on the eastern islands of the Aleutian chain. [C:78]

*The Russians make a kind of pastry of salmon-bellies, rice, eggs and such other things as may be at hand. When prepared in good style it is very nice, but when it has a few shreds of Attu garlic in it it is better to let it alone if you expect to entertain friends during the next several days. [C:111]

Black Lily, Chocolate Lily

Fritillaria kamtschalcensis [Hultén: 308, *Fritillaria camschatcensis*; Golodoff: 22]

There are several roots of native plants eaten by the Aleut. The principal of these is the bulb of the Kamchatkan Lily, (*Sarána* in Russian) which grows to a variable size depending on location and character of soil, usually little more than half an inch and one fourth in greatest diameter and somewhat flatly spheroid in form. The women dig these bulbs while the men are engaged in hunting geese in the fall of the year. The adherent soil is shaken from the bulbs and then placed where the latter will dry. They are gathered into heaps and then transported to the huts where they are either eaten raw or else boiled until they assume a pasty condition or resembling thick starch. This substance has a starchy taste and somewhat bitter; the latter is not objectionable after several attempts at eating it. When green the bulb tastes bitter and has a glutinous consistency that does not give palatableness to it. [208–209]

*The flower being small and of more greenish color. The natives of Norton Sound eat the bulb, but not to such a degree as the natives of the Aleutian Islands, where this plant is found in greatest abundance and size on all the islands. The natives (Aleuts) consume great quantities of the bulbs. During the months of September and August the women accompany the men who go out hunting the geese, which are making their autumnal migration. The women dig the roots of this lily and store them in huge grass sacks for winter's use. The bulbs are dug up with a copper or iron rod, the dirt shaken off and exposed to the air to dry the remaining dirt, which is then removed as much as possible. The bulbs are boiled with meat or simply in water; either way reduces them to a pasty consistency, having about as much taste as so much boiled starch. When eaten raw the bulblets have a bitter taste (the bitterness lies only in the thin skin which surrounds them), and is at first difficult to acquire a taste for. Those plants which grow in rich, loose soil form a bulb which is often 2 inches in diameter and an inch in thickness. This proves that by cultivation these bulbs could be produced of such size that they might be used as a substitute for the watery potatoes which are grown on some of the islands. The Russian-speaking people call this plant *sa ra ná*, meaning lily. [C:77–78]

Wild Cucumber, Watermelon Berry

Uvularia amplexifolia [Hultén: 311, *Streptopus amplexifolius*; Golodoff: 24]

Berries eaten. [79]

Crowfoot Family (*Ranunculaceae*)

Narcissus-Flowered Anemone

Anemone narcissiflora [Hultén: 464; Golodoff: 77]

Stalk eaten. [78]

*This species is abundant throughout the Aleutian Islands, attaining a height of 1 foot. The early spring growth on the upper end of the root is eaten by the natives of those islands. It has a waxy, farinaceous taste which is not disagreeable. [C:61]

Mustard Family (*Cruciferae* or *Brassicaceae*)

Scurvygrass

Cochlearia officinalis [Hultén: 500; Golodoff: 87. Spoonwart, Scurvy Weed]

Eaten raw. [78]

Rose Family (*Rosaceae*)

Pyrus sambucifolia Cham. & Schlecht.[2] [Hultén: 598, *Sorbus sambucifolia*]

Berries eaten. [78]

*A species of "strawberry"; grows abundantly on Akutan Island, the fruit being very fragrant and of excellent flavor. At Atkha Island the same species is found sparingly on the path from Nazan Bay to Old Harbor. I have eaten the fruit from both the localities named above, but could not obtain specimens of the plant at the proper season. It is not found on any other of the islands to my knowledge. [C:65]

Cloudberry

Rubus chamaemorus [Hultén: 602]

Berries eaten. [78]

*Very abundant at Saint Michael's and southward along the entire coast, including Aliaska and Unimak, Akutan, Attu and Agattu, of the Aleutian Islands. It is not found on Unalashka or any of the intermediate islands to Attu. The berries are slightly acid when fully ripe, and are eagerly sought for by the natives, who preserve them by putting them in water and allowing the mass to freeze. [C:65]

Nagoonberry

Rubus arcticus [Hultén: 603, *Rubus articus,* subsp. *stellatus*; Golodoff: 103]

Berries eaten. [78]

Large-leaved Avens

Geum macrophyllum. [Hultén: 625; Golodoff: 110]

*Obtained only at Attu and Unalashka. Not common at Unalashka, and but little more so at Attu. The semi-domesticated young of the white-cheeked goose devour the leaves of this plant so that it is difficult to obtain good specimens of it. [C:65]

Pea Family (*Leguminosae* or *Fabaceae*)

Nootka Lupine

Lupinus nootkatensis [Hultén: 636; Golodoff: 114–115]

The next most important root is that of a leguminous plant, *Lupinus*, termed *Zholtie koren* in Russian or Yellow-root in English. It grows on the low level tracts where there is not too much moisture. The root attains a size of two or three inches in diameter and a length of a foot or more. The root is very fibrous and contains so much woody matter that the consumer must exercise great caution in the parts eaten lest the quantity taken be so great that unless eaten with a liberal quantity of oil or fat the waste is liable to become impacted within the lower intestines and produce serious results. Measures of relief must be very prompt or inflammation sets in and the matter refuses to be dislodged even by heroic doses of Castor oil or Epsom salts. Several instances of death have resulted from indiscretion in eating this root. [209–210]

*This plant is called *zhóltia kóren* or "yellow-root," by the Russian-speaking people. About the middle of October the Aleuts dig great quantities of these roots for food. The roots are carefully scraped until the skin is removed, the interior possessing a slightly bitter but farinaceous taste and is eaten either raw or else boiled. When eaten in excess it is apt to produce disagreeable effects, and if oily food is not also eaten soon after the presence of so much woody fiber in the stomach and intestines, is likely to produce fatal inflammation. The roots are frequently the only food that the hunters can obtain during long-continued storms. Several such instances have occurred to my own knowledge. I am not aware that the natives of the mainland make use of this plant for food. A remark concerning the spread of this plant may not be out of place. Near the grave-yard of Iliuliuk village on Unalashka Island in 1878, but few stalks of this plant were to be seen; in 1881 the area was covered with a mass of vigorous stalks and were frequently referred to by others who had noticed their rapid growth. The cattle formerly collected there when they had eaten sufficiently, and their droppings may have favored the increased growth of these plants. [C:64]

Beach Pea

Lathyrus maritimus [Hultén: 673; Golodoff: 116]

*Grows abundantly throughout the coast line of Alaska, south of Cape Lisburne, and including the entire chain of Aleutian Islands.... There is no use made of this plant by the natives; neither is it eaten by the cattle or sheep. [C:64]

Parsley Family (*Umbelliferae* or *Apiaceae*)

Western Hemlock Parsley

Umbelliferae Conioselinum fischeri [Hultén: 704, *Conioselinum chinense*; Golodoff: 130]

*This species occurs throughout the Aleutian Islands, growing on the lowlands. It is regarded as highly poisonous by the natives. [C:67]

Wild Celery

Archangelica officinalis [Hultén: 705, *Angelica lucida*]

Leaf stalks eaten. [78]

*Among the Aleutian Islands it is very abundant, especially on the outskirts of the sites of ancient villages and in the excavations which formed the dwellings in those villages. It attains, in such localities, a height of several feet, 4 to 6 being common sizes, and of very thick stalks. This plant is one of the earliest plants to appear in the spring. The leaf stalk become very long. At Attu I have seen them 4 feet long, bearing a leaf as large as a palm-leaf fan. The tender leaf stalks and the main stalk are eaten by the Aleuts. During the months of May and June the women go and gather great bundles of these stalks and bring them to the village. The first finger is inserted into the hollow stalk and rapidly split open; the teeth are then used to assist the fingers to separate the tender parts from the exterior skin and strings of the stalk. It is an operation which requires much dexterity and practice to enable one to prevent the tender parts from breaking. The main stalk is stripped of its skin, which, when young and tender, is easily accomplished. The main stalk possesses a sweetish, aromatic taste; the leaf stalks are sweeter, but less aromatic. I have seen boys and girls eat these stalks by the yard at a time. A boy at Atkha received the nick-name of Poochka, the Russian name of this plant, because he devoured so much of it. On the approach of frost, the plant rapidly withers, and leaves the dry stalks standing until pushed out of the way for the next year's growth. When these stalks are in sufficient quantity near a village the people use them as fuel. The exterior bark of the dead stalk is impervious to the rain; hence when camping out a fire is easily started with these stalks if they are first broken open. They produce a fierce fire. [C:67]

Crowberry Family (*Empetraceae*)

Blackberry, Mossberry, or Crowberry

Empetrum nigrum [Hultén: 716; Golodoff: 139–140]

Berries eaten. Stems used as fuel. [79]

* Sitka, Saint Lawrence, Unalashka, Norton Sound, Point Barrow, Arctic coast. (This heather is found abundantly throughout all the treeless portions of Alaska. On the Aleutian Islands it obtains its maximum growth. The lower hills are covered with large patches of many rods in area with

this species. The berries are black in color, have a slightly acid taste when ripe, being produced in profusion on the stems, so much so that nearly a handful may be gathered at a time. Great quantities are gathered by the natives, who use them either raw or else cooked, though rarely in the latter manner. These berries form the food of several species of birds, such as geese, ptarmigans, and plovers. The natives of Aliaska and some of the eastern islands of the Aleutian chain use this heather for fuel. The women gather great bunches by pulling it from the ground and carrying it to their houses, where it is immediately used. In rare instances it is kept for a few days (but only because there is a sufficiency of other fuel to be used in its stead), until it is dried out. It is used in the following manner: The pot or kettle containing water or food to be boiled is placed on a small stick stuck in the side of the sod chimney of the hut; a few shreds of the plants are lighted, it burns rapidly, and has a quick, darting flame, like the branches of pine trees. The bunch of lighted fuel is held under the vessel, and, as fast as it is consumed by flame another wisp is lighted, until the boiling is finished. This work is usually performed by the smaller boys or girls. This kind of fuel is not used by the Attu people, the Atkan people being the farthest to the west who employ it for that purpose. The Attu people have never used it, and only those of Attu who have been to the eastward know how to use it, as it requires considerable skill to keep the heat properly applied to the vessel containing the water or food. [C:74–75]

FIG. 43. *Empetrum nigrum* growing at Unalaska, 2007.

Fig. 44. Woman carrying a load of *Empetrum nigrum* at Unalaska. Henry W. Elliott, "Illoolook, or Oonalashka," *Our Arctic Province.*

*At Atkha Island I saw several large patches, which had a deeper green and seemed to be of more vigorous growth. On inquiry I found that the people had in few years past taken the heather off from these areas, and that it was being renewed with a heavier growth. [C:75]

Heath Family (*Ericaceae*)

Lowbush Cranberry

Vaccinium vitis-idaea [Hultén: 731; Golodoff: 149. Lingonberry, Mountain Cranberry]

Berries eaten. [78]

**Ericaceae vaccinium vitis-idaea*. The berries are deep red and intensely acid, but of good flavor after a taste for it is acquired. The natives gather great quantities of the berries for food, and in some localities are in demand for preservation by putting them in pure water and kept for winter's use by the white people of Alaska. When cooked with a sufficient quantity of sugar they make a good pie or an excellent jelly or jam. [C:70–71]

Great or Bog Bilberry

Ericaceae *Vaccinium uliginosum* [Hultén: 734; Golodoff: 152. Alpine Blueberry, Bog or Lowbush Blueberry]

Berries eaten. [79]

*Plentiful at Unalashka and Attu: less common on the intermediate islands. Berries ripen in the latter part of August and early September. They are gathered in great quantities by the natives. [C:71]

Labrador Tea

Ledum palustre [Hultén: 717]

*A tea is made of the flowers of this plant. The infusion has a slightly terebinthine taste, which becomes pleasant enough after a time. Among some of the white people it has a reputed tonic effect on the system. [C:71]

Composite Family (*Asteraceae* or *Compositae*)

Dandelion

Taraxacum palustre [Hultén: 947, *Taraxacum trigonolobum*; Golodoff: 199]

Used medicinally. [78]

*Common throughout the Aleutian Islands, growing in the dry clefts of rocks on the hillsides and faces of cliffs. The flowers are rich golden-yellow and form of [sic] mass of bloom. The leaves are used by the Aleuts, who steam or wilt the leaves and apply them to indolent ulcers. [C:70]

Nightshade Family (*Solanaceae*)

Potato

[Turner, in describing the location of artifacts obtained at Attu, noted that they were gathered from a locality which for many years had "been the principal place for growing potatoes. The implements were brought to the surface as the natives were cultivating the ground preparatory to planting." (4)]

13

Origins: Evidence from Language and Folklore

When we come to consider the region as a habitation for man we are led to look upon the environment and from it deduce certain theories that cannot be supplied by other testimony. How long the ancestors of the present inhabitants have dwelt upon those islands is purely speculative unless evidence of a substantial character is brought to prove a greater or less time than has been assigned to them by modern writers who have had scanty opportunities for investigation and [have been] far-reaching in conclusions based on wildest speculations. [83–84]

The term Aleut applied to the people of the Aleutian Islands, formerly having a greater extension than at present, for reasons not necessary to discuss in this connection, is one of very unsatisfactory origin and similarly of signification. The earlier Russian navigators knew nothing of the language of these people and these nothing of the Russian speech so that when a remark or direction was given by the invaders to the simple natives they consulted among themselves as to the proper meaning of the order given for they soon found that promptness in obedience of the behests of the Russian was least likely to cause punishment to themselves. The word which they constantly repeated among themselves was *a'leu*, what? what is it? what did he say? what shall I do? what am I to do?[1] and in their conference time was so long taken up that the impatient Russian applied the word spoken by them to the people themselves and was afterward corrupted into Aleut with an extended signification to include people not belonging to the same branch as the Aleuts. [84–85]

The word Aleut is recognized among those people as one of unknown quantity. The Aleut word *Tai yá qukh* signifies person, man: *Tai ya ghun* signifies people: *Tai yá ghu ki thûkh* a multitude of people. [85]

The appellation *U nang an* of Veniaminof should be spelled *Unûn̗g ûn* for the reason that the Russian alphabet contains no sound equivalent to the short sound of *u (û)* and *a* had to be substituted for it. The word is in the plural (*u nûn̗g akh* being the singular) and is the name applied by the Aleuts of the eastern islands to themselves. That this term was afterward extended to include the western Aleut is not difficult to prove from a variety of circumstances which favored its extension and need not be referred to in this connection. [85–86]

The writings of recent authors would tend to lead the uninformed reader to conclude that the ancestors of the present Aleuts were as much native to those islands as the rocks that girt their shores and that their primitive condition was so low that they possessed not only the simplest means of conveyance but question the knowledge of the art of fire-making and ascribe to them a constant diet, which to this day is considered a delicacy even in their present advance toward a scale of civilization not equalled by any other natives of Alaska.[2] Series of statements are made upon flimsy evidence and deductions drawn out that have no more strength than the cobwebs over which those investigators trampled while searching for material to support predetermined conclusions. [86–87]

Every fact in the history of these people irresistibly proves that the eastern islands were first peopled from the mainland and that the western islands were successively inhabited by refugees from the eastern islands. All of the traditions of the Aleut point to the eastward and some refer to that unknown, dark-enveloped space to the westward. [87]

The names of many of the constellations are identical with those of the mainland Innuit and, furthermore, are of creatures which have never occurred upon any of the islands west of Unimak Pass. [88]

The linguistic affinities of the Aleut and the people of the mainland have been compared upon insufficient material[,] of which the greater part of either has been collected by different persons and often of different nationalities whose mother tongue did not permit those niceties of speech to be distinguished[,] and hence in the limited time given to the preparation of the vocabularies obtained many errors remained without opportunity for subsequent correction and verification. That upon these islands themselves an entire language has been swept away[,] until only a few traces of it remain at the present date[,] will be shown when the extreme western group is considered. [88–89]

Strangely enough wars were always waged from east to west and seldom did the western inhabitants retaliate by journeying to the eastward for they feared that direction and hesitated to attempt the attack upon those who compelled their ancestors to flee to the west. [89]

There were two recognized dialects or languages spoken formerly. They were as nearly related to each other as the modern Spanish and Portuguese or Norwegian and Swedish. These languages were known as the Unalashkan and Atkhan. The inhabitants of each island spoke some words differently from those not remote. In former times the people of Attu and the other islands of the Near Group spoke a language as dissimilar to the present Atkhan dialect as that of the mainland Malimyut differs from that of the Kaniagmyut, or people of Kadiak Island, and at present the Attu dialect is more nearly akin to the speech of the Umnak Aleut than to the Atkhans who are nearer the Attu people by some two hundred and forty miles by sea which means far more than the distance expressed by those figures would seem to imply. Certain it is, however, that the words of the Atkhans show a greater resemblance and identity to the mainland language than does that spoken at Unalashka, Umnak and Attu. There can be no dispute that the people of the Andreanof and Rat Islands were the first to pass from the mainland to the chain now termed the Aleutian Islands. Why they were driven from the eastward is a question that will be satisfactorily solved in another connection. The people of the eastern islands were subsequent to those termed Atkhans while the original inhabitants of the Nearer Group were an offshoot of the eastern people compelled by war to seek safety by flight beyond the Atkhans who fearing treachery caused them to journey to the islands to the westward. [89–91]

In the haste of flight resultant from a surprise mode of attack it is safe to infer that the retreating party was not forewarned in sufficient time to collect and pack their effects and then move calmly away and leave their habitations empty. That was not the manner of ancient Aleut warfare. Extermination was the only thought of the attacking party who fell upon the unsuspecting victims in the dead of night when drowsiness overpowered the vigils set for protection. It must be remembered that the Aleuts had no dogs or other domesticated creatures that might give warning. The umiak (*ni gíl yakh*) lay in a secluded spot and to it sped all who were fortunate enough to escape the death that awaited their capture or the state of captivity which was wholly at the pleasure of the leader of the victors. [91–92]

Is it any wonder that on all of the islands the greatest similarity of implements from the rough and uncouth flake of stone to the polished celt should be found? The pursued Aleuts had to begin anew on the uninhabited shore that now afforded him a retreat. The stones from the beach were employed to slay the hitherto unmolested creatures that dwelt on sea and land. [92]

It is impossible to account for the appearance of the Aleut on these islands without bringing in evidence from the mainland to support the assertion. In no instance do the mainland Innuit, anywhere in their distribution, make any reference to having come from the westward or the southward. All their traditions, legends and assertions point to the north and the east. The south is unknown and seldom referred to. The west is regarded in the same manner as we conclude the space beyond our atmosphere to be, dark, dreary and uninhabitable. The north is known to be a region of ice and cold while the east is bright and warm, the source of all things, the home of the light and heat principle anciently visiting the first created man in the form of a woman. [97–98]

One of the greatest obstacles in collecting traditions of the ancestors of the living Innuit is it [is] almost an impossibility to have the narrator, however reliable he may be, disassociate himself from the immediate vicinity of his birth-place. So persistently does he cling to that locality that all his information pertains only to that place. Many of the winter-night tales of the mainland people are identical with those of the Aleut, excepting that the various characters may be changed as beasts to birds and *vice versa*. [98–99]

The question naturally arises[,] which are the older people on their respective lands? If as is asserted by some writers that the Aleut came from the west we should find some linguistic trace or other indication to warrant such belief. No such evidence has been produced. [108]

The ancient population was far greater than when known from the accounts of the earliest discoverers. The history of the Aleut is better known since that date than any branch of the Innuit tribes whose territory occupy the shores of three oceans and extends many thousands of miles with a gap of only two or three hundred miles at the present date. [108]

So far as can be ascertained from the people of the present day[,] their earliest ancestors waged a perpetual war with the mainland Innuit. The character of this warfare was that marauding parties of few to many kaiaks (*Hiḱh akh* in the Aleut language) each containing one person assembled under the leadership of the principal man of the community sending out the party or else under the direction of one delegated by the chief of the villages (I use the word village advisedly) which contributed the force setting out. [109]

They were in turn attacked by the eastern or mainland people in the same manner. It is not difficult to believe that these wars were simply the continuation of those engaged in on the mainland when the overpowering hordes streamed from the north and drove the Aleut from the mainland along Aliaska to the Aleutian Islands for here the people constitute the only branch of the Innuit of the mainland. [109–110]

Those new-comers were again driven to the south and peopled the Kenai Peninsula and as far south as about latitude 58 degrees on the mainland. It is more than probable that the inhabitants of the latter portions of the mainland were compelled to move south at a date subsequent to the occupation of the Aleutian Islands by the Aleuts. [110]

While at Bristol Bay, on the north side of the Aliaskan Peninsula, in the summer of 1878, I questioned several persons and learned from them that that area was at one time neutral ground and that no one dwelt on it but that they traversed it in common. Also that the subsequent inhabitants of that region came from the north and occupied the land without molestation from people of their own kind. [110–111]

The Tugiagmyut assert that they came from the interior of the country. They were formerly settled in a village situated on the north side of the Kvikhpak (Yukon) River. One of the villagers possessed an ax which he valued so greatly as to refuse a small boy the use of it. The boy took the implement and when discovered by the owner the latter slapped (struck) the boy. (An action that is sufficient to cause the death of the one giving the blow.) The boy ran to his father and related what had happened. The father went out and said he and his people had always dwelt peaceably in the village and that if he could not be treated well he would go to another land. His friends espoused his cause and they journied [sic] to the south, coming to their present place of abode on the northern shore of Bristol Bay, where they form a community of less than three hundred souls. They are the cleanest, best dressed and good-natured people of Alaska. Their speech is dialectically distinct from those to the south and east of them and far more so from the inhabitants along the Kuskokwim River. [111–112]

All who have studied the Innuit tribes or people of Alaska acknowledge the abruptness of speech and customs that mark the people dwelling on the north and on the south of Unalakhlet, toward the head of Norton Sound. [112]

It was related to me, at St. Michael's (Norton Sound), that in ancient times the Unalit and the Innuit to the south of them were the only people of that region; and, that the Malimyut, and their kindred, came long after the Unalit had occupied the land from the head and southern side of the Kavyayak Peninsula far to the south. Other people, the Malimyut, came in great numbers to their country and attempted to dispossess the Unalit of it. Long wars followed, and finally when hostilities ceased the Unalit and Malimyut agreed to erect a village in common and that neither people should pass beyond it. The Malimyut were known to the Unalit as the *followers*, or those who came *second*, from the word *mal ik tok*, that which *follows*. It is the name of the *second* numeral and ordinal, but having different terminations. Unalakhlet is a word signifying *here shall it be*, referring to that place where the neutral village stands. The word Unalit signifies *here; in this place*. I may add that these people were noted for their proficiency in the use of the spear and that a spear is termed *ú nûk*, but the word is rarely applied to that weapon at this date. The Atlantic coast (Labrador) Innuit have the word *Unalit* to signify *murderer, destroyer*. [113–114]

There is every reason to believe that the Innuit inhabiting the eastern shore of Siberia were driven there, within the past three hundred years, by the people of the Alaskan shore, on the opposite side. [114]

It has been remarked on a previous page that the Aleut language is composed of two dialects each differing in important characters, yet not so much in the roots or stems of the principal words as in the terminations and in the names of objects which do not occur on both of the divisions. The Unalashkan dialect includes all the language spoken from Umnak eastward as far as the Aleut proper extend. The Atkhan dialect is more restricted and includes the speech of only the people of the island of Atkha. [115]

At the present time there is so much mixture of the speech of the Aleut that the distinctions would not appear to be so clearly defined as was existing previous to the cession of the territory to the United States. A total change in the method of capture of the sea-otter and the leasing of the Pribylof Islands has so nearly and intimately brought the people of the entire chain together as to cause many of the former differences of speech to disappear. [115–116]

A residence of four continuous months among the Atkhans convinced me that they were originally, previous to their occupation of the central islands of the Aleutian Chain, as much a sept of the Aleut branch of Innuit as they were after settlement of those Islands. Their dialect is more nearly related to the mainland Innuit, or contains a greater number of words having the same sound and meaning but with different terminations, than the dialect of the Unalashkans resembles that of the mainland people. This leads me to conclude that they occupied a more northerly position than the locality dwelt upon by the people now termed Unalashkans. When the wave of Innuit bore down from the north the ones termed Unalashkans moved first and followed the peninsular tract, retreating to the westward. The ones now termed Atkhans were in course of time compelled to take flight and were necessitated to follow the path taken by the other. On arriving at the chain of islands the Atkhans were driven past the islands dwelt upon by the eastern islanders and finally came to places not inhabited by the western-most of the Unalashkans. [116–117]

The longer contact with the northern Innuit enabled the Atkhans to adopt certain words from the Innuit which the Unalashkans had no opportunity to do. [117]

14

Governance

It is not probable that the Aleut adopted any special customs or originated any particular ceremonies after their arrival upon the islands than they had inaugurated before they left the mainland whence they came. Their laws and rulings were of a severe character as may be inferred from the writings of Veniaminof who first gave a true account of the people under consideration. Strangely enough the severity of the laws were tempered with teachings that rendered disobedience almost a crime and punishments were for only the gravest offences. Infractions of these were against the sentiment of the community and the offender incurred the contempt of the village people if for a slight disregard for the regulations, and for more serious offenses the punishment was mutilation, dismemberment or death. [117–118]

Submission to the sentiment or opinion of the people was the highest virtue of them and[,] while cruel and unsparing toward an enemy[,] he who did a noble act or performed a brave deed was the recipient of praise and good will from all. [118–119]

The rulings in their communal government were made by the elders who selected one of their number to act as the adviser of the people and to see that their wishes were carried out. Some of their rulers were revered through life and praised in song after death and their selection appears to have been wholly from the elder and wisest men of the community. Each dwelling had its principal man and he acted as the representative for the family in all its dealings. Each village selected, from the heads of the families, one who should direct the general actions of the community and again the inhabitants of an entire island chose a principal leader whose functions were that of a chief but only during war did he exercise the extreme authority delegated to him by the representatives of the entire population. [119–120]

This manner of delegating authority finally gave rise to two classes of people, the wise men and the common people. When the wise men convened to deliberate upon their affairs the common people were excluded and this gave rise to the erection of a special assembly-room to which none were admitted except upon donation of an amount of property commensurate with his ability which was determined by the sitting members. Male or female of any age was admitted at times and finally only the adult males who represented a certain number of people. [120]

Special ones were chosen to act as teachers and guides into the mysteries of the games and ceremonies springing from that system of government. [120–121]

In instances where cause gave rise to dissension and serious offense between the people of two villages the chief man of the island convened the sub-chiefs and they decided whether the cause was sufficient for war. If insufficient the offending party made satisfactory restitution which may have been imposed as a kind of tax upon the community and the sub-chief of that people was held responsible to the chief for the exactment of the penalty. Promptness in paying such debt and fulfilment of all obligations decided upon by the convention was the chief means of redemption of the position of the villagers giving offense. This led to a subdivision of the land into parcels apportioned to the amount of population. They were, in some instances, quite restricted and as their productiveness was well known each village had defined boundaries beyond the limits of which none must gather any character of food. The non-observance of this was the gravest offense and the culprit had to repay the robbed community fourfold value. [121–122]

The head chief was noted for his wisdom, bravery and ability to lead and direct all manner of hunting for the waters outside of defined and designated points of land was free to all. Certain hunters were skilled in the capture of whales and others in the sea-otter hunts or pursuit of sea-lions and other seals. The smaller marine creatures belonged to the captors but the larger whales were divided among the entire population. [122]

15

Internecine Wars and Slavery

As the population increased and the boundaries hitherto defined and limited became so small that it could not sustain the wants of the people[,] encroachments upon other islands led to war and these eventually caused strife amongst the two divisions of the Aleut. It is impossible to conceive the horrible cruelties practised upon an enemy but when he showed submission he was taken captive and his subsequent actions determined his life or death. As the subchiefs and the leader of the war-parties were the bravest men the greater number of captives fell to them and as they were consumers they were kept as hostages at first for a period of time and then as slaves having nothing of their own but those things which the master gave them. They married only female slaves and their children belonged to the owner of the male slave. [125–126]

Capital punishment was resorted to as a penalty for divulging the secret intentions of the conclave of wise men deliberating on the affairs pertaining to the community; also for extreme acts of disobedience on the part of slaves. The latter were well treated and misuse of authority over them brought disgrace upon him who owned them. Their lives were completely in the hands of the owner who could dispose of them by gift or sale as suited his will[,] and the wealth or importance of a chief or sub-chief was indicated by the number of slaves he was enabled to support; to deny them food was certain to bring contempt upon the master. The slave was expected to defend the life and property of his master with his life if necessary. [127]

The beginning of the system of slavery was doubtless instituted when the Aleut yet dwelt upon the mainland and continued after the occupation of those islands. It is not beyond belief that the idea of slavery amongst the Aleut was sprung from the mainland Indians near whom the Aleut dwelt, for the Thlinket are known to have had slaves from the earliest times. This view is supported from the fact that no other Innuit were known to retain the prisoners of war as slaves although hostages were kept and possessed greater liberties than the members of the community. Even the system of accepting hostages did not prevail north of the Kvikhpak (Yukon) River. [127–128]

There appears to be the best evidence, from tradition, that the cessation of hostilities between the islanders and mainland Innuit was followed by a second war resulting in the defeat of the ancestors of the Innuit now termed Aglimyut and scattering them from the Aliaskan peninsula to the eastward where their descendants now dwell. [128–129]

The suitableness of the Aleutian Islands for the support of a large population increased the number of people and wars sprang up among the two divisions represented there. The Unalashkans and Atkhans were at first on friendly terms but dissension sprang up and strife began to be waged with all the ferocity the nature of the combattants [sic] could summon. Total extermination was the rule and those escaping were compelled to relinquish their island to take refuge on another until the expanse of water between them was so great that the attacks could be made only once in a year[1] sometimes in two years and rarely less than every five years was a maurauding [sic] or scouting party fitted out to inspect the various uninhabited islands for enemies that might be lurking there and awaiting an opportunity to engage their opponents unaware. The scenes of the hardest strife were the smaller islands that lie between Umnak and Amlia [the Islands of Four Mountains]. The Atkhans were the most unrelenting in their wars seeming to care less for capture than for killing and pillage. [129–130]

The western islands had now become populated and the Atkhans waged war upon the Kiskans and nearly exterminated them, some of them were taken to the Atkhan group and incorporated among the Atkhans, others took to their boats and went to the more western islands and were safe from attack until one was observed to paddle his canoe on the water near Bouldyr Island. The Atkhan returned and reported the fact. A war party was organized and sent out, arriving at that island nothing could be discovered but traces of inhabitants. The party returned to Kiska and thence to Atkha. The next year they sent out a great number of people to the west; they found the Attu people and engaged them in war. The Atkhans retreated but some years after again came westward and fought the people of the three western islands. Struggles were carried on for many years and the western people were finally subdued. Not a trace of a man remained on either of the islands. A woman who happened to be on the mountains saw the fight and her people killed. She remained hidden hoping to discover some trace of an escaped person. The Atkhans scoured the hills and awaited all the summer for signs of a living person. They departed and in the meantime the woman subsisted upon such food as she could procure. Twice she walked around the island of Attu hoping to find a living being. She found none. The second summer she took a young gull as a pet and later she captured a young goose. These birds were her only companions and during this time she laughed only once. The gull and goose got to wrangling over a morsel of food she gave them and in their struggle the affair was so comical that she burst out laughing. [130–132]

Late that year a party of Atkhans visited the western three islands to discover whether anyone had escaped the massacre of the summer two years before. The woman saw the party approaching and went to meet them. They saw her and on landing they inquired if any men or other persons were yet on the island. She related that for two years she had wandered about the island and had seen none. The leader of the party had a number of prisoners taken from Umnak along with the war party. The leader determined to leave three men and two women on the island. He told the Attu woman to select a man for her husband. She took one of the Umnak men and the other four, two men and two women[,] were put on the land. The leader told them they should remain there. [133–134]

From the five Umnak people and the one Attu woman sprang all the inhabitants of the western islands. From then and to the present day the inhabitants of the Nearer Islands claim relationship only with the Umnak people. The present residents of Attu speak dialectically distinct from either the Atkhans or the Unalashkans and to my knowledge the speech is harsher, more guttural and not so pleasant in sound as that of the Atkhans. A great number of words are totally distinct and the plurals are formed by the ending *in*, and not *ng* and *an* of the Unalashkans, and *is* of the Atkhans. [134]

That the extermination of the people of the Nearer Islands, with the exception of the single woman referred to, took place long ago is indicated by the fact that the western islands were well populated at the time of their discovery, in September 1745, by Nevodchikov, and on the twenty-sixth of that month Chuprov with others went on shore to get water. They met many wild inhabitants, etc. (See *Chronological Hist. of Disc. of Aleutians Islands*; by V. N. Bergh; St. Petersburg; 1823. page 8.)[2] [135]

At this time the inhabitants were parcelled off in different localities each governed as related on previous pages. In 1880–'81 the only living person born on Agattu was the mother of the tyone at Attu [Chief Terrentii Prokopeuff]. She alone represented the number of people who dwelt in the thirty-four villages that formerly existed on Agattu, the names and positions of which are carefully located on an excellent map of Agattu Island prepared by myself and the natives of Attu.[3] Some of those villages contained many inhabitants and others were small. [135–136]

Wars were carried on between the people of Attu, Agattu and the Semichi Islands of the Nearer Group, each of which was ruled by a separate chief and sub-chiefs. When not content with waging battle among the other islands the people of one island fought among themselves on the merest pretext for pillage and murder. The slightest offense was sufficient to cause the people of one locality to attack another village. Their fights were always conducted at night. The attacking party stealthily moving under cover of darkness upon the unsuspecting people and at the hour when the Crested Auklet, *Simorhynchus cristatellus* (Pall.) [*Aethia cristatella*], uttered its morning notes the party began the attack. The manner of conducting these marauding parties was to await until the last sleep was upon the victims. The skin canoes and the umiaks lying on the stakes or scaffold were thrust into the skylight of the dwellings and then any inflamable [sic] material was used to set fire to and the people within either suffocated by the smoke or burned in the flames. All who attempted to escape were thrust back into the flames or struck with stone-headed cudgels. Seldom indeed did anyone escape from the habitations and the locality then belonged to the conquerors. [136–138]

[In the list of artifacts in] series twenty-four is a single object of stone of coarse texture, sandstone. There are numerous depressions cut into it for the reception of the finger-tips so that when held in the hand it will not slip. The function of this stone, four inches long three wide and the same thickness, giving it an ovoid form, is that of a killing stone. It was held by the hand and the victim [was] stealthily approached from behind and [was] struck on the head. It was employed in hand to hand combat. . . . [28]

Such pillaging and murder was carried on from time to time but under different conditions than prevailed among the eastern people of the islands, for the sub-chiefs appear to have not been subject to the authority of the chief except in matters pertaining to and affecting the entire island. [138]

Just when the interlocal struggles ceased is not possible to determine but that they long antedated the arrival of the Russians is without doubt. [138]

A tradition exists that a chief came into power and whose wisdom was so great together with his desire for peace that the entire people of the group revered him and obeyed his counsel. He was a very large man and this possibly accounted for the respect of the people under his rule. He instituted games and taught the people that hunting and fishing was more in accordance with their nature than massacre and plunder. [138–139]

16

Social Relationships

Just what the social relations of the two sexes were in former times are difficult to determine. It may be concluded that immoral degradation was not at a low stage previous to the occupation of the islands by the Russians.[1] It is only just to state that the horrible cruelties perpetrated by the white invaders was solely in retaliation of the resentment of the Aleut against the Russians for rape of their women and the little value [the Russians] set upon the females torn from the families of nearly every village. [211]

How the marriage ceremony was conducted in former times there is but a shadow of information. That chastity and continence were virtues may be inferred from several writings of the earlier voyagers and sojourners in the region. [211–212]

It was not to be expected that certain acts could under the conditions of dwelling be kept from a common knowledge of the people. The garments were so arranged about the body that exposure of person could not always be obviated. It is related in one of the stories of ancient times that a man in descending, into his dwelling, by means of the notched post exposed himself in such manner as to excite those below to laughter. He well knew the cause and merely inquired if they had never before seen such a sight. The women present begged him to take no offense at their merriment over the affair. The women were expected to conceal their person or at least not become notorious in her [sic] actions. [212]

It was generally known throughout the community who were the parties contracting the ceremony of intended marriage for even to this day the large stone lamps are referred to [as] the lamps given by the young women to the daughter of the chief when she married the person of her choice. This donation was made to show the approval of the others and to afford her with the means of continuing the fire that was to welcome her husband to his home. These lamps were filled with oil and a lighted wick placed in it so that while the party sat within the hut the burning lamps were placed before them. A young man placed a small, lighted lamp before the woman of his choice and if she continued to feed the flame her affection for him was shown; but, if it was extinguished or left to burn out was an indication that his attentions were disregarded. [213–214]

This ceremony may be considered as having a direct connection with the mainland legends referring to the origin of light and the sun and moon and is simply in commemoration of those events in the mythic lore of the Innuit. [214]

Licentiousness was considered a crime and the unfortunate girl bearing a child out of such acts was compelled to undergo severe punishment and infanticide brought misfortune upon the community. [214]

To dream of a white bird was to become pregnant while to dream of a dark colored bird was an evil omen that could be dispelled only by undergoing a punishment of death to [the] offender so bringing the dream into the community for it had the signification that the child born was illegitimate. Incest was the gravest crime that could be brought upon a person. The degree of relationship prohibiting cohabitation was about the same as obtains among civilized nations. [214–215]

Special ceremonies were instituted to discover the perpetrator of the following grave crimes: murder with cause, often not a serious cause either; incest, infanticide and defilement of person. [215]

Strangers were received as friends and so long as they conformed to the rules governing the settlement they were treated with consideration. It was deemed a great breech of trust that any stranger or visitor should return and reveal the secrets of the place where he had been received. The people of his own village being unwilling to hear the reports[,] except those pertaining to the hospitality for the place from which he returned[,] for the repetition of those secrets was often a prime cause of war between the neighboring settlements. [215–216]

Each individual (male only) was supposed to be able to take such steps in his own affairs that would endure to his credit and there seems to have been social disgrace if an insult was not avenged and as each community had its own ideas of right and wrong it was often a matter of difficulty that one knew at what moment he might trespass upon the privilege accorded

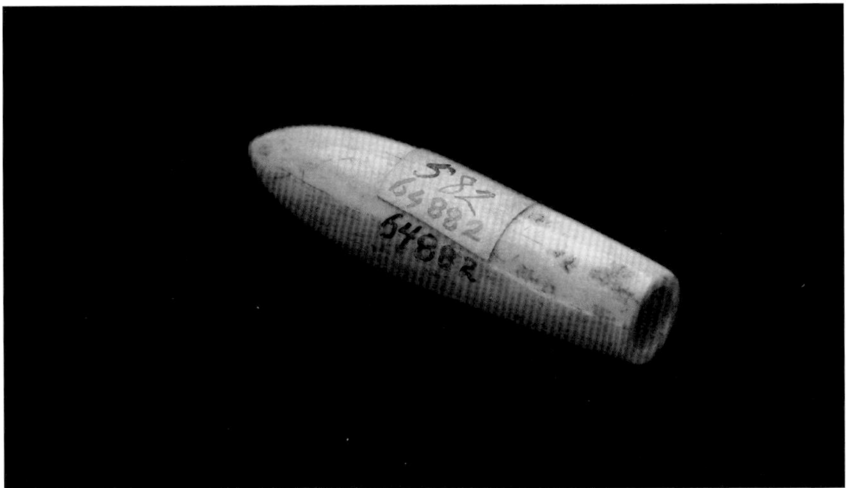

Fig. 45. Blunted spear point, Attu. *Department of Anthropology, Smithsonian Institution (NMNH A64882) (T582).* This blunted point was used in a winter competition when people engaged in games in order to "forget their hunger." Spears tipped with these points appear to have had another use. While on Attu in 1936, Alan G. May was told, "The bullet-shaped points that I have been finding were used by children to practice harpooning." (May, *1936 Expedition to the Aleutian Islands: Complete Journal*, p. 121. Box 15, folder 6, Alan G. May Papers. Archives & Special Collections Department, University of Alaska Anchorage.)

only to the one and not to the other so that the guest was bound to observe a strict course of conduct. [216]

During the winter season when the ground was covered with a crust of snow[,] the Aleuts diverted themselves, *forgetting their hunger* as it was termed, by casting a dart or arrow at an object set upon the snow-crust at a distance from the players. The object was that the shaft should strike not on this side but *near* or beyond the target and skip by a series of bounds beyond and he whose shaft made the greatest number of leaps was declared the winner. It often happened that the inequality of the surface diverted the shaft from a straight line and this mishap was the source of many shouts of laughter from the participants and spectators. If, by chance, the point stuck in the snow and did not skip[,] the person was taunted with lack of skill and this often led to contests between the tormentor and the other until the shaft of the first failed to accomplish the intention. A boaster was always held to his word until he proved his ability to perform or failed so signally as to acknowledge his incompetency. . . . Number 590 is three and three-eighths inches long and seven-eighths of an inch in diameter at the base. The cavity is half an inch across and thirteen-sixteenths of an inch deep. The form is long and conical, largest at base and regularly tapering to a blunt cone tip. [35–36]

17

The Yearly Cycle

The divisions of the year were almost innumerable for each specific pursuit had a term and each occupation had its season, so that there were on each island a term applicable that did not obtain in other localities. [140–141]

The long and short days had the effect of dividing the year into two parts. The recurring changes of the moon again subdivided the year and the appearance or disappearance of beasts, birds, and fishes again separated the weeks and months. The time of appearance of certain plants and their fitness for food determined other divisions of time. In other words their seasons were marked by well defined times of beginning yet not accurate as to date according to our system.[1] [141]

The names of the months and seasons are here given to indicate, in a clearer manner[,] the meaning of the sentence above and also to show what class or character of objects was deemed of importance as divisions of time. [141–142]

Seasons

Spring is termed *Khá ni kińga* or when snow ceases. The time includes May and part of June. [142]

Summer is termed *Cyuk hú thak* or when birds and butterflies come, referring to the breeding of the adult birds, the appearance of their young and the coming of lepidoptera and other insects and plants. [142]

I may add that the word for summer is identical with the name of the the [sic] plant *Archangelica officinalis* [i.e., *Heracleum lanatum*; see Chapter 12] the leaf-stalks of which are so greedily devoured by the people of all ages and sexes. [142]

Autumn (or Fall) is termed *Syakhu tha king a* or the time when summer ceases. [143]

Winter is termed *Khá nakh*[,] a word whose meaning could not be determined. Another term is applied more frequently to that period and refers to the cold or freezing weather in the same manner that the word for Spring includes the thaw or melting; the word is *khing í nakh*. The latter begins from late October and lasts to May or late April. The year really began about the last of January or the middle of February. [143]

Months

The first month of the twelve months was termed *Á nul ghi likh*, Cormorant. The Cormorant (of several species) formerly abounded on the Aleutian Islands and formed an essential part of the food of the Aleut. The birds were captured by stealthily approaching them when sitting on the solitary rocks, above the swash of the waves, and knocking them off with a club or pole. The tail-feathers were prized highly not only for vanes on the shafts of spears [,] darts and arrows but also for use in many of the ceremonies and games among the people. [143–144]

The next month was named *Khí sa gú nakh*; the time when from necessity the people ate sealskin thongs and such like food. *Khí sak* is the Aleutian word for sealskin thongs used for any purpose requiring such fastenings. [144]

The next month was termed *Úl yam*; the time when the people ate their food within their huts; that is it was too cold and stormy for them (as was their custom) to eat outside of the dwellings. [144–145]

The next month was termed *Sa thû gan–Khá ghikh*, or when the people eat outside of their huts. *Sa thû gan* signifies outside, without the hut. [145]

The following month is named *Sa ghá úl yuk*, or when the people sleep but little; from the word *Sá ghakh*, sleep. [145]

The next month is termed *Cha gha li lim–tu gi thû*, or the month when seals and other marine amphibians are born. It is derived from *Cha gha likh* denoting the young of seals, sea-otters, etc. [145]

The next month is termed *Sa thig nam–tu gi thû*, the time when mammals become fat; (presumably when they have ceased to give birth to their young). [146]

The next month is termed, *Ukh nam - tu gí thû*, or the time when vegetation begins to decay and mammals lose their fat. [146]

The following month is named *Chngu likh*, or the time when mammals shed their pelage; or in other words, the new hair appearing. [146]

The following month is termed *Ki máth gim–tu gí thû*, or the time when mammals are hunted for their fur; specially referring to the Fur-seal. [146]

The next month is termed *Á gal gál yuk*, or the time when people are employed in catching mammals for their fur. [147]

The following and last month was named *Tu gi the ga mûkh*, or the principal (long) month, month of months. It embraced a variable period possibly from and including December to the beginning of February. According to the elder people the sea was then still, a condition that does not obtain at present. [147]

That the seasons may have changed somewhat in their character is not beyond belief. [147]

When the Russians had converted the natives of the Aleutian Islands to Christianity, the people were necessitated to remind themselves of the frequently recurring holidays observed by the Greek Church. In order to do this a flat piece of bone was prepared 2 ¾ inches long and an inch and a

Fig. 46. Bone calendar, Attu. *Department of Anthropology, Smithsonian Institution (NMNH A64947) (T647)*. This weekly calendar was not located in the collection. The drawing is based on the illustration in the original accession book. Peg calendars usually covered a month.

half wide; seven holes were pierced through the longitudinal center and into these a peg was slipped for each successive day of the week. When the peg was inserted into the last hole the Christian knew it was Saturday and that night begun the Sunday continuing until the noon of the day following the one when the last peg-hole was filled. [53]

18

Assorted Beliefs and Traditions

One of the greatest obstacles in collecting traditions of the ancestors of the living Innuit is it [is] almost an impossibility to have the narrator, however reliable he may be, disassociate himself from the immediate vicinity of his birth-place. So persistently does he cling to that locality that all his information pertains only to that place. Many of the winter-night tales of the mainland people are identical with those of the Aleut, excepting that the various characters may be changed as beasts to birds and *vice versa*. [98–99]

The superstitious nature of the Aleut evinces itself even to this day after a hundred years of religious teaching has been pressed upon them. Every thing in nature was supposed to be endowed with life and that this life was active or passive according to its nature. Some of the passive objects were possessed of active spirits and active objects with passive spirits so that there were no less than four classes of spirits. Some of these were excessively hurtful to man and some were not possessed of either harm or good. [124]

Evil spirits lurked on every path ready to pounce upon the unwary or those who had performed some act not yet known to the people. Propitiations and offerings were made by the one under such influence until he unburdened his mind by making offerings to the spirit which held him under control. [124–125]

Talismans and charms were worn to prevent evil, disease and death. The form of shamanism was highly developed amongst these people but appears to have not had that oppressive character that is so evident among the mainland Innuit. Each great hunter had special objects which he supposed insured success in the chase and immunity from perils in all his undertakings. The different parties setting out on hunts or war were made to undergo certain observances that have now been forgotten. [125]

*The narrative is, in substance, as follows: We always had the umiak as a boat for general purposes, used as a vessel for a community or several families. Later, when strife became common, the umiak was made smaller, and only a man and his own family entered it and made it their home for days at a time. They were thus exposed to the inclemency of the weather, and a cover was made over the front as a protection for the family. The place of the man was now drawn nearer the centre, and that left space behind in which could be stored the effects that also required protection. By the act of covering at each end a small space was finally left in which the man could sit, and it was then found that the accompanying members of the family were unnecessary to comfort and speed. [R:749]

*A shaman, who had attained a degree of reverence from his people and whose decree was law, decided that the women and children should no longer accompany the man in the covered boat, and that the length of the vessel should be that of the fin of the large whale; hence the development of the kaiak, which is essentially a vehicle employed by the men, and not by women and children. [R:749–750]

Strangely enough the evidence of belief that all marine mammals had their origin from spirits of human form[,] some from males and some females[,] is paralleled on the opposite side of the North American continent, and nearly the same degree of latitude, where the creatures of the sea sprang from the fingers of a poor woman who was so impoverished as to be a charge upon the community with whom she dwelt. They cast her overboard and as she clung to the side of the boat to regain it her fingers were cut off and were transformed into the various mammals that live in the ocean. Her curses upon her people yet linger in the beasts that attack the slayer of their original form. [174]

The mighty contentions and struggles that fill the Aleut folk-lore and traditions of men and beasts of long bygone times show how they braved the dangers of the deep [and] the dark recesses of frowning cliffs in order to master the foes that beset their every pathway by water and land. [174–175]

Some of these monsters were of hideous form and terrible mien having the power to transform their bodies into various conditions that would enable them to successfully elude the attacks of the mighty hunters whose kind have long since gone; but, their traces yet remain, and, are found in the caves and recesses of the mountainsides scarcely to be gazed upon lest the talismanic power worn on breast or arm fail in its efficacy to prevent harm and the unlucky finder become insane or blind and wander to the face of the cliff to plunge to the depths below and there be a lifeless victim of his own temerity. [175–176]

Certain ones of the whales were possessed of a particularly vindictive spirit and these sought to destroy the hunter and his craft the moment it came in view. Charms of most potent character were worn to ward off the attack of those whales (the genus Orca is mostly referred to here) and divert them from the course of the hunter. [176]

The seals and sealions were under the protection of a special spirit which must be propitiated by addresses and offerings before the hunter might slay them. The sea-otter that gave such beautiful robes was once a delicate woman who fled from the approach of man and took refuge in the sea, permitting no man contaminated by contact with woman to see her. Even to this day no woman unclean must touch the sea in which dwells the chaste sea-otter. [176]

In order to obviate the danger of the sea and disaster to the life of the hunter[,] charms and other objects were worn about the body to dispel any evil besetting the hunter or his family. In place of the hunter watching for his prey on the hillside[,] he erected a shelter from the storm[;] and in his solitary musings the place became devoted and when left by the hunter his spirit remained within and guarded the spot now consecrated to special purposes[,] finally receiving adoration and worship in which was placed the same charms that had shielded him from all harm. Here the votary implored the sky to quietude, the winds to abate, the sea to calm and his craft to swiftness, his arm and spear to unerring aim and immunity from the lurking spirits of evil thwarting every step. In after time all the spirit worship took material form in the shape of a specialized idol or *Khu gá thûkh* the omniscient, (see list of words appended for idol, shaman, devil, idolatry, grave[1]) that bore all power for good and evil according to its mood. The devotee addressing soft words besought the gifts it controlled and tore it from its seat on failure to grant the desire of the hunter if its mood was contrary to his wishes or withheld the benefits of its office to provide and protect. While man endeavored to keep this idol in good-humor yet it did not fail to receive the wrath of the hunter who cursed, beat and trampled upon it as an enemy to him that relented only when the anger of the person had been appeased by some fortunate undertaking accomplished during absence from the abiding place of the object which was now deemed in humor to be controlled again by its master. [177–178]

*This bird [bald eagle] is undoubtedly the origin of the "*bayglei*" [outside man] of the Eastern Aleuts, as it sometimes sits on a hill top or open space and opens its wings to air them, or sits in such a strange position that it is, at a distance, scarcely recognizable as a bird. The timid Aleut imagines it to be some strange beast, which entices the victim within reach and disappears with it; and, according to their story, this beast turns out to be a man, who keeps the captive as his servant. The *bayglie* stories of the Aleuts are a wonderful mixture of cunning and superstition. I think, however, the earliest Russians made use of the expression (for in the Russian language the word means deserter, runaway) in all its subsequent meanings, in order to deter their women, whom they had, in most instances, forced from their homes and compelled to live with their hated mates, from deserting them and returning to their own people. At the present day it is used as a "bugbear" to prevent the small children from wandering away. Many of the adults stoutly maintain that they have seen these apparitions. The Attu people do not use the expression only as they have heard of it from their eastern relatives. [C:159]

19

Miscellaneous Remarks

1. The greater number of the middle-aged and younger people, of both sexes, are able to read and write the Alyut characters (Slavonic or Church text) and many thus correspond by letter or read their catechisms. [V:3499]

2. *Liçaq*—A term applied when one person annoys, pesters, teases etc. another. The one who does so is spoken to by the word *Liçaq* for the purpose of causing him to desist but not spoken ill-naturedly. [V:3545]

3. #625. This represents a charm. The wide large pieces are worn on a frame which fits the head in such a manner that when the frame is on the head, these spread out like the wings of a bird and are intended to represent the wings of a gull. The other large pieces are to represent the head of the gull and are worn above the temple of the head and pointing downward as does the gull. The heads of the walrus are to be hung to the frame so that one will hang over each eye of the wearer. The wearer is supposed to be able to skim the surface of the water as the gull flies through the air. The head of the gull enables him to see at a great distance. The heads of the walrus enable him to see in [sic] under the water. This is used while seal hunting. It is considered a great charm. They are very rare. I am told that there are but four or five along this part of the coast. It is handed down from father to son as an heirloom and seldom sold or otherwise disposed of. [Natural History Archives. Ms. and Pamphlets. Box 45a. Misc.][1]

4. The forty-third series includes two wooden carvings, representing sea otters on land. They are faithfully executed and when the age, 14 years, of the boy, who carved them, is taken into consideration the skill displayed is remarkable. [60]

5. So many errors have crept into the few words collected into vocabularies, of the Aleutian language, published that I cannot refrain from adding a number of words to show the proper meanings to them. The speech is, in composition, similar to that of the mainland Innuit. The inflexions and terminations are not so numerous. The compass of the language is restricted and not so rich in words as that of the other branch of the Innuit. [220][2]

6. The twenty-first series embraces six pieces of bone. They are thin flakes and for the purpose of this paper may be termed cutting boards. Their use is as follows. When the hair of the head was so long as to need trimming it was cut by means of a stone having a sharp edge. The bone piece was placed under the hair and the stone edge cut the hair on the surface of the bone. The edges are concave more or less and serve to fit the various curves of the skull. Number 641 [E64941] and 642 [E64942] are perfect types of these implements. Numbers 98 [E64398] and 643 [E64943] are less perfect examples of the same character of specimens. Numbers 609 [E64909] and 9 [E64309] are very old pieces of bone used for the same purpose. [25]

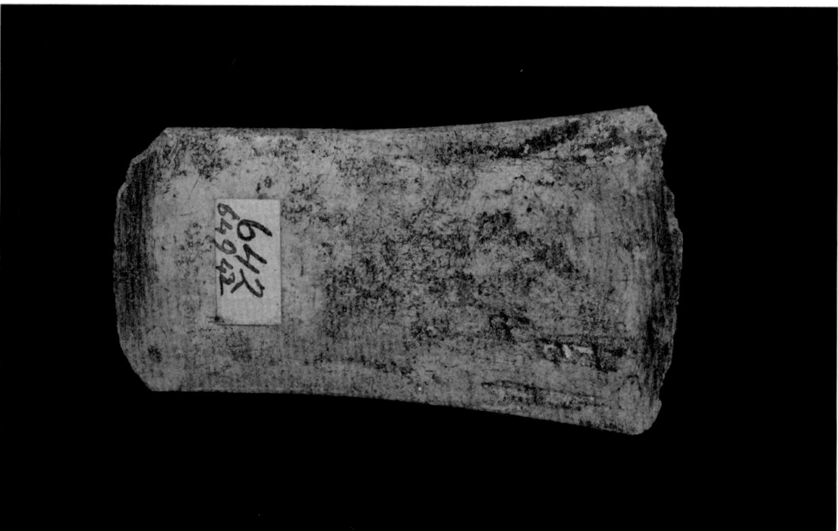

Fig. 47. Bone used for cutting hair, Attu. *Department of Anthropology, Smithsonian Institution (NMNH A64942) (T642).* This flat thin piece of bone was placed under strands of hair, which were then cut by pressing a sharp knife against it.

7. The twenty-third series embraces three objects employed as mullers for grinding various hard or soft substances into a condition to be used as pigments. These stones are of hardest character. Number 411 [A64711] is a circular disc three inches in diameter and one inch in thickness. Both sides are perfectly smooth and yet contain traces of pigments adhering to the sides and rim. Number 400 [A64700] has but one grinding surface and is a rounded, irregularly so, boulder of the same character of stone as 411 [A64711]. Like the latter it also contains traces of the pigments yet adhering to the side of the muller. No. 413 [A64713] is an egg-shaped, hard stone but little used for the purpose of grinding. It shows wear on the under side and traces of adherent ferruginous rock used as pigment. [27]

8. It is not to be supposed that the effect of contact with civilized beings for the past century and a half has not had its influence upon the Aleut. The history of invasion and aggression of the Russian promishlenyks has wrought a wondrous change upon the fearless Aleut of two hundred years ago. Instead of strife and pillage now reigns quiet and submission worked doubly well by the American trader who pursues his vocation upon the strict business principles of thrift and enterprise. The latter employs them so much of their time that the former follows in course of events that when but a quarter of a century ago was squalor and disease are now comfortable homes and many of the evidences of prosperity and cleanliness. [167]

Appendix 1

Three Charts of the Near Islands

Mt Carmel Illinois
Oct 28 1881

My Dear Mr Dall,

I have this day mailed and registered the Charts of which I spoke to you.

The Chart of Attu is excellent. I judge all of it by the part over which I have traveled marked with a red line and know it to be sufficiently correct to assert that the rest of it is correct. I have not visited the islands of Agattu but many natives of Attu spoke in highest terms of the Charts of all of those three islands.

The Chart of the neighborhood of St Michael's was made by the native who is now interpreter on the Jeanette. You are able to judge of it yourself. It represents the coast from Unalachhlet to just below the lower mouth of the "canal."

The native names of the principal localities occur on the Charts of Attu and St Michael's.

Should you choose to have them copied or any other disposition made of them you are at liberty to do so save that I should like at some future time to copy the native names of the places on them.

Please accept my best wishes.

Sincerely yours,
Lucien M Turner
Mt Carmel
Wabash Co
Illinois

To
Wm H Dall
Asst US C & G S
US Coast Survey Office
Washington D C

During Turner's stay on Attu he had one or more unnamed residents draw charts of Attu, Agattu, and the Semichi Islands. (In the *Catalogue* he wrote that the Agattu map had been drawn with the aid of "natives of Attu." The mother of Chief Terrentii Prokopeuff was the only person then living who had been born on Agattu.) In October 1881 he sent them to Dall, who published the Agattu chart in 1896 as an example of the meticulous workmanship of Aleut cartographers.[2] In his article Dall acknowledged the contributions made by Aleuts in the production of the Teben'kov atlas. He also knew of the assistance Davidson and others had received from charts prepared by such Aleut navigators as Paul Lemasheffsky and Illarion Archimandritov, after whom a shoal in Kachemak Bay was named. The charts that Turner obtained, however, were of a different order. They were drawn not by navigators or sailors, but by kayakers. "These maps lay down with the greatest detail every bend of the shore-line and every rock or reef where sea otters resort or a kayak might suffer injury," Dall explained. "Topography is not attempted or is but rudely indicated, but everything which bears on the canoe life of these amphibious people is carefully set down." He described the process by which the Agattu chart was prepared for publication by Bradley and Poates of New York. "The original sketch was in pencil on a large sheet of brown manila paper. From this a tracing was taken on linen and this reduced by photography."

The original maps have not been located. Shortly after receiving the charts, Dall had cyanotype (blueprint) copies prepared. He glued greatly reduced copies of them into his scrapbook for 1881.[3] The Semichi Islands chart is very dark and the one of Attu has faded in some areas. Blueprint copies of all three maps also reside in the Library of Congress. Although a few details and names remain obscured, the charts are an eloquent testimony to the knowledge of Unangan kayakers.

The Agattu chart shows a "Landing for Skin Boats," a "Boat Landing," and a "Harbor for Small Craft." The details are remarkable and include twenty-seven "ancient village sites" and three portages across the island.

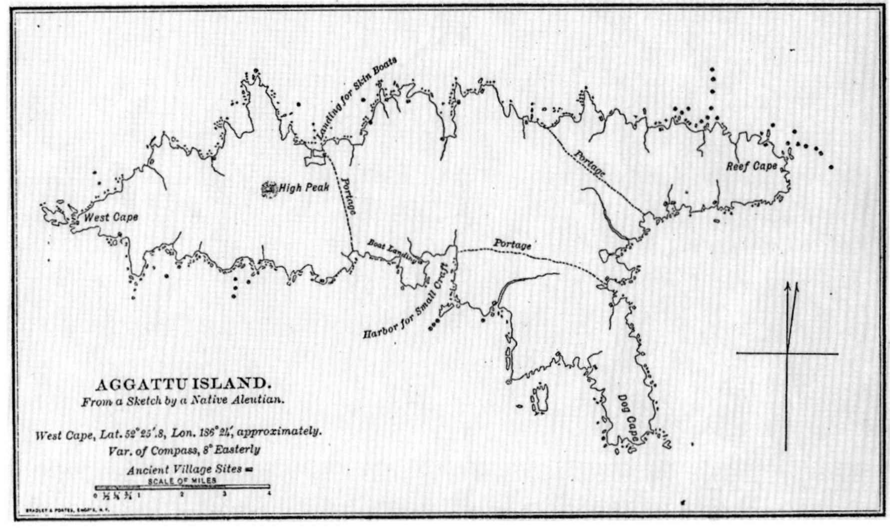

Fig. 48. Chart of Aggattu Island. Prepared by Dall from Turner's original and printed in "Geographical Notes in Alaska," *Bulletin of American Geographical Society* XXVIII(1).

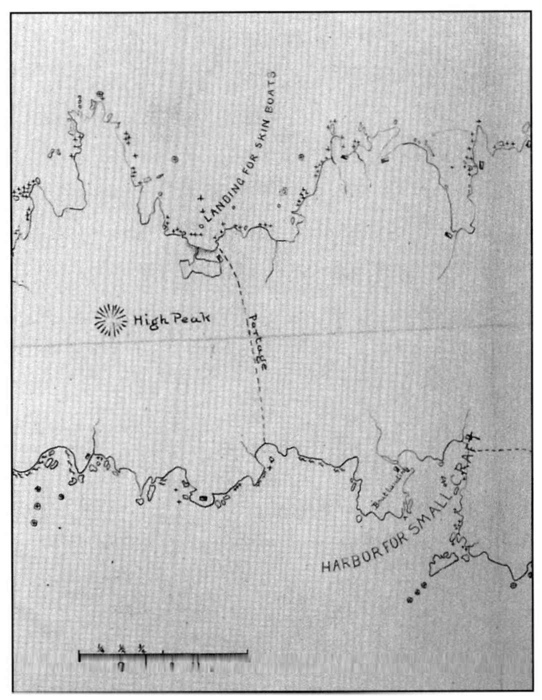

Fig. 49. Detail from Turner's Agattu chart showing the "Landing for Skin Boats" in Armeria Bay, on the north side of Agattu, and the "Harbor for Small Craft" in Karab Cove in Otkriti Bay, on the south side. Village sites are shown by shaded rectangles. This and subsequent maps and details are from blueprint copies in the Geography and Map Division, Library of Congress (Alaska. Aleutian Islands, Near Islands, 18--? 1:85,000).

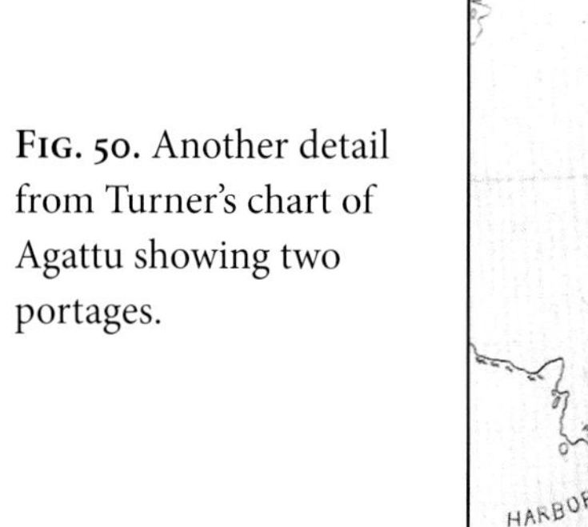

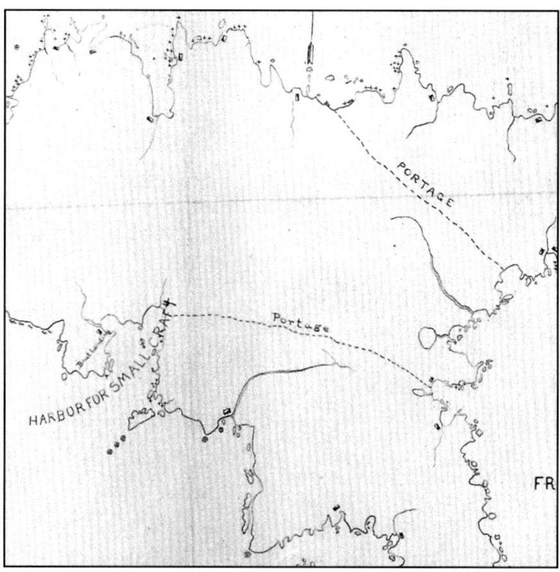

Fig. 50. Another detail from Turner's chart of Agattu showing two portages.

The chart of the Semichi Islands is similar to the Agattu map in that it shows an abundance of coastal features, but little of the interior. What is unusual is that Alaid and Nizki islands are shown as a single body, connected by a very narrow tongue of land. The 2003 *U.S. Coastal Pilot 9* describes this as "a shifting sandspit."[4] The name "Alaid" was used in the nineteenth century (Teben'kov listed it as *Alaidskaya Pupka*). Nizki (although derived from the Russian for "low") was not formally adopted by the U.S. Board on Geographic Names until 1938.

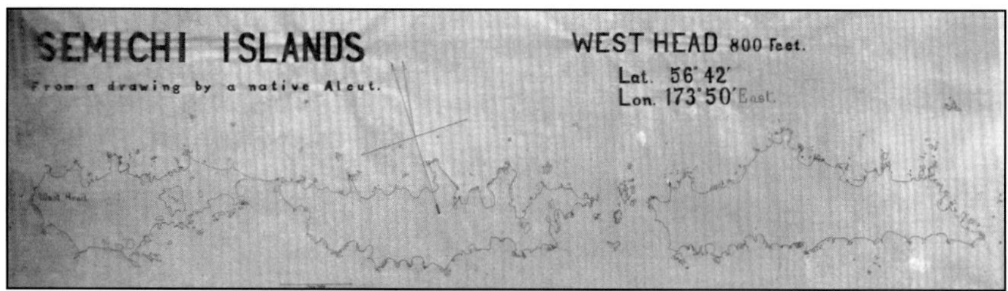

Fig. 51. Chart of the Semichi Islands.

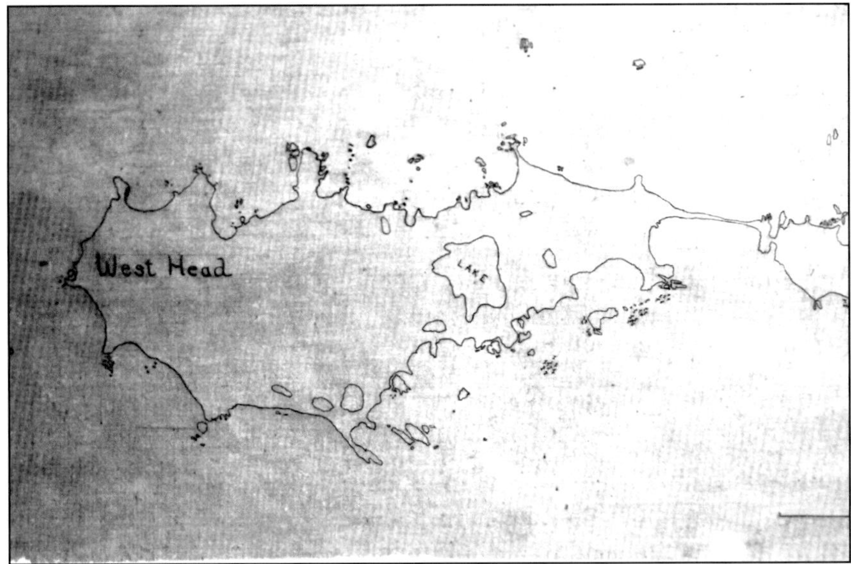

FIG. 52. Detail of the Semichi Islands chart showing Alaid Island and the narrow connection with Nizki Island.

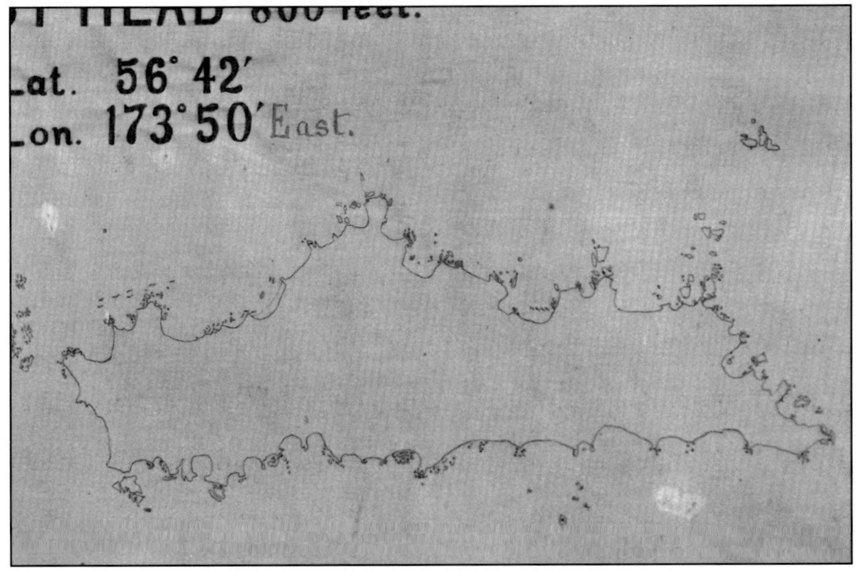

FIG. 53. Detail of the Semichi Islands chart showing Shemya Island with Hammerhead Island in the upper right.

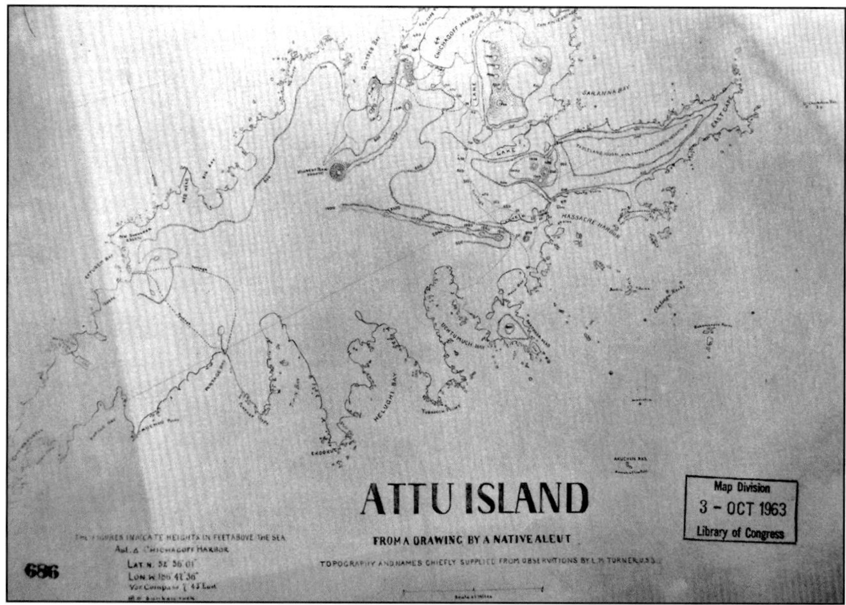

FIG. 54. Chart of Attu Island.

The chart of Attu is a remarkable document, drawn with breathtaking detail. The map's legend states that the topography and names were supplied chiefly by Turner. Taking what was perhaps immodest advantage, he named the ridge west of the village Cape Turner. Today it is the west arm of Fishhook Ridge.

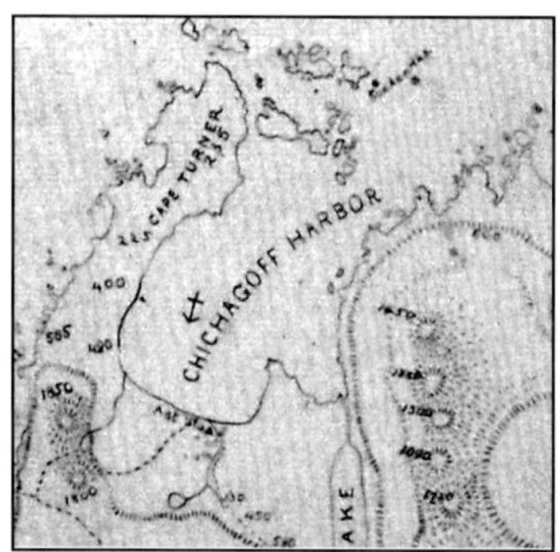

FIG. 55. Detail of the north end of Attu showing Chichagof Harbor, where the village was located, and Cape Turner.

This map provides a number of nineteenth-century Aleut place-names that were recorded nowhere else. Bergsland does not appear to have studied the names on this map, although Orth consulted it for his *Dictionary of Alaska Place Names* (1967) and included most of the Aleut names as variants of established names. In the *Aleut Dictionary* and in *Aleut Dialects of Atka and Attu,* Bergsland provides six definite place-names and eleven unidentified names from various texts, only one of which corresponds to a named location on the Turner map.

Table 4: Place-Names on the Attu Chart

Current Name	Turner	Remarks
Chichagof Harbor	Chichagoff Harbor	Main village site
Khlebnikof Point	Cape Khliebnikoff	
Sarana Bay	Saranna Bay	
	East Cape	Site of Chirikof Point
Alexai Point	Nanikakaya Point	Bergsland indicates an ancient village near here called Nanikax̂ (1994: 653, location 1066)
Massacre Bay	Massacre Harbor	Turner indicates a "rocky shore" at the head of the bay.
	Southeast of Massacre Bay are five groups of rocks with names or warnings:	
	Sootin Rocks	
	Chalooga Rocks	
	Bashmakoff Rocks	
	[unnamed] "Awash at low [tide]"	
	Akuchin Rocks "Awash at low tide"	
Casco Bay	Hulu Bay	
Murder Point	Akachaga Head	
Temnac Bay	Uchtumuch Bay	
Theodore Point	Tubkooch Point	
Nevidiskov Bay	Helughi Bay	
Chuniksak Point	Ekookuch Point	
Abraham Bay	Tipin Bay	
Mikhail Point	Portage Point	
Etienne Bay	Portage Bay	
Etienne Head	Muchoo Point	
Unnamed bay between Etienne Head and Cape Wrangell	Kapsoo Bay	

Current Name	**Turner**	**Remarks**
Small cove off Cape Wrangell	Amna Bay	
Cape Wrangell	Cape Wrangell	
	Mayach (?) Bay	
Earle Cove	Eftugem Bay	Turner names the north side of this bay "N.W. Shoulder."
Red Head	Red Head	
Steller Cove	Big Bay	
The northern shoreline	N.E. Bluff	
Holtz Bay	Goltseb Bay	
Chichagof Point	Cape Turner	

Three portages and several trails are shown. The numerous elevations along the trails and one of the portages suggests Turner himself hiked these routes. In his letter to Dall he said he had marked his routes in red;

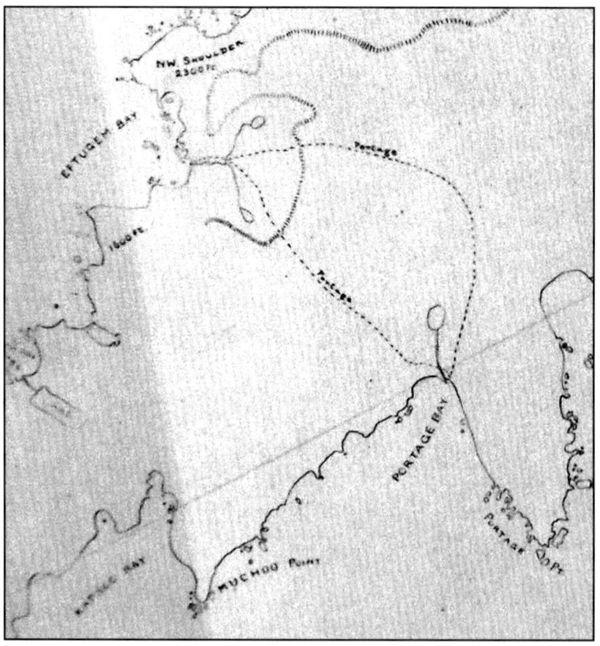

Fig. 56. Detail of the Attu map showing dual portages between Etienne Bay/Portage Bay and Earle Cove/ Eftugem Bay.

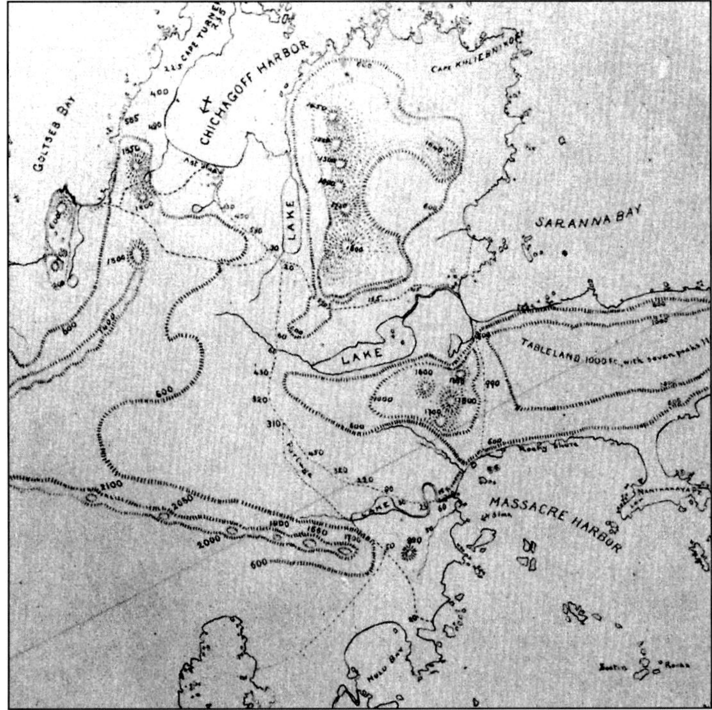

FIG. 57. Detail showing the extensive trail systems from Chichagof Harbor to Sarana Bay and Temnac Bay/Uchtumuch Bay.

the blueprint does not show that color. Two portages connect the head of Etienne Bay/Portage Bay with Earle Cove/Eftugem Bay.

This map also shows a circular trail leading into the mountains from behind the village in Chichagof Harbor. Another route branches from this trail and leads to Sarana Bay (indicated as a portage) and to the south side of the island, where it eventually reaches the east shore of Temnac/Uchtumuch Bay.

The knowledge Unangan had of island coastlines was unparalleled. (This continued well into the twentieth century, when the military employed Unangan like Henry Swanson as pilots for ships during mapping and resupplying missions.) That they also had extensive knowledge of the interior of their islands is reflected by trail systems. On Unalaska, three historical trails are known. One was taken by the young chief who led John Ledyard from English Bay to Iliuliuk in 1778. In 1805 Rezanov, von Langsdorff, and others were guided by Unangan from Ugadaga Bay in

Beaver Inlet to Iliuliuk. An established trail from Captains Bay was used to reach Makushin Bay by Sarychev in 1790, by Innokentii Shaiashnikov in the 1860s, and it continued to be used by Unangan well into the twentieth century. The trails Turner recorded on maps of Attu and Agattu confirm a similar knowledge of the Near Islands.

Appendix 2

Gut Bags—A Preliminary Survey

There are forty-four gut bags listed in the *Descriptive Catalogue* (numbers 284 to 319 and 1409 to 1416). All are ascribed to Atka, where Turner lived from May 4 to August 29, 1879. The variety of patterns, their unused condition, and, in some cases, the delicacy of the material suggest they were commissioned pieces, purchased to exhibit the range of patterns, sewing stitches, and decorative techniques then in practice. Turner described them as "articles made of the intestines of the Sea lion and Seal. These objects are used for containing small affairs of cloth etc. They are of various sizes, designs and patterns" [70]. The transparency of the gut suggests the material had been prepared during the summer. Gut processed during the winter and left outside in freezing weather turns white and opaque.

The Smithsonian's current in-house list has twenty-seven gut bags (within accession numbers E65244 to E65279, E65299 to E65305, and E129324). E129324 is identified as being from Unalaska, but may be the missing E65304 as it resembles the drawing for that bag in the original accessions book. E65267 bears the note "exchanged New York museum, 2/20/1901." Two of the catalog numbers have multiple "parts"; that is, there are two bags in E65259 and four in E65279. A preliminary comparison of these with the accession sketches suggests the following:

E65259 1 of 2	is	E65258 in the original accessions book
E65259 2 of 2	is	E65259 in the original accessions book
E65279 1 of 4	may be	E65279 in the original accessions book
E65279 2 of 4	is	E65278 in the original accessions book
E65279 3 of 4	is	[illegible] in the original accessions book
E 65279 4 of 4	may be	E65256 in the original accessions book

Although the accession book sketches were done quickly, they provide details, such as drawstrings, that may now be missing from the items. They are not, however, always accurate, and consequently the above identifications must be considered tentative. (See E65266 for an example of a poorly drawn entry that may be compared with the bag itself. The drawing depicts seven panels where the bag actually has only five.)

There are two gut bags collected by Turner that are now at the Peabody Museum at Harvard. Both the "wallet of intestine" (88-51-10/50018) and the "bag of intestine" (88-51-10/50019) differ from those in the Smithsonian in that neither has a drawstring. The bag has a braided or twisted carrying cord. These may have been items that Turner sold after the end of his tenure at the Smithsonian.

Sewing Stitches and Decorative Techniques

A detailed study of stitches and design elements in late-nineteenth-century Unangan garments and gut-manufactured items remains to be done. A cursory look at the Atka bags shows several stitches, including the common running stitch and a type of chain stitch. There is also the frequently used technique in which a running stitch of sinew is overlaid with a strand of cotton or wool embroidery thread (a type of blanket stitch).[1] Extensive deterioration of the embroidery threads has left only faint remnants of this stitch, requiring a careful reconstruction to determine exact patterns. (This was not attempted in the pattern representations in this appendix.) Frequently the seam between two pieces of gut was reinforced with a narrow strip of gut painted red or black. Colored tabs of gut or tufts of yarn, individual delicate white feathers, and fine white hairs were sewed into seams. The remarkable appliqué seen on cuffs and collars of festive kamleikas from a few decades earlier is absent although remnants appear on at least one bag (E65279 1 of 4). Design was also produced by alternating the colors of thread. White, black, and red were the most common although green and blue also appear. Turner wrote that "the root of a kind of grass or vine" was used to decorate gut items but that it "was purely ornamental, having insufficient strength to support the strain of the bodily action of the wearer" [199].

Gut Container Patterns

Bags were made using from two to six panels of gut. These were sometimes folded at the bottom so that one continuous piece was used on both sides. In other bags, two matching sides were made and then sewed together around the perimeter of the sides and bottom. In still other bags, the two identical sides were joined by a third piece of gut, which was folded and sewed around the perimeter of the sides and bottom, giving the bag greater volume. The mouths of bags were usually finished with a single piece of folded gut containing a drawstring, but here also there were variations. The following drawings were made from photographs in the collection with the exception of those marked "from the original accessions book."[2]

FIG. 58
Gut Bags with Two Panels

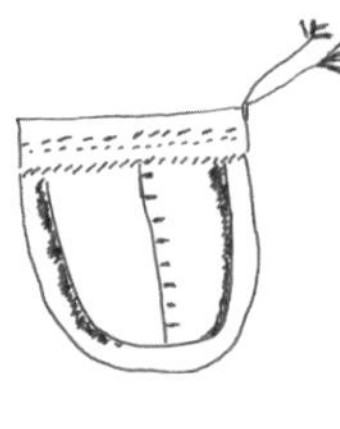

E65245
Drawing from the original accessions book.

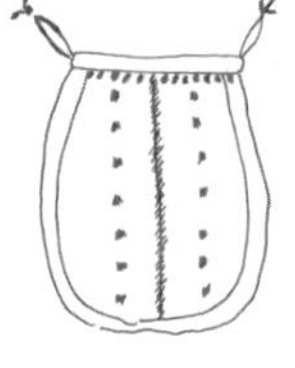

E65261
Drawing from the original accessions book.

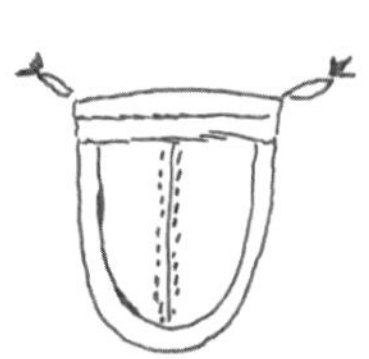

E65276
Drawing from the original accessions book.

Gut Bags with Three Panels

E65248
Outer panel folded over. Brown thread blanket stitch.

E65249
Center panel folded at bottom. Sides sewed. Red gut strip at internal seams.

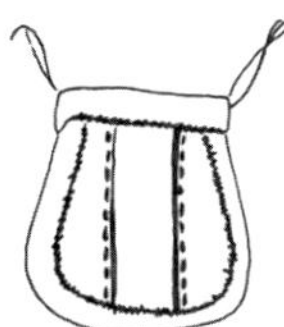

E65255
Drawing from the original accessions book.

E65257
Drawing from the original accessions book.

E65258
Drawing from the original accessions book.
May be E65259 1 of 2

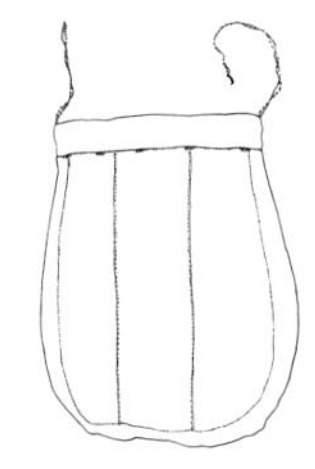

E65259 1 of 2
Transparent gut. Red, green, and brown thread. Outer panel folded over.
May be E65258

E65260
Drawing from the original accessions book.

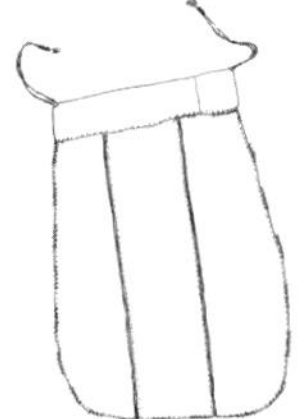

E65262
Black and red blanket stitches. Black gut strip at internal seams. Sides and bottom sewed.

E65264
Panels folded at bottom. Sides sewed.

E65268
Sides and bottom sewed. Black and red blanket stitches. Black gut strip at internal seams.

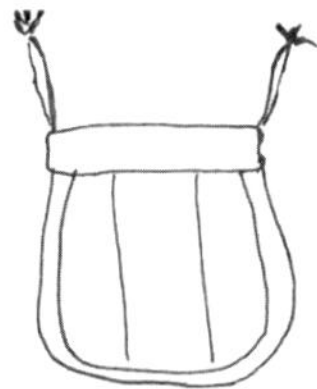

E65273
Drawing from the original accessions book.

E65274
Drawing from the original accessions book.
May be E65279 3 of 4

E65275
Red gut strip at internal seams. Outer panel folded over.

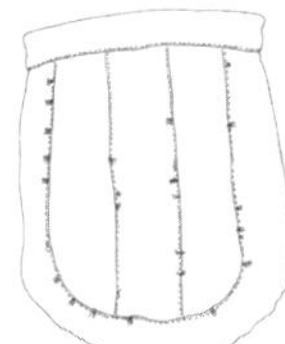

E65279 3 of 4
Outer panel folded over. Green and red wool tufts in the internal seams. May be E65274

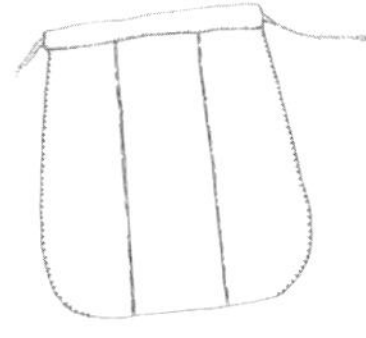

E65305
Red gut strip at internal seams. Panels folded at bottom. Sides sewed.

Gut Bags with Four Panels

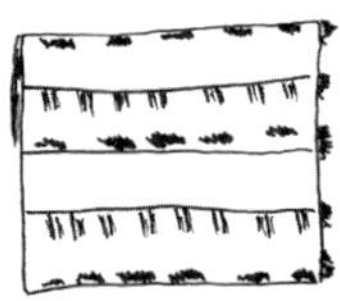

E65247
Drawing from the original accessions book.

E65250
Drawing from the original accessions book.

E65251
Panels folded at bottom. Sides sewed. Red and black blanket stitches on outer edges.

E65252
Outer panel folded over. Heavily decorated with green or blue blanket stitches.

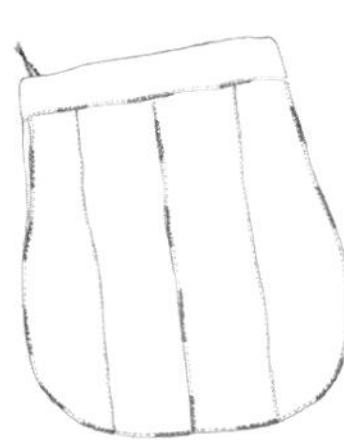

E65254
All edges sewed. Heavy green blanket stitching.

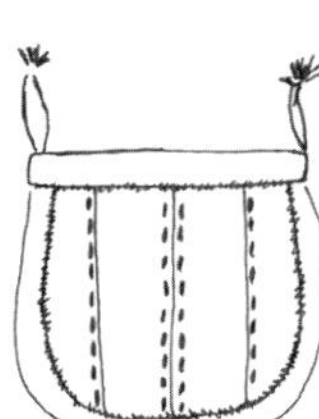

E65263
Drawing from the original accessions book.

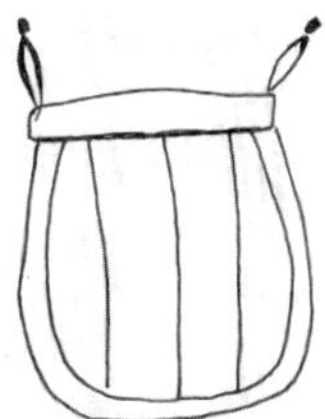

E65267
Drawing from the original accessions book.

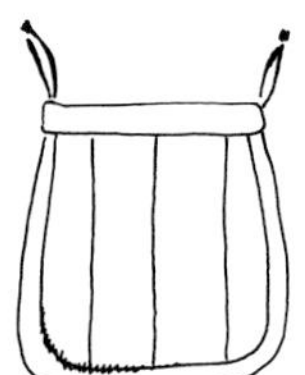

E65269
Drawing from the original accessions book.

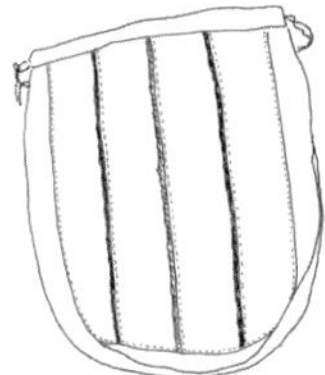

E65270
Red gut strip at center internal seam. Black gut strip at outer two internal seams.

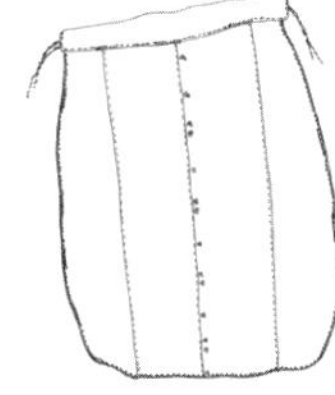

E65271
Light and dark blanket stitches around perimeter. Brown tufts of decoration on center seam.

E65272
Outer panel folded over. Extensive green or blue blanket stitching on all seams.

E65277
Red gut strip at center internal seam. Black gut strip at outer two internal seams. Brown tufts (fur?) on center seam.

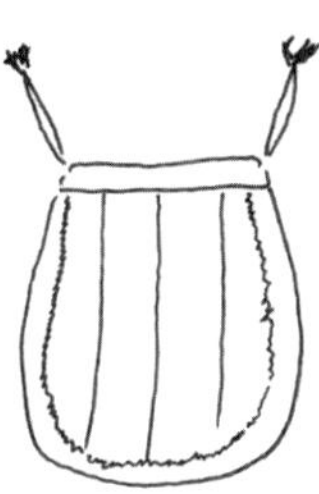

E65278
Drawing from the original accessions book.
May be E65279 2 of 4

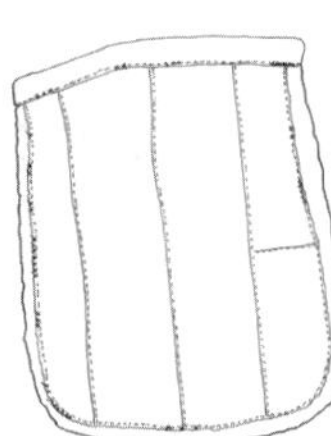

E65279 2 of 4
Blue, red, and dark threads. Outer panel folded over.
May be E65278

E65299
Black gut strip on internal seams. Brown tufts of decoration.

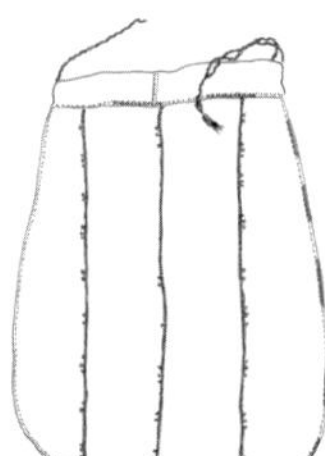

E65301
Red gut strip on internal seams with dark wool tufts inserted.

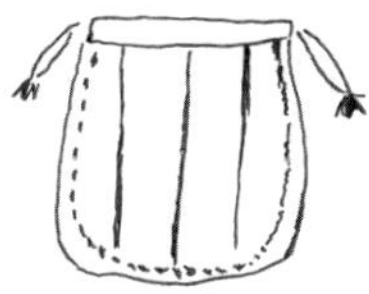

E65303
Drawing from the original accessions book.

Gut Bags with Five or More Panels

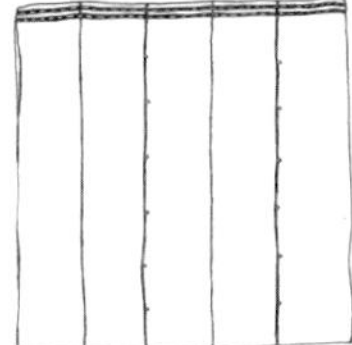

E65244
Black gut strip on internal seams and on each side. Black and green tabs on 2nd and 4th seams.

E65246
Drawing from the original accessions book.

E65253
Drawing from the original accessions book.

E65256
Drawing from the original accessions book.

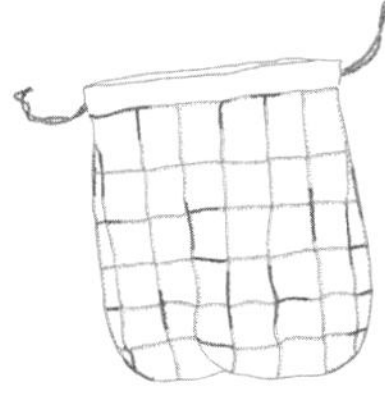

E65259 2 of 2
Panels folded at bottom. All the surface covered with squares of blanket stitching. May be E65259

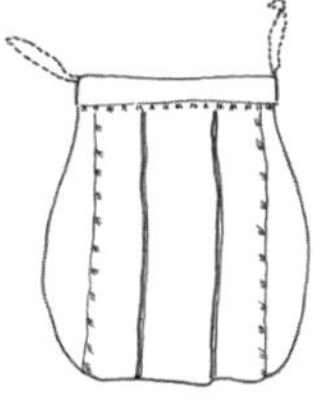

E65265
Drawing from the original accessions book.

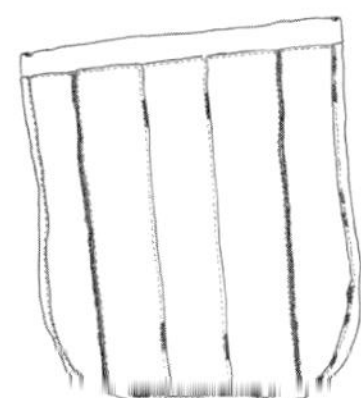

E65266
Red gut strip on seams 1 and 4. Green and red blanket stitch on seams 2 and 3 and on seam attaching outer wrapped panel.

E65279 1 of 4
Top contains black strip with traces of appliqué.
May be E65279

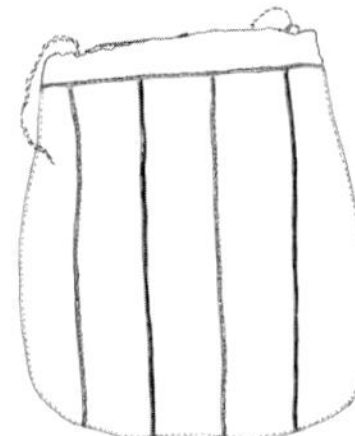

E65279 4 of 4
Red strip of gut on seams 1 and 3; black, on seams 2 and 4. Red gut strip across top seam. Outer edges sewed.
May be E65256

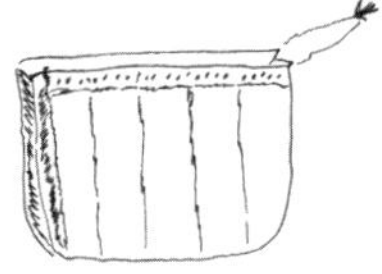

E65300
Drawing from the original accessions book.

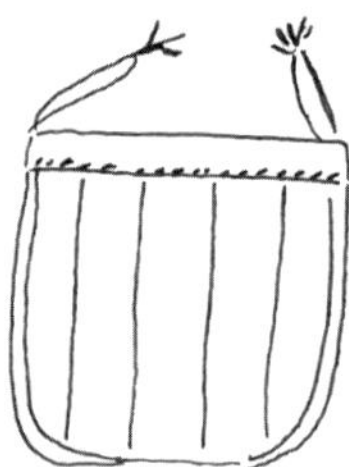

E65302
Drawing from the original accessions book.

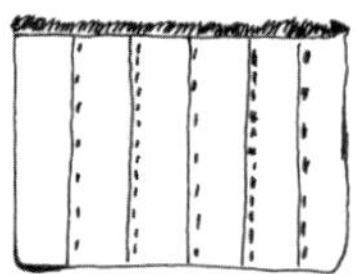

E65304
Drawing from the original accessions book.
May be E129324

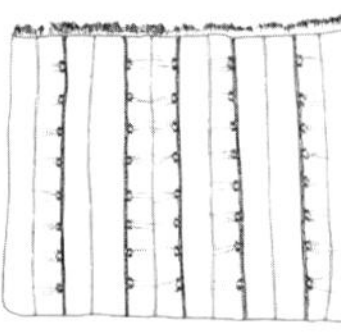

E129324
The current listing ascribes this to Unalaska.

Notes

Notes to "A Note on the Term *Aleut*"

1. Donna Matthews, *Unangam Hiitnisangin/Unangam Hitnisangis/Aleut Plants*, ed. Barbara Svarny Carlson (Association of *Unangan/Unangas* Educators, 2002), 5.
2. Moses Dirks has suggested this derivation is more accurate than "people of the shore or coast" as was earlier held. See Bergsland and Dirks, *Unangam Ungiikangin kayux Tunusangin/Unangam Uniikangis ama Tunuzangis/Aleut Tales and Narratives*, collected 1909–1910 by Waldemar Jochelson (Alaska Native Language Center, University of Alaska Fairbanks, 1990), 2.
3. Knut Bergsland, *Aleut Grammar: Unangam Tunuganaan Achixaasix̂*, Research Paper No. 10 (Alaska Native Language Center, University of Alaska Fairbanks, 1997), 1; Roza G. Liapunova, *Essays on the Ethnography of the Aleuts*, trans. Jerry Shelest, Rasmuson Library Historical Translation Series, Vol. IX, ed. Marvin W. Falk (Fairbanks: University of Alaska Press, 1996), 4, note b (Lydia T. Black). Lydia Black, *Russians in Alaska, 1732–1867* (Fairbanks: University of Alaska Press, 2004), 90.

Notes to Introduction

1. Lucien Turner, *Contributions to the Natural History of Alaska* (Washington, DC: Government Printing Office, 1886), 48.
2. Turner wrote to Spencer Baird that he arrived at Unalaska on May 6 (letter August 22, 1878). The 1881 *Report of the Secretary* notes he arrived May 10. He sailed from San Francisco on the *Eustice* and may have transferred to another vessel at Sitka or Kodiak. The schooner *LaGironde*, with Captain B. C. Genereaux, arrived on May 5 after a voyage of twenty-eight days from San Francisco. The company steamer *St. Paul* arrived on the 8th, following a trip of eleven days. *A.C. Company Log*, January 1878–June 1879. Archives and Manuscript Collections, Alaska and Polar Regions Department, Elmer E. Rasmuson Library, University of Alaska Fairbanks.
3. Turner, *Contributions*, 48.
4. Turner, *Descriptive Catalogue of Ethnological Specimens Collected by Lucien M. Turner in Alaska* (Lucien Turner papers, Bureau of American Ethnology collection, National Anthropological Archives, National Museum of Natural History, Smithsonian Institution, Washington, DC, manuscript [illegible]), [illegible].
5. Eric Hultén, *Flora of the Aleutian Islands* (New York, J. Cramer, Hafner Publishing Co., 1960), 13.

6. Hultén, *Flora of the Aleutian Islands*, 238. Here Hultén's statement is based on a mistaken reading of Turner. Referring to the cloudberry, *Rubus chamaemorus*, he wrote, "Its occurrence at Unalaska, Akutan and Unimak, based on reports of Torrey & Gray and Turner should be checked." Turner, however, did not assign this plant to Unalaska. Hultén, on the other hand, when questioning Turner's annotations about another plant wrote, "Although Turner's reports have not always proved to be reliable I think that one has no right to doubt that the specimens were collected at Atka" (161).
7. I am indebted to Turner's grandson, L. Wayne Turner, for much of this biographical information.
8. Smithsonian Institution, "Necrology: Robert Ridgway" (*Annual Report of the Board of Regents of the Smithsonian Institution . . . for the year ending June 30, 1929*, Publication 3034, 1930), 20–21.
9. Baird to Dall, March 7, 1874, Smithsonian Institution Archives (SIA), Record Unit (RU) 7073, box 7.
10. Turner to Baird, April 16, 1874, SIA, RU 16, incoming correspondence, box 34.
11. On this occasion Turner and Nelson collected "some ivory dolls and small parkies" (Nelson, Alaska Journal, May 26, 1877–May 13, 1878, SIA, RU 7364, Series 2, box 11, folder 2. See also Stephen Loring, "Introduction to Lucien M. Turner and the Beginnings of Smithsonian Anthropology in the North," in Turner, *Ethnology of the Ungava District, Hudson Bay Territory*, xiii (Washington, DC: Smithsonian Institution Press, 2001).
12. Turner to Baird, Sept. 1, 1881, SIA, RU 16, incoming correspondence, box 37, #17,822.
13. Turner, *Contributions*, 9.
14. George Bailey, "Condition of Affairs in Alaska: Report of U.S. Revenue-Steamer 'Richard Rush', October 1879" (46th Congress, 2d Session. Senate. Ex. Doc. No. 132. 1880), 16.
15. William Healy Dall, *Diary 1873–74*, SIA, RU 7073, box 20A, folder 4.
16. Bailey, "Condition of Affairs in Alaska," 16.
17. Both Alfred and his brother Louis removed an "e" from the spelling of their surname, Greenebaum. (Louis, who worked for the company, later changed his to Greene. He was the author of *310 Sansome Street*, an account of the early years of the Alaska Commercial Company.)
18. Theodore C. and Caryl Hinckley, "Ivan Petroff's Journal of a Trip to Alaska in 1878," *Journal of the West* 5, no. 1 (1966): 38.
19. Turner to Ridgway, Nov. 10, 1878, Blacker-Wood Library, McGill University.
20. *A.C. Company Log*, January 1878–June 1879; July 6, 8, 10, 20, 1878. Archives and Manuscript Collections, Alaska and Polar Regions Department, Elmer E. Rasmuson Library, University of Alaska Fairbanks
21. Turner to Baird, Nov. 11, 1878, SIA, RU 26, incoming correspondence, 1878–1879, vol. 181, box 96.
22. Hubert Howe Bancroft, *Literary Industries, The Works of Hubert Howe Bancroft*, vol. XXXIX (San Francisco: The History Company, Publishers, 1890), 557.
23. Hinckley, "Ivan Petroff's Journal," 26.
24. See Knut Bergsland, *Aleut Dictionary/Unangam Tunudgusii* (Alaska Native Language Center, University of Alaska Fairbanks, 1994), xli.
25. Turner to Baird, Nov. 25, 1879, SIA, RU 28, incoming correspondence, box 19, #8595.

26. Turner to Ridgway, June 20, 1879, Blacker-Wood Library, McGill University.
27. Turner to Ridgway, Sept. 1, 1882, Blacker-Wood Library, McGill University.
28. The chief from Makushin Village had arrived on the 15th with pelts from seven red foxes and one cross fox. *A.C. Company Log,* January 1878–June 1879.
29. Turner to Baird, Nov. 25, 1879, SIA, RU 28, incoming correspondence, box 19, #8595.
30. Turner to Baird, May 6, 1879, SIA, RU 28, incoming correspondence, box 9, #4234.
31. Pirjo Varjola, *The Etholén Collection: The Ethnographic Alaskan Collection of Adolf Etholén and His Contemporaries in the National Museum of Finland* (National Board of Antiquities, Finland, 1990), 274–75.
32. Lydia Black, *Aleut Art, Unangam Aguqaadangin,* second revised and expanded edition (Anchorage: Aleutian/Pribilof Islands Association, 2003), 96–97.
33. Accession record for catalog number E358970.
34. *Alaska Appeal,* 1, no. 9 (July 30, 1879): 5.
35. Turner to Baird, Nov. 25, 1879, SIA, RU 28, incoming correspondence, box 19, #8595.
36. Turner to Ridgway, June 20, 1879, Blacker-Wood Library, McGill University.
37. See *Contributions,* 143.
38. Turner to Ridgway, June 20, 1879, Blacker-Wood Library, McGill University.
39. Turner to Baird, Nov. 25, 1879, SIA, RU 28, incoming correspondence, box 19, #8595.
40. Turner to Baird, Dec. 5, 1881, SIA, RU 28, incoming correspondence, box 37, #17,826.
41. Hudson, "Designs in Aleut Basketry," in *Faces, Voices & Dreams: A Celebration of the Centennial of the Sheldon Jackson Museum*, ed. Peter L. Corey, 78–86 (Division of Alaska State Museums and the Friends of the Alaska State Museum, 1987), 78–86.
42. *Alaska Appeal* 1, no. 14 (Oct. 15, 1879): 4.
43. Bailey, "Condition of Affairs in Alaska," 7–8.
44. Turner to Ridgway, June 20, 1879, Blacker-Wood Library, McGill University.
45. Turner, *Contributions*, 177.
46. Turner to Baird, Nov. 25, 1879, SIA, RU 28, incoming correspondence, box 19, #8595.
47. King died at Sannak in 1885.
48. Turner to Ridgway, June 20, 1879, Blacker-Wood Library, McGill University.
49. Mary E. Turner to Baird, March 24, 1880, SIA, RU 7002, box 34, folder 29.
50. Baird to Mary E. Turner, March 27, 1880, SIA, RU 7002, collection division 2, private outgoing correspondence, vol. 25.
51. Dall, entry for July 27, 1880, *Diary July 25–August 31, 1880,* SIA, RU 7073, box 21.
52. Statement by Rudolph Neumann, June 17, 1895, Unalaska, Alaska. Alaska Commercial Company Records, JL006, Dept. of Special Collections, Stanford University Libraries, Stanford, California. In this statement Neumann says he began work at Unalaska on July 15, 1880, but Dall's diary indicates the date must have been later.
53. Isabel Shepard, *The Cruise of the U.S. Steamer "Rush" in Behring Sea* (San Francisco: The Bancroft Company, 1889), 121, 59.
54. Molly Lee, "Context and Contact: The History and Activities of the Alaska Commercial Company, 1867–1900," in *Catalogue Raisonné of the Alaska Commercial Company Collection*, ed. Nelson H. H. Graburn et al., 16 (Berkeley: University of California Press, 1996). I have benefited from conversations with [illegible] about the early history of the A.C. Company.
55. Turner, *Contributions*, 15.
56. For example, information from Neumann about furs in the Aleutians arrived too late to be incorporated into the text but Nelson mentioned it in his introduction. *Report*

upon Natural History Collections Made in Alaska between the years 1877 and 1881 (No. 3, Arctic Series of Publications, issued in connection with the Signal Service, U.S. Army. 49th Congress, 1st Session, Senate Misc. Documents 156. Serial 2349, 1886), 229.

57. Turner, *Descriptive Catalogue,* 4.
58. Turner to Baird, Sept. 1, 1881, RU 28, incoming correspondence, box 37, #17,822.
59. Turner, *Contributions*, 49.
60. There is a discrepancy about the date. The monthly abstract says the *Czar* arrived the evening of May 12 and anchored the next morning. In the text (*Contributions*, p. 178), Turner dates the ship entering the harbor on May 14.
61. Turner, *Contributions*, 178–79.
62. Turner to Baird, May 14, 1881, SIA, RU 28, Office of the Secretary, 1879–1882, incoming correspondence, box 37, #17,821.
63. Turner mentioned that there were people from Attu with him on Amchitka. *Contributions*, 129.
64. National Archives and Records Administration (NARA), RG 27, box 4. Weather Bureau, Unalaska. Monthly Mean Reports from S. Applegate, October 1881–May 1886.
65. Turner to Baird, Sept. 1, 1881, SIA, RU 28, Office of the Secretary, 1879–1882, incoming correspondence, box 37, #17,822.
66. Turner, *Contributions,* 172–73.
67. Turner, *Descriptive Catalogue*, 58.
68. Smithsonian Institution, *Annual Report of the Board of Regents of the Smithsonian Institution,* 1881:21. During his years in the Aleutians, Turner periodically received checks from Spencer Baird to defray costs of collecting. In 1878 he received $399.64. This was followed by $607.07 in 1879 and $1319.72 in 1880. In 1881 he received $704.32. He recorded receiving a total of $3030.75 during his stay in Alaska. The A.C. Company cashed the checks, usually charging 25 or 50 cents per check. (Information in a notebook owned by L. Wayne Turner.)
69. May 14, 1882, L. Wayne Turner Collection.
70. Franz Boas, *The Central Eskimo* (Washington, DC: Government Printing Office, 1888), 420; John Murdoch, *Ethnological Results of the Point Barrow Expedition* (Washington, DC: Government Printing Office, 1892).
71. Turner to Baird, Aug. 20, 1886, SIA, RU 29, incoming correspondence, box 6.
72. Turner to Baird, Sept. 13, 1886, SIA, RU 29, incoming correspondence, box 6.
73. Turner to Baird, Dec. 24, 1886, National Museum of Natural History accession record 19248. In late February 1887 the museum purchased the collection. An invoice lists 147 items for sale at $559.85. On June 8, Turner wrote O. T. Mason, curator of ethnology, concerned that the collection had not been cataloged and fearing many items could be damaged by insects. The accession card (for 156 items) was dated the next day (Smithsonian Institution, registrar's file).
74. J. W. Powell, *Eighth Annual Report of the Bureau of Ethnology, 1886–1887* (Washington, DC: Government Printing Office, 1891), xxviii.
75. His review of Rink's paper on east Greenlanders is dated Smithsonian Institution, April 11, 1887 (*American Naturalist*, August 1887).
76. Loring, "Introduction to Lucien M. Turner," xxii.
77. The Peabody received two ivory toggles, one in the shape of a seal (88-51-10/50020) and the other in the shape of a paired sea otter on land (88-51-10/50021). They also

received two examples of gut sewing, probably from Atka (88-51-10/50018 and 50019). At the same time material was received collected by Nelson, Dall, and Applegate.

78. L. W. True to G. B. Goode, July 30, 1890, SIA, RU 189, box 133, folder 10.
79. Loring, "Introduction to Lucien M. Turner," xxii.
80. Memorandum attached to a letter from Turner to Goode, Jan. 30, 1894, SIA, RU 189, box 133, folder 10.
81. In an August 1888 review, R. W. Shufeldt praised the books coming from work sponsored by the U.S. Signal Service and noted, referring to Turner's work, "The last one of these, very recently issued, is now before us." Shufeldt, "Turner's Explorations in Alaska," *Science* XII, no. 287 (August 3, 1888): 59.
82. "Alaska: Dr. William H. Fall [sic] Speaks of Its Resources and People," *Sunday Chronicle* (San Francisco), Nov. 14, 1880, SIA, RU 7073, box 4, folder 3.
83. Soter A. Mousalimas, "… If Reports Can Be Believed, Russian Priests Destroyed All the Masks They Could Find," *Études/Inuit/Studies* 14, no. 1–2: 191–208. See also Dall's undated "Veniaminoff Address" in which the fur traders are described as "greedy, faithless, unmerciful and sensual." Aleuts became "poor, diseased and ignorant slaves; stolid, sullen, and except for gleams of sensuality plunged in the apathy of despair." Veniaminov was praised highly in this address. National Anthropological Archives, William Healey Dall papers, box 1.
84. "Explorations in the Aleutian Islands," *Weekly Bulletin* (San Francisco), Nov. 21, 1873.
85. Dall, "Deserted Hearths," *Overland Monthly* 13, no. 1 (July 1874): 25–30.
86. H. B. James, chief of customs, to Dall, Dec. 1 and 3, 1879, SIA, RU 7073, box 12, folder 19.
87. Dall, *On Masks, Labrets, and Certain Aboriginal Customs with an Inquiry into the Bearing of Their Geographic Distribution,* Bureau of American Ethnology, Third Annual Report for 1881–1882 (Washington, DC: Smithsonian Institution, 1884), 38.
88. "In spite of their great trust in Father Ivan [Veniaminov], it was only with difficulty that he could obtain any knowledge as to their former practices." Frederic Litke, *A Voyage Around the World 1826–1829*, vol. 1, *To Russian America and Siberia*, trans. from the French 1835 edition by Renée Marshall, ed. Richard A. Pierce (Kingston, ON: The Limestone Press, 1987), 101.
89. Dall, *On the Remains of the Later Prehistoric Man Obtained from Caves in the Catherina Archipelago, Alaska Territory, and Especially from the Caves of the Aleutian Islands*, Smithsonian Contribution to Knowledge no. 318 (Washington, DC: Smithsonian Institution, 1878), 7.
90. "Prehistoric Remains," *Daily Evening Bulletin* (Nov. 6, 1872), SIA, RU 773, box 47, folder 2. Turner described an item in his collection (number 597) as "a fragment of tooth, employed as a blunt for an arrow or spear." *Descriptive Catalogue,* 40.
91. Baker to Dall, Aug. 23, 1876, SIA, RU 7073, box 7.
92. Elliott to Paul Bartsch, U.S. National Museum, June 13, 1927, SIA, RU 73, 1, general correspondence, 1858–1982, box 32, folder 7.
93. Elliott to Dall, April 22, 1872, Ounalaska, SIA, RU 7073, box 10, folder 10.
94. Elliott to Dall, July [illegible], SIA, RU 7073, box 10, folder 10. Elliott made the indelicate suggestion to Dall that "If you have any lonely feelings, my dear old friend, just come up here for a few days at least, and weeks if you can, we will make a regular excursion for you to all the lions of the Island."
95. [illegible] to Dall, Aug. [illegible], SIA, RU 7073, box 9 (bound correspondence). Lydia Black (*Russians in Alaska*, [illegible]) wrote that Dall refused to attend Elliott's wedding

to Alexandra Milovidov and suggests this was because of Dall's racism. Although recorded in the Unalaska vital statistics (1872, vol. 16, p. 26), the wedding took place at St. Paul, not at Unalaska. ("In the evening Assistant Treasury Agent Henry W. Elliott was joined in marriage to Miss Alexandra Melovedoff according to the rites of the Greek Church of which the bride is a member." NARA, Pacific Alaska Region, Anchorage. RG 22, U.S. Fish and Wildlife Service, Official Log, St. Paul Island, July 21, 1872.) Dall was not at St. Paul and learned of the wedding through Gustave Niebaum and from Elliott's letter of July 22, 1872 (SIA, RU 7073, box 10, folder 10).

96. Samuel Falconer, 1829–1915, was appointed deputy Collector of Customs for Alaska on Dec. 14, 1868.
97. Dall to Baird, Nov. 14, 1873, SIA, RU 7073, box 4 (outgoing correspondence II, letterpress, 1871–1873).
98. Bryant to Dall, Oct. 4, 1875, SIA, RU 7073, box 8, folder 20.
99. Baird to Dall, April 6, 1874, SIA, RU 7073, box 7.
100. *Boston Daily Advertiser*, July 15, 18, and 20, 1875.
101. Baird to Dall, Oct. 11, 1874, SIA, RU 7073, box 7.
102. Dall to B. W. Evermann, U.S. Bureau of Fisheries, Dec. 7, 1910. NARA. RG 22, U.S. Fish and Wildlife Service. File 290.
103. Lisa Marie Morris, "Keeper of the Seal: The Art of Henry Wood Elliott and the Salvation of the Alaska Fur Seals" (unpublished PhD thesis, University of Alaska Fairbanks, 2001), 74, note 13.
104. Henry W. Elliott, *Our Arctic Province: Alaska and the Seal Islands* (New York: Charles Scribner's Sons, 1886), 190.
105. *Investigation of the Fur-Seal and Other Fisheries of Alaska*, 50th Congress, 2d Session, House Report No. 3883, Serial 2674, 1889, pp. 135, 162.
106. They were featured in a 1982 retrospective at the Anchorage Historical and Fine Arts Museum. Robert L. Shalkop, *Henry Wood Elliott, 1846–1930, A Retrospective Exhibition* (Anchorage Historical and Fine Arts Museum, 1982).
107. *Alaska Commercial Company*, 44th Congress, 1st Session. June 3, 1876, Serial 1712, p. 76.
108. In 1879 Petroff wrote to Dall that he was among the "citizens by purchase" of the territory and hoped that if he were appointed as a "Russian-speaking Secretary" for a new territorial government this appointment would be "a good answer to Mr. Stanhouse's sweeping charge, that the former Russian subjects are 'a very undesirable element of population.'" Letter, July 18, 1879, SIA, RU 7073, box 15, folder 3.
109. Richard Pierce, "Archival and Bibliographic Materials on Russian America Outside the USSR," in *Russia's American Colony*, ed. Frederick Starr, 355–56 (Durham, NC: Duke University Press, 1987). See also Morgan B. Sherwood, *Exploration of Alaska, 1865–1900,* Yale Western Americana Series 7 (New Haven, CT: Yale University Press, 1965), 57–69.
110. Elliott, *Biographical Sketches of Authors on Russian America and Alaska* (written in 1915), Occasional Paper no. 2 (Anchorage: Anchorage Historical and Fine Arts Museum, 1976), 27. On April 10, 1879, Petroff wrote to Dall that he had "been engaged off and on since 1875" in Alaskan research for Bancroft. SIA, RU 7073, box 15, folder 3.
111. Petroff to Dall, April 10, 1879, SIA, RU 7073, box 15, folder 3.
112. Veniaminov, *Notes on the Islands of the Unalashka District* (Fairbanks: The Elmer E. Rasmuson Library Translation Program, University of Alaska, Fairbanks, and The Limestone Press, 1984), 17.

113. Dall, "A New Volcano Island in Alaska," *Science: An Illustrated Journal* III, no. 51 (Jan. 26, 1884): 91.
114. Ivan Petroff, *Population and Resources of Alaska,* preliminary report dated December 28, 1880, p. 19.
115. Petroff, *Early Times on the Aleutian Islands; Life of Peter Kostromitin, 1798–1878,* Bancroft Library. Contrast the length and detail of this production with Petroff's statement that he found it "next to impossible to arouse his slumbering faculties of recollection." *The Alaska Appeal,* (April 22, 1879). In the travel diary Petroff wrote that Ruf Bourdukofsky, the Unalaska chief, accompanied him to Makushin to translate and that Kostromitin gave him "a detailed statement of what he knew."
116. Petroff, *Report on the Population, Industries, and Resources of Alaska,* 47th Congress, 2d Session, House Miscellaneous Document 42, vol. 13, no 42, part 8 (Washington, DC: Government Printing Office, 1884), 92.
117. Bancroft, *History of Alaska,* 683–84.
118. Black, *Russians in Alaska,* 214.
119. Ledger owned by Larry Shaishnikoff, translated by Lydia Black. This may have been written by Vasilli Shaiashnikov, chief of Unalaska from 1887 to 1902.
120. Pierce, "Archival and Bibliographic Materials," 356.
121. Black, "The Daily Journal of Reverend Father Juvenal: A Cautionary Tale," *Ethnohistory* 28, no. 1 (Winter 1981): 33-58.
122. Pierce, "New Light on Ivan Petroff, Historian of Alaska," *Pacific Northwest Quarterly* 59, no. 1 (January 1968): 8. The Alaska Commercial Company Records, Kodiak Station, Outgoing Letters, 1868–1891, and the Kodiak Station Log, April 1, 1889–April 1, 1890, record Petroff's presence on Kodiak Island at Eagle Harbor and Old Harbor from October 1883 to April 1884, possibly in May 1885, in November and December 1886, and again from October 1887 to May 1888. Alaska and Polar Regions Collections, University of Alaska Fairbanks. In 1888 A. B. Alexander on the steamer *Albatross* met Petroff at Old Harbor, where he reported catching three hundred barrels of fish in three weeks. Petroff said he had caught cod at Cold Harbor in 1883 and shipped them to San Francisco. A. B. Alexander, "Narrative of the Voyage from San Francisco to Unalaska," 1888: 66, 67. NARA. RG 22, #62, box 2, folder "Albatross."
123. There is a photograph dated 1890 of Petroff recording field data at Kodiak (photograph no. 351 in the Sheldon Jackson Papers, RG 239, Presbyterian Historical Society).
124. Elliott, *Biographical Sketches,* 29.
125. Petroff to John W. Foster, Nov. 11, 1892. U.S. Government, *Fur Seal Arbitration: Proceedings of the Tribunal of Arbitration,* vol. VII (Washington, DC: Government Printing Office, 1895), 153–54.
126. *The Times of London,* April 4, 1893, 3.
127. On Feb. 1, 1980, Lydia T. Black addressed a letter to the American Anthropological Association cautioning all researchers about any use of the "Petrov file."
128. "The Russians in Alaska," *New York Times,* March 23, 1880, 1.
129. Anonymous, but attributed to Dall, "Bancroft's History of Alaska," 292. (For Dall's authorship see Bartsch et al, *A Bibliography and Short Biographical Sketch of William Healey Dall,* Smith. Misc. Coll., vol. 104, no. 15, 1946, p. 51.)
130. Morris, "Keeper of the Seal," 78. Morris noted that Elliott "took some authorial license and altered his itinerary a bit, intimating that he traveled as far as Point Barrow." She suggests this book was based on his 1874 tour.

131. "Reply to George M. Dawson's 'Elliott's Alaska and the Seal Islands,'" *Science* VIII, no. 202 (Dec. 17, 1886): 566.
132. Anonymous, but attributed to Dall, "Elliott's Alaska and the Seal Islands," *Science* VIII, no. 200 (Dec. 3, 1886): 523. (For Dall's authorship see Bartsch, *A Bibliography and Short Biographical Sketch,* 52.)
133. See, for example, his "Statement . . . in reference to the Fur Seal of Alaska made to the Secretary of the Treasury, Feb. 25th, 1870," SIA, RU 7073, box 31.
134. Elliott, *Biographical Sketches*, 27.
135. Elliott, *Our Arctic Province,* 121–22; Petroff, *Population and Resources of Alaska*, 23.
136. Elliott, *Our Arctic Province,* 171–72; Petroff, *Population and Resources of Alaska*, 19.
137. Petroff, "An Alaska Centennial," *Alaska Appeal*, March 22, 1879. In this article Petroff claimed to have visited English Bay on Oct. 3, 1878, the exact centenary of the day Cook arrived there.
138. Elliott, *Our Arctic Province,* 176.
139. Petroff's journal (Hinckley, "Ivan Petroff's Journal," 36) dates the visit Sept. 10, 1878, and this is confirmed in the *Alaska Commercial Company Log*, Unalaska. January 1878–June 1879, Sept. 9–10, 1878.
140. Petroff, *Report on the Population, Industries, and Resources of Alaska*, 22.
141. Elliott, *Our Arctic Province,* 179.
142. Petroff, *Population and Resources of Alaska*, 10.
143. Elliott, *Our Arctic Province*, 164.
144. Petroff, *Report on the Population, Industries, and Resources of Alaska*, 20.
145. Elliott, *Our Arctic Province*, 165.
146. George M. Dawson, "Elliott's Alaska and the Seal Islands," and Elliott's reply, *Science* (Dec. 17, 1886): 565–66.
147. Walter Hough, "Fire Making Apparatus in the United States National Museum," *Report of the U.S. National Museum, Annual Report of the Smithsonian Institution* (Washington, DC: Government Printing Office, 1888), 531–87.
148. Turner to Ridgway, April 28, 1883, Blacker-Wood Library, McGill University.
149. Turner to Ridgway, Jan. 26, 1886, Blacker-Wood Library, McGill University.
150. Turner, *Descriptive Catalogue*, 135; Bancroft, *History of Alaska*, 103 and xxiv.

Notes to Chapter 1

1. Turner included tables of meteorological data for both St. Michael and the Aleutian Islands in *Contributions to the Natural History of Alaska*. However, he addressed only weather phenomena at St. Michael. In addition to his own Aleutian observations, he included those made by Veniaminov from 1825 to 1834 and by Innokentii Shaiashnikov from October 1866 to April 1867.
2. The Semichi Islands include three islands: Alaid, Nizki, and Shemya. On the chart Turner and his Attuan companions prepared, Alaid and Nizki are connected by a low and narrow strip of land. On contemporary charts, this "shifting sandspit" is below water. See NOAA chart number 16435.

Notes to Chapter 8

1. When describing the short-tailed albatross, Turner wrote, "When a native kills one he saves only the wings, from which to take the sinew for wrapping round his spear heads." [C:128–129]

Notes to Chapter 10

1. The Spectacled or Pallas Cormorant, weighing twelve to fourteen pounds, was hunted to extinction by 1852.
2. Turner frequently used the common nineteenth-century term "Duck Hawk" for this bird.

Notes to Chapter 11

1. Note that Turner used the Russian name for king salmon (perhaps confusing *chavícha* with *chouicha*), but Latin names for the others.

Notes to Chapter 12

1. Turner here repeats an erroneous local tradition. Veniaminov himself dated the planting to "around 1805" (*Notes on the Islands of the Unalashka District*, 1984:27).
2. This plant was almost certainly misidentified by Turner. The one he describes was possibly *Fragaria chiloensis*, beach strawberry (Hultén: 606).
3. Both Turner and Hultén, in their description of people eating this plant, confuse it with *Heracleum lanatum* (Hultén: 707), the famous putchki or wild celery. See Golodoff p. 131 for *Angelica lucida* and pp. 133–134 for *Heracleum lanatum*.

Notes to Chapter 13

1. In Eastern Aleut the interrogative "what?" is *alqu-x̂*.
2. Turner is referring to sea urchins. See Chapter 11.

Notes to Chapter 15

1. The sentence was probably intended to end here where Turner has a comma, and a new sentence was to begin with the next phrase.
2. Pages 4–5 in the modern translation by Dmitri Krenov, edited by Richard A. Pierce (Kingston, ON: The Limestone Press, 1974).
3. See Appendix 1.

Notes to Chapter 16

1. Based on his subsequent statements, I think Turner meant that immoral conduct was *not* prevalent prior to the arrival of the Russians.

Notes to Chapter 17

1. "Rather than 'the usual four seasons,' the Aleuts may once have distinguished six or seven seasons of the year, according to the vegetation and the general weather conditions." Knut Bergsland, *Aleut Dictionary/Unangam Tunudgusii* (Alaska Native Language Center. University of Alaska Fairbanks, 1994), 572.
2. See Chapter 1 where "March is known as the snow month."

Notes to Chapter 18

1. None of these words appear in the Golodoff's [illegible] pages [illegible].

Notes to Chapter 19

1. This object may or may not have been from the Aleutian Islands. For the use of seagulls in shamanistic practices, however, see Gerald D. Berreman, "Aleut

Shamanism in the Twentieth Century? An Assessment of Evidence," in Bruno Frohlich, Albert B. Harper, and Rolf Gilberg, eds., *To the Aleutians and Beyond: The Anthropology of William S. Laughlin*, 25–50 (Publications of the National Museum Ethnographical Series, Volume 20. Department of Ethnography. The National Museum of Denmark. Copenhagen, 2002).

2. On pages 221–235 of the *Catalogue* is a list of 175 vocabulary words.

Notes to Appendix 1

1. Smithsonian Institution Archives, RU 7073, box 13, folder 39.
2. William Healy Dall, "Geographical Notes in Alaska," *Bulletin of American Geographical Society* XXVIII(1): 1–20.
3. SIA, RU 7073, box 48.
4. *U.S. Coastal Pilot 9. Alaska: Cape Spencer to Beaufort Sea*, 21st ed., (Annapolis, MD: ProStart Publications Marine Division, 2003), 420.

Notes to Appendix 2

1. For diagrams of two variations of the blanket stitch and a type of couching stitch, see the explanations by Agnes Sovoroff (born at Unalaska in 1907 and died at Nikolski in 1995) and Sophia Pletnikoff (born at Chernofski in 1907 and died at Unalaska in 1982) in Raymond Hudson, ed., *Unugulux Tunusangin, Oldtime Stories* (Unalaska School District, 1992), 82–86, 96. For the running stitch with overlaid thread, see Edna Wilder, *Secrets of Eskimo Skin Sewing* (Fairbanks: University of Alaska Press, 1998), 94–95, where it is described as a decorative stitch on rain parkas.
2. Except for E65269, all bags marked "From the original accessions book" are currently absent from the collection.

Bibliography

Works by Lucien M. Turner

n.d. *Descriptive Catalogue of Ethnological Specimens Collected by Lucien M. Turner in Alaska.* Lucien Turner papers, Bureau of American Ethnology collection, National Anthropological Archives, National Museum of Natural History, Smithsonian Institution, Washington, DC, manuscript 7197 [c. 1886–1887].

1878 *Alyut-English Vocabulary, Collected at Unalaska Island, Alaska, 1878–1879.* National Anthropological Archives, National Museum of Natural History, Smithsonian Institution, Washington, DC, manuscript 2505-c.

1885 "Notes on the Birds of the Nearer Islands, Alaska." *The Auk*, II(2) (April 1885).

1886 *Contributions to the Natural History of Alaska. Results of investigations made chiefly in the Yukon District and the Aleutian Islands; conducted under the auspices of the Signal Service, United States Army, extending from May, 1874, to August, 1881.* Washington, DC: Government Printing Office.

1887 Review of Dr. H. Rink's Paper on the East Greenlanders. *Recent Literature,* August 1887: 748–55. Extracted from *The American Naturalist*, August 1887.

1894 "Ethnology of the Ungava District, Hudson Bay Territory." *Eleventh Annual Report of the Bureau of Ethnology*, 1889–90, edited by J. W. Powell, 159–350. Washington, DC: Government Printing Office. Reissued in 2001 with an introduction by Stephen Loring as part of the Classics of Smithsonian Anthropology Series.

Manuscripts

Turner: Smithsonian Institution Archives [**SIA**], Record Units 16, 26, 28, and 29. Also consulted were letters at the Blacker-Wood Library, McGill University, Montreal, Quebec, and material in the collection of J. Wayne Turner.

Dall: Smithsonian Institution Archives, Record Unit 7073, William H. Dall Papers.

Nelson: Smithsonian Institution Archives, Record Unit 7364 – Series 2. Edward William Nelson and Edward Alphonso Goldman Collection.

National Archives and Records Administration [NARA], Record Group 22, Records of the U.S. Fish and Wildlife Service, 1868–2005. Record Group 27, Records of the Weather Bureau.

Two collections of Alaska Commercial Company manuscripts were used. The January 1, 1878, to June 30, 1879, Unalaska log book (Box 152, Folder 1577) and the Kodiak Station records, both at the Archives and Manuscript Collections, Alaska and Polar Regions Collections, Elmer E. Rasmuson Library, University of Alaska Fairbanks. The statement by Rudolph Neumann, June 17, 1895, Unalaska, Alaska, is in Alaska Commercial Company Records, JL006, Dept. of Special Collections, Stanford University Libraries, Stanford, California.

Works Cited

Bailey, George

1880 "Condition of Affairs in Alaska. Report of U.S. Revenue-Steamer 'Richard Rush', October 1879." 46th Congress, 2d Session. Executive Document No. 132. Senate.

Bancroft, Hubert Howe

1886 *History of Alaska, 1730–1885. The Works of Hubert Howe Bancoft.* Vol. XXXIII. San Francisco: A. L. Bancroft & Company, Publishers.

1890 *Literary Industries. The Works of Hubert Howe Bancroft.* Vol. XXXIX. San Francisco: The History Company, Publishers.

Bergsland, Knut

1994 *Aleut Dictionary/Unangam Tunudgusii.* Alaska Native Language Center. University of Alaska Fairbanks.

1997 *Aleut Grammar: Unangam Tunuganaan Achixaasix^.* Research Paper Number 10. Alaska Native Language Center. University of Alaska Fairbanks.

Bergsland, Knut, and Moses L. Dirks

1990 *Unangam Ungiikangin kayux Tunusangin/Unangam Uniikangis ama Tunuzangis/Aleut Tales and Narratives.* Collected 1909–1910 by Waldemar Jochelson. Alaska Native Language Center. University of Alaska Fairbanks.

Berreman, Gerald D.

2002 "Aleut Shamanism in the Twentieth Century? An Assessment of Evidence." In *To the Aleutians and Beyond: The Anthropology of William S. Laughlin* edited by Bruno Frohlich, Albert B. Harper, and Rolf Gilberg, 25–50. Publications of the National Museum Ethnographical Series, Volume 20. Department of Ethnography. The National Museum of Denmark. Copenhagen.

Black, Lydia

1981 "The Daily Journal of Reverend Father Juvenal: A Cautionary Tale." *Ethnohistory* 28(1):33–58.

2004 *Russians in Alaska, 1732–1867*. Fairbanks: University of Alaska Press.

Boas, Franz

1888 *The Central Eskimo*. Sixth Annual Report of the Bureau of Ethnology, 1884–85. Washington, DC: Government Printing Office.

Dall, William Healy

1870 *Alaska and Its Resources*. Boston: Lee and Shepard.

1874 "Deserted Hearths." *The Overland Monthly* 13(1):25–30.

1878 *On the Remains of the Later Prehistoric Man Obtained from Caves in the Catherina Archipelago, Alaska Territory, and especially from the Caves of the Aleutian Islands*. Smithsonian Contribution to Knowledge, No. 318. Washington, DC: Smithsonian Institution.

1884 "A New Volcano Island in Alaska." *Science: An Illustrated Journal* III(51):89–93.

1884 *On Masks, Labrets and Certain Aboriginal Customs with an Inquiry into the Bearing of Their Geographic Distribution*. Bureau of American Ethnology, Third Annual Report for 1881–1882. Washington, DC: Smithsonian Institution.

1896 "Geographical Notes in Alaska." *Bulletin of American Geographical Society* XXVIII(1):1–20.

Elliott, Henry W.

1875 *A Report Upon the Condition of Affairs in the Territory of Alaska*. Washington, DC: Government Printing Office.

1886 *Our Arctic Province: Alaska and the Seal Islands*. New York: Charles Scribner's Sons.

1976 *Biographical Sketches of Authors on Russian America and Alaska*. (Written in 1915.) Occasional Paper No. 2. Anchorage: Anchorage Historical and Fine Arts Museum.

Golodoff, Suzi

2003 *Wildflowers of Unalaska Island: A Guide to the Flowering Plants of an Aleutian Island*. Fairbanks: University of Alaska Press.

Hinckley, Theodore C. and Caryl

1966 "Ivan Petroff's Journal of a Trip to Alaska in 1878." *Journal of the West* 5(1):25–70.

Hough, Walter

1888 "Fire Making Apparatus in the United States National Museum." In *Report of the U.S. National Museum, Annual Report of the Smithsonian Institution*, 531–87. Washington, DC: Government Printing Office.

Hudson, Raymond L.

1987 "Designs in Aleut Basketry." In *Faces, Voices & Dreams: A Celebration of the Centennial of the Sheldon Jackson Museum,* edited by Peter L. Corey. Division of Alaska State Museums and the Friends of the Alaska State Museum.

Hudson, Raymond L., ed.

1992 *Unugulux Tunusangin, Oldtime Stories.* Unalaska City School District.

Hultén, Eric

1960 *Flora of the Aleutian Islands.* New York: J. Cramer; Hafner Publishing Co.

1968 *Flora of Alaska and Neighboring Territories; a manual of the vascular plants.* Stanford, CA: Stanford University Press.

Lee, Molly

1996 "Context and Contact: The History and Activities of the Alaska Commercial Company, 1867–1900." In *Catalogue Raisonné of the Alaska Commercial Company Collection, Phoebe Apperson Hearst Museum of Anthropology* edited by Nelson H. H. Graburn et al., 19–38. Berkeley: University of California Press.

Liapunova, Roza G.

1996 *Essays on the Ethnography of the Aleuts.* Translated by Jerry Shelest with the editorial assistance of William B. Workman and Lydia T. Black. The Rasmuson Library Historical Translation Series, Vol. IX, Marvin W. Falk, editor. Fairbanks: University of Alaska Press.

Litke Frederic

1987 *A Voyage Around the World, 1826–1829.* Vol. I, *To Russian America and Siberia.* Translated from the French 1835 edition by Renée Marshall. Edited by Richard A. Pierce. Kingston, ON: The Limestone Press.

Loring, Stephen

2001 "Introduction to Lucien M. Turner and the Beginnings of Smithsonian Anthropology in the North. In Turner, *Ethnology of the Ungava District, Hudson Bay Territory.* Pp. vii–xxxii. Washington, DC: Smithsonian Institution Press.

Matthews, Donna

2002 *Unangam Hiitnisangin/Unangam Hitnisangis/Aleut Plants.* Edited by Barbara Svarny Carlson. Association of *Unangan/Unangas* Educators.

Morris, Lisa Marie

2001 "Keeper of the Seal: The Art of Henry Wood Elliott and the Salvation of the Alaska Fur Seals." Unpublished PhD thesis. University of Alaska Fairbanks.

Mousalimas, Soter A.

1990 "... If Reports Can Be Believed, Russian Priests Destroyed All the Masks They Could Find. ..." *Études/Inuit/Studies* 14(1–2):191–208.

Murdoch, John

1892 *Ethnological Results of the Point Barrow Expedition*. Ninth Annual Report of the Bureau of Ethnology, 1887–88. Washington, DC: Government Printing Office.

Nelson, Edward W.

1886 *Report upon Natural History Collections Made in Alaska between the years 1877 and 1881*. No. 3, Arctic Series of Publications, issued in connection with the Signal Service, U.S. Army. 49th Congress, 1st Session, Senate Misc. Documents 156. Serial 2349.

Petroff, Ivan

1878 *Early Times on the Aleutian Islands: Life of Peter Kostromitin.* Hubert Howe Bancroft Collection. Bancroft Library, Berkeley, California. Ms. BANC MSS P-K 14, 16p.

1880 *Population and Resources of Alaska*, 46th Congress, 3rd Session, House Executive Document No. 40. January 15, 1881. Serial 1968. (This was the preliminary report, dated Washington, DC, December 28, 1880.)

1884 *Report on the Population, Industries, and Resources of Alaska*. 47th Congress, 2d Session. House Miscellaneous Document 42, vol. 13, no. 42, Part 8. Serial 2136. Washington, DC: Government Printing Office. (Dated Washington, DC, August 7, 1882.)

Pierce, Richard

1968 "New Light on Ivan Petroff, Historian of Alaska." *Pacific Northwest Quarterly* 59(1):1–10.

1987 "Archival and Bibliographic Materials on Russian America Outside the USSR." In Starr, ed., *Russia's American Colony*, pp. 355–56.

Powell, J. W.

1891 *Eighth Annual Report of the Bureau of Ethnology*, 1886–1887. Washington, DC: Government Printing Office.

Shepard, Isabel S.

1889 *The Cruise of the U.S. Steamer "Rush" in Behring Sea, Summer of 1889.* San Francisco: The Bancroft Company.

Sherwood, Morgan B.

1965 *Exploration of Alaska, 1865–1900*. Yale Western Americana Series, 7. New Haven, CT: Yale University Press.

Shufeldt, R. W.

1888 "Turner's Explorations in Alaska." *Science: An Illustrated Journal*, XII (287), p. 59.

Smithsonian Institution

1881 *Annual Report of the Board of Regents of the Smithsonian Institution, showing the operations, expenditures and condition of the institution for the year 1881*. Serial Set vol. no. 1994, session vol. no. 2, 47th Congress, 1st Session, S. Misc. Doc. 109.

1929 "Necrology: Robert Ridgway." *Annual Report of the Board of Regents of the Smithsonian Institution . . . for the year ending June 30, 1929*. Publication 3034. Pp. 20–21.

Starr, S. Frederick, ed.

1987 *Russia's American Colony*. Durham, NC: Duke University Press.

U.S. Government

1895 *Fur Seal Arbitration. Proceedings of the Tribunal of Arbitration*. Volume VII. Washington, DC: Government Printing Office.

1964 *United States Coast Pilot 9: Pacific and Arctic Coasts*. 7th edition. U.S. Department of Commerce and Coast and Geodetic Survey. Washington, DC: Government Printing Office.

2003 *U.S. Coastal Pilot 9: Cape Spencer to Beaufort Sea*. 21st Edition. Annapolis, MD: ProStart Publications Marine Division.

Varjola, Pirjo

1990 *The Etholén Collection: The Ethnographic Alaskan Collection of Adolf Etholén and His Contemporaries in the National Museum of Finland*. With contributions by Julia P. Averkieva and Roza G. Liapunova. National Board of Antiquities, Finland.

Veniaminov, Ivan

1984 *Notes on the Islands of the Unalashka District*. Translated by Lydia T. Black and R. H. Geoghegan. Edited, with an introduction by Richard A. Pierce. Published jointly by: The Elmer E. Rasmuson Library Translation Program, University of Alaska, Fairbanks, and The Limestone Press, Kingston, Ontario.

Wilder, Edna

1998 *Secrets of Eskimo Skin Sewing*. Fairbanks: University of Alaska Press. First published 1976 by Alaska Northwest Books.

Newspapers and Periodicals

Alaska Appeal, 1879
Boston Daily Advertiser, 1875
Daily Evening Bulletin (San Francisco), 1872
New York Times, 1880
Science, 1886, 1888
Sunday Chronicle (San Francisco), 1880
Times of London, 1893
Weekly Bulletin (San Francisco), 1873

Index

Page numbers in italics refer to figures.
Turner's alternative spellings for place and proper names are in brackets.